Sociology and socialism
in contemporary China

International Library of Sociology

Founded by Karl Mannheim

Editor: John Rex, University of Warwick

Arbor Scientiae
Arbor Vitae

A catalogue of the books available in the **International Library of Sociology** and other series of Social Science books published by Routledge & Kegan Paul will be found at the end of this volume.

Sociology and socialism in contemporary China

Siu-lun Wong

Routledge & Kegan Paul
London, Boston and Henley

First published in 1979
by Routledge & Kegan Paul Ltd
39 Store Street,
London WC1E 7DD,
Broadway House,
Newtown Road,
Henley-on-Thames,
Oxon RG9 1EN and
9 Park Street,
Boston, Mass. 02108, USA
Set in Times New Roman, 10 on 11 point
and printed in Great Britain by
Thomson Litho Ltd, East Kilbride, Scotland
© Siu-lun Wong 1979

British Library Cataloguing in Publication Data

Wong, Siu-Lun

Sociology and socialism in contemporary
China—(International library of sociology)
1 Sociology—History—China
I Title II Series
301'.0951   HM22.C6   78–40832

ISBN 0 7100 0089 8

iv

Contents

80- 0738

Tables

Preface

This is a case study of the state of sociology in a non-western, non-capitalistic society. My interest in the present topic was first aroused by the wave of critical self-examinations of the discipline in the late 1960s and early 1970s, represented by Alvin W. Gouldner's book *The Coming Crisis of Western Sociology* (1971). These radical assessments of sociology raised two questions to me: Is sociology inherently tied to a bourgeois social order? As an intellectual product of western industrial civilization, how far is sociological inquiry culture-bound and thus not applicable to the understanding of Asian societies? In my consideration of sociological research as a possible vocation, these are salient and recurrent problems. As a student and then a teacher of sociology in the Colony of Hong Kong, I am keenly conscious that the subject is still very much a western transplant with shaky roots. It is necessary, I feel, to evaluate and redefine the meaning of sociology in an Asian context.

But why China? There are academic as well as personal reasons for my choice. In the first half of this century, China was a centre of flourishing sociological activities. But since the victory of the Communist Revolution in 1949, sociology has become a problematic pursuit and its status has been a sensitive issue in the People's Republic of China. The re-emergence of sociology in the USSR and other East European countries in the last decade or two has given rise to quite a number of studies on the development of this discipline in these socialist societies. But, to date, there are no similar studies for China. A more systematic review of the waxing and waning of sociology in China may fill a gap in our knowledge of the sociology of sociology, and may shed some light on the nature of both sociology and contemporary Chinese society. As for the personal reason, though I was born and educated in the British Crown Colony without direct experience of life on the Chinese mainland, I have always felt an emotional attachment to China. International developments in the early 1970s have terminated a period of isolation of China from world affairs, and have shattered many long-held attitudes and stereotypes. It has become important for me to have a realistic understanding of how the sociological profession is being regarded in socialist China.

During the early stage of this study, I was mainly engrossed in the demise of professional and institutional sociology in the People's Republic. I devoted most of my attention to the reasons for and implications of its decline. But in a seminar where I presented my preliminary thoughts on the subject, I was struck by the comment of a visiting American sociologist to the effect that if a group of people were shut together in a room and given the task of under-standing modern, industrial societies, they would invent some kind of sociology on their own. I did not agree with this completely, but it led me to ask whether there are 'functional substitutes' for insti-tutional sociology in China. I was able to identify several forms of social inquiry which are quite similar to sociology, namely the studies on the minority nationalities, *tiao-ch'a yen-chiu* or investi-gation and research, and the 'four histories'. Then at the suggestion of Professor C. K. Yang, I did more research on these varieties and developed my rudimentary observations into separate chapters.

As I went deeper into the subject, I became more and more interested in the pre-1949 development of Chinese sociology. What was once a sketchy description intended as a backdrop to the main story was expanded into a more lengthy chapter. But still, this has hardly done justice to the efforts of the first generations of Chinese sociologists. Their works describing and analysing a crucial phase of China's transformation deserve full critical reviews. Their contri-butions should be recorded and appreciated. In the process of this study, my respect for these sociologists has increased and gradually I formed my opinions on the abolition of sociology in contemporary China. I believe it to be a regrettable event. Many promising careers have been ruined. It is particularly painful to witness former sociolo-gists engaging in repeated denigrations of their past. One possible justification is that revolution is not a feast. It will necessarily involve violence and sacrifice. After all, it may be argued, what are stunted careers compared to death and mutilation? But I would ask: How would it contribute to socialist construction to force sociologists to give up their chosen profession? In the name of sacrifice, has there not been an unnecessary wastage of talents? Then, perhaps, the abolition of sociology can be justified in terms of developmental priorities. But China is a huge country and it is hardly convincing to argue that no human and material resources can be spared for sociological research which will actually involve a tiny proportion of the population. The last possible defence is that sociology is not important and useful for industrialization and modernization. This, I think, reflects a failure to adopt a longer view of socio-economic development. The practical import of sociological research, like that of basic and theoretical research in the natural sciences, may not be readily apparent. Furthermore, an intellectual subject should not be judged solely by its immediate utility. In this connection, Professor Maurice Freedman's view on the value of studying other cultures, though addressed primarily to an audience of western anthropologists, may have a message for China: 'We have to further the study of oriental civilizations among us, not simply because it is a matter of national security that we have people equipped in Asian languages and cultures, but because our own title to civilization must be kept alive by our capacity to view the world impartially' (1963, p. 12).

After stating where I stand, let me make clear some of the more technical matters on the methods adopted in this study. First, a delimitation of the scope of my inquiry: 'Sociology' is the key term, and by it I mean what Alex Inkeles has called 'the study of systems of social action and of their interrelations' with a set of rules and norms accepted by the participants in this activity to govern the validation of observations and the making of inferences. Needless to say, this definition is broad and vague, but it is unavoidable since it is symptomatic of the present state of sociology. I have also tried to identify sociology as what is socially designated as such or as its equivalent in contemporary China. I have relied on several institutional indicators such as the existence of teaching departments in academic institutions, and works produced which are classified as sociological. By 'contemporary China', I refer to the society on the Chinese mainland under the jurisdiction of the government of the People's Republic of China. Sociology carried out in Taiwan or practised by Chinese scholars outside China will not be discussed because, significant and valuable as it is, it lies beyond the scope of this study.

As for data, I depend primarily on information that is available in the publications of the People's Republic. Periodicals and books are the major sources, and those that have been consulted are listed in the bibliography. Owing to the lack of specialized journals of sociology in contemporary China, more attention has been paid to two periodicals—*Hsüeh-hsi* (*Study*) and *Hsin chien-she* (*New Construction*)—to provide indications on the state of sociology in contemporary China. Besides being more accessible and complete, these two periodicals are chosen for greater attention because the former was the theoretical official organ of the Chinese Communist Party in the 1950s from which the prevailing official views on philosophical and social scientific matters can be sampled, and the latter was a more academic journal carrying many articles on the social sciences. In addition to the periodicals and books produced in China, reports and comments on sociology in China by outside scholars are also consulted and used.

There are obvious limitations in relying on Chinese publications as sources of information. As Michel Oksenberg has pointed out, one's perspective will be affected by the sources employed. According to him, four broad methodological problems will have to be confronted in the use of the Chinese press: 'its ideological and cultural worldview, its deliberate distortions, its discontinuity in coverage, and its unintentional inaccuracy' (1969, p. 586). These problems exist elsewhere, but they are more acute in the case of China with its selective publication and controlled communication of information. Therefore, from these books and periodicals, no more than the tip of the iceberg can be seen. And the information is often couched in an ideological language that cannot be easily interpreted and understood by an outsider without direct experience of life in China. Thus elements of subjectivity on the part of the observers will inevitably exist since there is no sure way of checking the validity of an interpretation. These are well-known methodological problems in the study of contemporary China. As long as the chances of first-hand observation are difficult to come by, these problems, endemic to the use of secondary sources, have to be accepted as necessary constraints due to the lack of better alternatives.

This book grew out of my master's thesis presented to the Board of Studies in Sociology, the Chinese University of Hong Kong, in 1973. In the preparation of the thesis, I have benefited from the guidance of my supervisor, Dr Ambrose King, and my advisers, Dr Geoffrey Guest, Mr Wong Sou-lam, and Mr Michael Palmer. The encouraging and penetrating remarks of my external examiner, Professor C. K. Yang, provided me with the motivation and direction for rewriting. During a two-year sojourn in England, I have collected more material and have done further thinking on the subject. I began several revisions of the thesis after my return to Hong Kong in 1975. For the revisions, I am indebted to the late Professor Maurice Freedman, Professor P. M. Worsley, Dr Klaus Jäcklein, Dr Graham Johnson, Mr A. R. Sanchez, Mr Steve S. K. Chin, Mr T. S. Wong, and Mr Yu Fong-ying for their comments and assistance. At the last stage of revision, I had the good fortune of meeting Professor Sydney L. Greenblatt who read the entire typescript for me and made many valuable suggestions. I am grateful to my wife, Yeuk-lin, for stylistic improvements and for typing an early draft. The typing of the revised manuscript has been expertly done by Mrs Hilda Chan. Parts of this study have been presented as seminar papers in the University of Manchester, the University of Oxford, and the Centre of Asian Studies of the University of Hong Kong. I wish to record my thanks to the participants in these seminars for giving me the benefit of their criticisms.

Finally, a note on the transliteration of Chinese terms and the compilation of the bibliography: except for familiar place-names such as Canton, all Chinese terms are transliterated according to the Wade–Giles system of romanization. Idiosyncratic transliterations of personal names, such as Lin Yüeh-hwa, Fei Hsiao-tung, are retained in bibliographical references but replaced by standard romanizations, Lin Yao-hua, Fei Hsiao-t'ung, in the text. Chinese personal names are cited according to the Chinese convention with surnames first. The bibliography is divided into two sections, one containing works in Chinese and the other works in English. Chinese authors who have written in both languages will have their works listed separately.

Hong Kong   S. L. Wong

Abbreviations

CB	Current Background
CSPSR	The Chinese Social and Political Science Review
HCS	Hsin chien-she (New Construction)
HMTHHP	Hsia-men ta-hsüeh hsüeh pao, she-hui k'o-hsüeh pan (Journal of Amoy University, Social Sciences edition)
JMJP	Jin-min jih pao (People's Daily)
KMJP	Kuang-ming jih pao (Bright Daily)
NCNA	New China News Agency
SCMM	Selections from China Mainland Magazines
SCMP	Selections from China Mainland Press

1 The growth of sociology in pre-Liberation China

Sociology is not indigenous to China. The intellectual ancestry of the first generation of Chinese sociologists was clearly marked in their major publications. The Chinese Sociological Society, founded in 1930, inaugurated its *Journal of Sociology* with articles commemorating William Graham Sumner, while Yenching University's *Sociological World* ended with the final volume dedicated to 'The London School of Anthropology'. Respects were paid to Alfred Reginald Radcliffe-Brown in the form of a special issue of the *Sociological World*, and to Robert Ezra Park in a collection of essays.[1] But no Chinese thinker had been similarly honoured.

At first sight this might appear strange as social and inter-personal relationships had long been the dominant area of Chinese intellectual concern. The long tradition of social commentary should, it would seem, have genealogical links with the Chinese students of sociology who were well aware of this cultural heritage. In fact, they had tried to find intellectual predecessors among their past sages for their field. They scrutinized Confucius, Mencius, Lao Tzu, Hsün Tzu, etc. and found in them only fleeting resemblances to modern sociological theorists of the environmental or functional schools. They explored China's literary records and caught glimpses of an apparently rich mine of sociological ore in ancient classics such as the *I Li (Book of Etiquette and Ceremony)*, the *Li Chi (Book of Rites)*, and *Shih Ching (Book of Odes)*; in historical works such as the *Twenty Four Standard Dynastic Histories*; in encyclopaedias such as *T'ung Tien, T'ung Chih* and *T'ung K'ao*; in local documents such as provincial and prefectural gazetteers; as well as in novels and fiction (see L. K. Tao, 1925). Yet in spite of the existence of abundant insights and materials on the subject of social relationships, they failed to identify anyone who could truly be claimed as

1

their indigenous progenitor. The search usually ended in disappointment. With frustration one of them wrote (*ibid.*, pp. 52–3):

> one suffers from having too many and too few books on Chinese sociology—too many because it is almost beyond the power of one single man to peruse all the books in search of sociological data and determine their genuineness, and too few because there are few books that can be definitely called sociology.

About the social thinkers of the Chinese past, another student observed that 'the limits of their culture and civilization debarred them from the analytical method and focused their social interest on the pattern of what ought to be instead of on the scientific study of actualities. Social ethics they had, but not social science' (Wang Yü-ch'üan, 1938, p. 346). What constituted the 'limits of their culture' is a complex subject that cannot be dealt with here, but it is almost certain that one of the major limitations was the firm grip of confucian orthodoxy on Chinese thinking since the Han Dynasty. According to Joseph Needham, confucianism was characterized by an ambivalent attitude towards science (1954, vol. 2, pp. 12–16; 26–9). On the one hand, it was basically rationalistic and agnostic, thereby favouring the emergence of a scientific method. But on the other hand, its interest in man's social life was 'too humanistic' in that the value of knowledge was judged by whether it could benefit people and bring quick improvements to their livelihood. Thus the practical efficacy of social techniques was extolled while the value of developing a scientific logic was dismissed and the importance of theoretical investigation denied. Such an attitude was best exemplified by Hsün Tzu who influenced subsequent confucians in this respect. In a famous passage, he rebuked the taoists for their disinterested inquiry of natural phenomena (quoted in *ibid.*, p. 28):

> You depend on things and marvel at them;
> Why not unfold your own abilities and transform them?
>
> You meditate on what makes a thing a thing;
> Why not so order things that you do not waste them?
>
> You vainly seek into the causes of things;
> Why not appropriate and enjoy what they produce?

He asserted the confucian position in such a way that it left little room for science (quoted in *ibid.*, p. 29):

> All those things which have nothing to do with the distinction of right and wrong, truth and falsehood, good government and misrule, or with the ways of mankind, are things the knowledge

of which does not benefit men, and ignorance concerning which does no harm to men . . .. They belong to the speculations of unruly persons of a degenerate age . . ..

This mentality became the dominant intellectual outlook for centuries, buttressed by two pillars of the Chinese imperial structure—the examination system and the administrative bureaucracy. With the emphasis on the exegesis of the confucian classics, the competitive examination system impelled generations of scholars to accept a fairly uniform mode of thinking. Successful candidates were rewarded by official positions in the imperial bureaucracy. Assuming administrative duties, the attention of the scholar–officials was necessarily drawn to practical affairs and the effects of policies. The result was a reinforcement of the confucian pragmatic attitude towards knowledge. Of course there existed deviants and heretics who rejected confucian teachings. But it appears that most of them, being men of letters, were primarily interested in the 'great tradition' of ideal and normative behaviour. Few of them actually extended their curiosity and imagination to understand the mundane realities of the way of life of the common people. Some might have challenged the content of confucianism, but basically they shared a similar approach devoid of an empirical and quantitative method of study. Thus limited, they failed to engender a proto-sociology.

The nineteenth century brought a drastic change to the political fortune and intellectual climate of China. On a downturn in the dynastic cycle, the Ch'ing government was heavily jolted by the intrusion of the West. Beaten by Britain in the Opium War of 1842, China entered into what Hsün Tzu might have called 'a degenerate age'. A series of defeats at the hands of western nations ensued. At first the disturbed Chinese literati remained confident in their confucian worldview. They believed it was possible to arrive at a compromise such as the one proposed by Chang Chih-tung in his famous statement 'Chinese learning as the substance and western learning for application'. However, this hope was dashed when China lost the 1894–5 war with Japan, another Asian competitor in modernization. The psychological blow to the Chinese literati was tremendous. With their confucian faith deeply shaken, they were forced by the course of events into a process of intellectual self-doubt and self-examination. Attempts were made by scholars such as K'ang Yu-wei to find justifications for political changes through a radical re-interpretation of confucian classics. These efforts were inadequate to rescue the traditional social order as its main pillars began to collapse one after the other.

The abolition of the examination system in 1905 was quickly

3

followed by the destruction of the dynastic monarchy and its bureaucracy in the 1911 Revolution. A frontal attack was then launched on confucianism during the May Fourth Movement of 1919. As the Chinese broke loose from the confucian mode of thinking, they had open to them a chaotic but free market for thought. Chinese intellectuals began to look for alternative formulas to revitalize their country. Then followed passionate debates on the relative merits of various imported doctrines ranging from constitutional monarchism, democracy, socialism and communism, to anarchism and nihilism. The focus of these debates was on the nature of Chinese society, often as contrasted with that of other countries. The style of discussion was governed by a new scientific spirit. Scientism, or the belief in the omnipotence of science, emerged as the new faith (D. W. Y. Kwok, 1965). It became both logical and appealing to advocate the application of scientific principles to the study of social reality. A receptive mood was emerging for the introduction of sociology.

Adoption: translations

If we have to date the adoption of sociology in China, the year 1897 could be chosen as it marked the appearance of the first Chinese translation of a western sociological work—Yen Fu's rendering of two chapters of Herbert Spencer's *The Study of Sociology* for a Chinese newspaper. This event, however, did not indicate the beginning of sociological investigation on Chinese soil. That had already been carried out by several outstanding European scholars in the latter half of the eighteenth century. Notable among these scholars were J. J. M. de Groot (1854–1921), a Dutch civil servant who later became a professor in ethnography and in Chinese, and Marcel Granet (1885–1940), a French sociological sinologist. Influenced by the ideas of Spencer and Durkheim respectively, de Groot and Granet made significant contributions to the analysis of Chinese civilization especially in the field of religion.[2] Yet their important writings were largely unknown to their Chinese contemporaries for a variety of reasons. Their stays in China, mostly of short duration, not exceeding a few years, were probably too brief for them to gain access to local intellectual circles. Moreover, the Dutch and French languages they wrote in were understood by very few Chinese scholars. At any rate, their sociological approach to the study of Chinese society was so unconventional at that time that the Chinese historians and sinologists of the mainstream would not have taken notice of their works (see Yang K'un, 1942, p. 34). Therefore, the sociology they used remained a stranger to the Chinese academic scene.

4

The debut of sociology had to await a new breed of Chinese intellectuals—the student who had studied abroad. This breed might be divided into two major groups—the *Tung-yang* (East Seas) group educated in Japan; and the *Hsi-yang* (West Seas) group trained in Europe and the United States. Both groups brought back sociology at the same time, but with different labels. Among the East Seas group, Chang Ping-ling in a 1902 translation first used the Japanese term *she-hui-hsüeh* for sociology. Other translated texts which followed included Wu Chien-chang's 1903 re-rendering of a Japanese version of a minor work by F. H. Giddings and Ou-yang Chün's compilation of the lectures and writings of a Japanese scholar, Professor Tofuchi.[3] Representing the West Seas group, Yen Fu coined the term *ch'ün-hsüeh* (literally, the study of collectivities)[4] and used it in the title of his full translation of Spencer's *The Study of Sociology* published in 1903. He derived the name from classical sources, specifically in Hsün Tzu's statements such as '[Man's] strength is not equal to that of a bull; his running is not equal to that of a horse; yet the bull and the horse are used by him. How is that? Men are able to form collectivities [*ch'ün*], the former are not able to form collectivities'; and 'if men are to live, they cannot get along without forming collectivities.'[5] In choosing the name, Yen Fu was aware of the Japanese term *she-hui* which stood for society, but he thought it should be subsumed under the more general concept of *ch'ün* or collectivity: 'There are several types of human collectivities. A society is a collectivity governed by norms [*fa*].... When men aggregate and form an organization with a common purpose and aspiration, it is called a society' (Ssu-pin-sai, 1927, p. 2). But such fine conceptual distinctions and care in the choice of terms did not save *ch'ün-hsüeh* from falling into oblivion. It was *she-hui-hsüeh* that gained currency and became the standard translation. This was probably a reflection of the temper of that time. Japan, fresh from a resounding military victory over China, was regarded by many Chinese as the new model for imitation. Facilitated by relatively cheap transportation, students flocked there and returned full of Japanese loan-words. According to an estimate, of all the foreign terms that slipped into the modern Chinese vocabulary, more than half were borrowed from Japan (Li Yu-ning, 1971, pp. 108–9). At the same time, traditional scholarship was regarded by most Chinese youths as out of tune with the modern age, and *ch'ün-hsüeh* carried too many classical overtones to be fashionable.

The initial reception of the new science had its fair share of confusion and misunderstanding. Many terms and ideas, being novel, were not readily accepted and assimilated.[6] For the mixed reception, most of the translators were at least partly responsible.

5

With more enthusiasm than understanding, some of them simply converted their readings or their lecture notes into Chinese and rushed them into print.[7] Their own knowledge of the subject was often not very impressive. One translator–compiler, for instance, defined the aim of sociology as 'the attempted improvement of material life and the reform of family, state and international relationships' (quoted in Wang Yü-ch'üan, 1938, p. 351). In their eagerness to gain intellectual acceptance, they committed the familiar mistake of resorting to jargon. This led F. L. K. Hsu to comment that (1944, p. 16):

> some of our sociologists prefer long and obscure terms such as
> Euphoria and Disphoria, Synchronization and Dyachronization
> to short and simple ones. They do so not primarily to clarify
> their thought (such terms generally being used to disguise
> muddled thinking), but to augment the aura and respectability
> of their science.

But the greatest weakness of these early translators was the lack of well-considered and systematic plans. Most of their efforts were haphazard, producing raw fruits that no sooner appeared than they perished.

A small number of works endured the test of time. These were mostly done by Yen Fu, the scale of whose translation enterprise dwarfed all contemporary endeavours and placed him as the leading pioneer of Chinese social science. He selected the finest in modern western scholarship for his Chinese readers. His translation of Thomas Huxley's *Evolution and Ethics and Other Essays* appeared in 1898, followed by Adam Smith's *An Inquiry into the Nature and Causes of the Wealth of Nations* in 1902, Herbert Spencer's *The Study of Sociology* and John Stuart Mill's *On Liberty* in 1903, Edward Jenks's *A History of Politics* in 1904, and C. L. S. Montesquieu's *The Spirit of the Laws* in seven volumes between 1904 and 1909. Besides introducing these substantive writings on various social science subjects, he also called attention to the importance of scientific methods by translating the first half of John Stuart Mill's *A System of Logic* in 1905, and W. S. Jevons's *Logic the Primer* in 1909 (Wang Shih, 1976, pp. 98–106).

But the high reputation enjoyed by Yen Fu in modern Chinese intellectual history was built not on the magnitude of his labours alone. More important was the spirit infusing his translations and associated commentaries which articulated the concern of his era and shaped the outlook of his and subsequent generations. In many respects, he typified the rapid transformation undergone by the Chinese literati at a critical historical juncture. Two motifs stood out clearly in his life (1854–1921). First, he was the vanguard of the modern Chinese who had direct exposure to western culture. His initial contact with foreign learning started in China itself when he entered the newly-established Naval School of the Foochow Shipyard in 1866 for his secondary education. There he was taught English together with other novel subjects in the Chinese curricula: mathematics, physics, chemistry, geology and astronomy. After graduation, he was selected as a member of the second group of students sent by the Ch'ing government to study abroad. Between 1877 and 1879, he received his education in England at Portsmouth and the Greenwich Naval College. His knowledge of the English language and his personal experience of English society seemed to have helped him develop insights into the dominant questions preoccupying his country—what made Great Britain the exemplar of national wealth and power? And, in comparison, what were the reasons for the weakness of China? He looked beyond the material trappings of western weaponry and industry and found the answers in a set of political, economic, and social ideas, the product of a certain kind of mentality. Therefore in England, while nearly all of his fellow students received military training and served on warships, he alone stayed in the academies all the time and read widely. His reading in this period lay the foundation for his later translations. But his keen interest in western thought was paralleled by a strong attachment to traditional Chinese values which formed the second motif of his life. He straddled two cultural worlds, frequently nagged by doubts as to where he belonged. Born into a declining scholar–gentry family in Fukien, he had a traditional education under a tutor that provided him with a solid grounding in the classical and historical literature. The conventional examination path leading to an official career opened before him until his father, a village medical practitioner, died when he was fourteen. Financial difficulties forced him to enrol in the Foochow Naval School which gave economic aid to its pupils. The school was one of the emergent training institutions that prepared its graduates for the far less prestigious vocation of *yang-wu* (western affairs). Though later Yen Fu distinguished himself as the foremost expert in this field, in his personal ambitions he remained an aspiring mandarin. The lure of high officialdom was strong enough to make him smart under the still widespread disdain for 'barbarian' studies among the educated. His fame as a translator apparently failed to compensate for his regret at having strayed into a deviant track. In his middle age, he made several attempts to compete in the civil service examinations, but without any success. He died a frustrated minor official (see Wang, Shih, 1976; Schwartz, 1964).

Yen Fu made a great impact in popularizing the doctrine of social darwinism. In the writings of Huxley and Spencer, he found the attractive idea of evolution, and the illuminating image of the 'social organism' which said to him that a society must adapt and struggle in order to survive. By proposing this new perspective of China's malaise, he helped to effect a basic shift in the self-conception of the Chinese. China as the *t'ien hsia*, a cultural world unto itself, was replaced by China as a nation-state existing in a ruthless universe populated by other social organisms. From this angle, cultural values and social arrangements could no longer be seen as sacred and immutable. Constant modification was both beneficial and necessary to the transformation of the mentality of the people and to the release of the 'Promethean spirit' which Yen Fu identified as the source of western power. The comprehensive vision offered by social darwinism stunned the Chinese intellectuals in the opening epoch of the twentieth century. In 1911, a YMCA secretary in China by the name of John Stewart Burgess sampled with a questionnaire the impression of educators on what Chinese students were reading. Most of them thought that Huxley's *Evolution and Ethics* and Spencer's *The Study of Sociology* were the most influential books among students. Other popular writers they named included Darwin, Mill, Rousseau, Jenks and Kidd (D. W. Treadgold, 1973, p. 127). Some of these students under the spell of Yen Fu's translations later emerged as eminent politicians and writers of the next generation. Poring over these books was a young man called Mao Tse-tung who studied on his own for half a year in a Hunan provincial library (E. Snow, 1972, p. 169). Another teenager who came to be known as Lu Hsün devoured the Chinese version of *Evolution and Ethics* in his spare time (Lu Hsün, 1958, pp. 54–5). In his reminiscences, Hu shih recalled vividly the impact of social darwinism on the popular imagination (1931, p. 248):

> Rich men gave money for new editions [of Yen Fu's version of *Evolution and Ethics*] to be made for wider distribution...
> because it was thought that the Darwinian hypothesis, especially in its social and political application, was a welcome stimulus to a nation suffering from age-long inertia and stagnation. In the course of a few years many of the evolutionary terms and phrases became proverbial expressions in the journalistic writings of the times. Numerous persons adopted them in naming themselves and their children, thereby reminding themselves of the perils of elimination in the struggle for existence, national as well as individual.
>
> Even my own name bears witness to the great vogue of evolutionism in China. I remember distinctly the morning when I asked my second brother to suggest a literary name for me. After only a moment's reflection, he said, 'Survival of the

Fittest?' I agreed and, first using it as a *nom de plume*, finally adopted it in 1910 as my name.

Ironically, Yen Fu did not intend to translate for such a wide audience. He selected an elegant but difficult 'ancient style' of classical Chinese to convey modern western ideas. Though he was working before the movement for 'vernacular' Chinese writing had gathered momentum, the 'ancient style' was already regarded as anachronistic by his peers. Liang Ch'i-ch'ao, who otherwise admired his books, took exception to his style which Liang considered so 'concerned with profundity and elegance' that 'those who have not read many ancient books found his translations most difficult to comprehend' (quoted in Schwartz, 1964, p. 93). In his reply to Liang's criticism, Yen Fu was emphatically elitist: 'the books with which I concern myself are profound and abstruse. They are not designed to nourish schoolboys and I have no hopes of their deriving profits from them. I have translated precisely for those Chinese who do read many ancient books' (*ibid.*, p. 94). In addition to the elitism of his style, he showed an aversion to political involvement. The bold thinker of westernization, contrary to expectation, was never an active participant in political movements. Many of his Chinese biographers and critics regarded both his style and politics incongruous with the modern thought he championed. They interpreted this incongruity in terms of a retrogressive development undergone by Yen Fu from a forward-looking thinker into an obstinate reactionary. But as Schwartz has perceptively pointed out, the paradox might lie in the eyes of the beholders who too easily assumed that a westernizer was necessarily an anti-traditionalist, and a modern thinker necessarily a radical politician. At least to Yen Fu himself, his stylistic and political ideas formed a logical and consistent whole with his belief in the social theory of evolution. He stated his position very clearly in his translation of Spencer's *The Study of Sociology*. He praised this book as the most illuminating one he had ever read because he found in it affinities to the confucian classics of *Great Learning* and *Doctrine of the Mean* in two basic respects. First, Spencer argued that social life must be studied objectively with the method of science, and to Yen Fu this was compatible with the confucian idea that a scholar–official must first cultivate himself by analysing matters to gain knowledge before he was fit for the task of governing people. This apparent compatibility confirmed Yen Fu's belief that the traditional political structure of China could and should be preserved, only that the cultivation of the leading stratum of scholar–officials must be injected with a new content. An essential subject for the education of an enlightened elite in the modern age was sociology, which Yen Fu defined in a way probably too pragmatic for Spencer's liking as 'aiming to understand the causes of social stability and chaos, prosperity and decline', and 'providing precepts for good government' (Ssu-pin-sai, 1927, 'Introduction', p. 1). Second, since changes were cumulative events occurring over a long period of time, evolutionism implied a scepticism towards sudden transformations. Yen Fu found this to be in line with the 'doctrine of the mean' which abhorred excesses. In Spencer's evolutionary theory, therefore, Yen Fu discovered the ideal compromise for the conflict then raging between the reformists and the traditionalists in China. If the various partisans would just study sociology, he wrote, they would soon realize that they were fighting over a non-issue since political and religious systems, be they old or new, had their proper places in the evolutionary process. He cautioned the radical reformers in particular not to tamper too rashly with the intricate, organic structure of society. Reform was such a complicated task, he said, that 'contemplating to change A inevitably leads to the modification of B; and to modify B necessarily entails a further change in C' (quoted in Wang Shih, 1976, p. 49). Therefore, he prescribed sociology as an antidote to political radicalism (Ssu-pin-sai, 1927, 'Introduction', p. 1):

> In recent times, vast changes are taking place in our country. We are about to reap the harvest of whatever seeds our forefathers had sown. But the superficial men among us do not realize that our present predicament has extensive and deep roots in the past. Raising their arms and rushing about, they proclaim that they can avert decline and bring about rejuvenation of the country with immediate, whimsical changes. Fighting an opponent much stronger than they are, they cannot but fail. Then they wail and hail, attempting to rally the whole world for a blind charge of destruction. Destruction is easy, but the replacement may not be what they want. In view of this, why not be more cautious and take counsel in serious studies first?

With his idea of sociology, intertwined with elitism and political gradualism, Yen Fu set the tone for later Chinese sociology, particularly of the Anglo-American variety.

During this period, the imported sociology was more read than taught. It was first mentioned as an academic subject in Liang Ch'i-ch'ao's 1901 biography of his teacher, K'ang Yu-wei. K'ang had established a private academy in Kwangtung in 1891 to tutor his disciples, and Liang listed *ch'ün-hsüeh* as a subject in the academy's curriculum (Liang, 1976, p. 13). But the curriculum could have been only an idealized one drawn up by Liang himself. If the subject had actually been taught, then this would mark the beginning of sociological instruction in China. In the institutes of higher learning established by the Ch'ing government, sociology first appeared in the 1906 prospectus of the National Political College of Peking as one of the topics in the first-year course on political studies. Four years later, the curriculum of the National University of Peking included a course in sociology as a subject for the junior class throughout the year (Sun Pen-wen, 1931, pp. 5–6; 1949, p. 248). But these were only requirements recorded in the regulations of these institutions. It is not certain whether these courses were really offered. If they had been, we know nothing about who taught them or what textbooks were used.

Infancy: American missionary sociology

In the next two decades (1910–30), the study of sociology developed such distinct foreign and religious features that it might be named American missionary sociology. It was reared almost exclusively in the Christian colleges established by missionary bodies from the USA. Shanghai College was the first to have it taught in 1913 by several American professors from Brown University including J. A. Dealey, D. H. Kulp II, and H. S. Bucklin (Sun Pen-wen, 1949, p. 248). Generally, the curricula of the Christian colleges in China were by no means heavily tilted towards the social sciences. In 1925–6, they had devoted only 14 per cent of their total instruction to social science subjects, and they provided less teaching in economics and politics than both the leading non-Christian universities in China and the small colleges in the USA (J. G. Lutz, 1971, p. 189). But they showed particular favour towards sociology.

TABLE 1.1   *The teaching of sociology in ten Christian colleges in China, 1925*

College	No. of courses offered	No. of semester credits offered
Shanghai College	6	18
St John's University	2	—
Nanking University	8	40
Fukien Christian University	2	9
Hangchow Christian College	2	9
Shantung Christian University	11	26
Yale in China	5	21
Ginling College	3	12
Canton Christian College	6	18
Yenching University	31	102

Source: derived from L. S. Hsu (1927b, p. 374).

In 1925, J. S. Burgess surveyed the teaching of sociology in the ten leading Christian colleges for the China Association of Christian Higher Education, and found that all of them offered courses on the subject with Yenching University giving as many as thirty-one courses (see Table 1.1). Most of the colleges said that they would like to provide more courses, but they had difficulty in recruiting suitable staff. This attitude contrasted sharply with the apparent lack of interest among the government universities, none of which except the National Institute of Political Science at Woosung had a separate department of sociology (L. S. Hsu, 1927b, pp. 373–5).

Virtually all the sociology teachers in the colleges were Americans. A sample of these people showed that many of them had had a religious upbringing. In Hangchow University, it was a Rev. Frank D. Scott who taught sociology. He was a graduate of Waynesburg College, Auburn Theological Seminary (C. B. Day, 1955, p. 32). The Lingnan University had western teachers provided by the American Maryknoll Mission, and among them was Father George N. Putnam who taught sociology (C. H. Corbett, 1963, p. 150). In Soochow University, Rev. Wesley M. Smith was in charge of sociology courses from 1910 to 1917. He was succeeded by T. C. Chao, who 'co-operated effectively with Z. T. Kaung, then pastor of St John's Church in a very remarkable "Religious Emphasis Week".' Then came M. O. Williams Jr, a graduate of the School of Religion, Vanderbiet University, who was 'Professor of Religion and Sociology and Director of Religious Activities for ten years' (W. B. Nance, 1956, pp. 116–17). Prominent among these missionary sociologists was John Stewart Burgess (1883–1949). His father was an elder in the Presbyterian Church in New York and an active member of the YMCA. Burgess, after graduation from Princeton University in 1905, studied briefly at Oberlin and Union Theological Seminaries. After a two-year stay in Japan where he taught English and worked for the YMCA in Kyoto, he went to Columbia University for his graduate training in sociology (MA, 1909; PhD, 1928). He returned to East Asia in 1909, this time to Peking under the sponsorship of Princeton students and alumni as a YMCA secretary. There he began teaching sociology and Christian ethics in the School of Theology at Yenching University. He then set up the department of sociology and helped to build it into one of the foremost centres in the country (P. West, 1976, pp. 32–4).

Burgess was also the pioneer of the social survey method which became the most favoured technique employed by the western sociologists in China. They modelled their work on the examples set by the French sociologist, Le Play, and the British investigators, Charles Booth and F. S. Rowntree. The earliest survey appeared in 1914–15. It was a small-scale statistical study of 302 rickshaw pullers carried out by the Society for Social Improvement in Peking, a Christian organization (Wang Yü-ch'üan, 1938, p. 360). This was followed in 1917 by an analysis of the household expenditures of 195 peasant families near Peking, under the direction of C. G. Dittmer who was teaching at Tsinghua University (H. C. Yen, 1936, p. 65). The majority of these early surveys were concerned with urban poverty and other social pathologies caused by industrialization in the large coastal cities. Household budget survey was the favourite means of assessing the standard of living of various social groups. From 1917 to 1930, no fewer than eighty studies using this technique were conducted (*ibid.*, pp. 62–9). One of the most important large-scale social surveys of this period was undertaken jointly by Sydney D. Gamble and John Stewart Burgess between 1918 and 1919 on the city of Peking. It dealt with every conceivable aspect of social life, ranging from population, government, health, education, commerce, entertainment, prostitution, poverty, prison conditions, and Christian activities. The report was published in the United States in 1921 as *Peking: A Social Survey*, and the authors characteristically dedicated their book to 'The Missionaries whose work has made this study possible'.

Why was sociology nourished by the American missionaries but neglected by the Chinese government? One of the most important factors was the cultural extra-territoriality enjoyed by the missionaries in China during the first quarter of the twentieth century. The colleges they established were beyond the jurisdiction of the Chinese educational authorities, as illustrated by the Shanghai Baptist College (later known as the University of Shanghai) which was incorporated under the laws of Virginia rather than those of China (Lutz, 1971, p. 111). They were therefore able to design the curricula as they saw fit. Their interest in sociology was a natural outgrowth of their evangelistic activities. Since Chinese traditional values and social arrangements were the major obstacles to their attempt to convert the Chinese to Christianity, they had no hesitation in adopting the sociological perspective to dissect Chinese culture 'objectively' in order to loosen its hold on the population. At a more practical level, the Christian communities in China had long been engaged in the provision of medical services, education and recreational facilities. By this time, they had reached the point where they had to explore 'new ways to apply their principles to the social life of the people' (D. W. Edwards, 1959, p. 167). Sociological activities offered just such a field for them to expand their work. The growth of the department of sociology at Yenching University was an example. In the 1910s, Princeton University sent out annually two or three graduates for a two-year term of service with the YMCA in Peking. But as the YMCA developed a Chinese staff and a

13

Chinese constituency, these American staff members were not needed and a new outlet for them was sought. The solution was found in strengthening the teaching and research work that Burgess had begun in Peking. Princeton offered to supply two scholars annually to teach in the department of sociology at Yenching University provided Yenching would appoint two full-time staff of their own (Edwards, 1959, pp. 168–9). The social environment of the treaty ports in which most of the missionaries found themselves was also fertile for sociological investigations. Social changes were so disruptive and social problems so glaring in the coastal cities that a historian of the Soochow University was led to comment that conditions in Shanghai were particularly favourable to the expansion of the university's department of sociology (Nance, 1956, p. 109). The Christian sentiment of sympathy towards the weak and the downtrodden was quickly awakened. Social investigations were carried out with the aim of reform and amelioration. This resulted in a close association between survey research and social work, as expressed by Burgess in his famous study of the guilds of Peking (1928, p. 7):

> Interest in research inevitably follows participation in social
> work in China. The intricacies and difficulties of the adjustments
> made imperative by contemporary changes in the social
> structure of that ancient nation become increasingly clear to
> those who have a practical part in facilitating such adjustments,
> and constitute a challenge to gain a clarifying knowledge of the
> underlying social, economic, and political situation.

Thus the missionary interest in sociology was decidedly practical and not theoretical, an attitude not unlike the confucian emphasis on the use of knowledge. The President of Soochow University, reporting the teaching of sociology to the Trustees, gave the clearest statement of such a conception (Nance, 1956, p. 110):

> Our prime emphasis is not so much on social theories as on
> the training of social workers. Here, of course, the theoretical
> and the practical cannot be separated. But our aim is not so
> much to train theorists who can write essays on social
> problems, but practical workers who will plan and direct
> programs of social service . . .. What we are aiming at is a school
> for the training of Christian social workers, somewhat like the
> New York School of Social Work, where several of our
> teachers received their training.

The final factor that made American missionary sociology possible was the availability of strong financial support. Besides the resources of the missionary bodies themselves, funds were forthcoming from several sources. A number of American universities were interested in co-operation with their Chinese counterparts. As already mentioned, Princeton was instrumental in founding the sociology department at Yenching. As early as 1906, it established Princeton-in-Peking, a centre for its graduates to conduct social service and to study urban social conditions. The centre transferred its base to Yenching University in 1923, leading to the formation of the Princeton–Yenching Foundation in the 1930s which fostered a vigorous research programme in political science and sociology (Lutz, 1971, pp. 312–13). Harvard University initiated another well-known effort in 1925 by setting up the Harvard–Yenching Institute with funds derived mainly from the estate of Charles M. Hall, a Harvard alumnus. It gave support to research, instruction and publication in the field of Chinese culture (*ibid.,* p. 314). As for funding by individuals, the most influential was the Rockefeller Foundation. Although its early interest was mainly in medical and scientific education in China, it also provided grants to the social sciences from the Laura Spelman Rockefeller Memorial Fund (*ibid.*, p. 312). Later in the 1930s it shifted its focus and strengthened its support for social research and reform activities in rural China. Governmental funds were apportioned by the China Foundation for the Promotion of Education and Culture. The money came from the Boxer Indemnity Funds[8] paid by the Chinese government to the USA. The USA returned the first portion of the Indemnity to China to establish the Tsinghua College to prepare Chinese students for further studies in the USA. The College later grew into the Tsinghua University with a prestigious department in sociology. In 1924, the USA government agreed to return the second portion of the Indemnity in twenty annual instalments to create the China Foundation administered by Chinese and American trustees. This Foundation, together with donations from the Institute of Social and Religious Research of New York, financed from 1926 onwards an Institute of Social Research in Peking. It produced studies mostly on the standards of living and household budgets[9] (W. W. Yen, 1928, pp. 426–9; W. Y. Chyne, 1936, p. 133). But, among these funding agencies, the most important one for sociology during the first half of this century was the Institute of Pacific Relations (IPR). Set up in Hawaii in 1925 by a number of people associated with the YMCA movement there, its aim was to bring together leaders of different countries involved in the Pacific region for regular discussions and to 'study the condition of the Pacific peoples with a view to the improvement of their mutual relations'. The IPR began with six national councils including the United States, Canada, Australia, New Zealand, China, and Japan, and each council was to be

15

financially self-supporting. But from the start, the American council was the best funded and exerted the greatest influence over the international IPR. The research committee of the IPR, under the leadership of Edward C. Carter and Owen Lattimore, encouraged ventures in the then underdeveloped field of Asian research. It gave a great push to sociological research in China and sponsored a large number of publications (see J. N. Thomas, 1974, pp. 3–35).

This type of imported missionary sociology had obvious short-comings. In the Christian colleges, American textbooks were used to teach the subject with little modification to suit Chinese con-ditions. Teachers were entrusted with an impossible task. The linguistic hurdle of reading in English, which the Chinese students had to overcome, was difficult enough for Leonard S. Hsu, once head of Yenching's department of sociology, to observe that 'over one-half of the class read an American text, not as a treatise in sociology, but as a book in English literature and composition' (1927a, p. 14). Worse still, they had to lead their students through the maze of foreign examples and experiences on which the American textbooks were based. Fei Hsiao-t'ung, who was educated in Yenching and Tsinghua Universities, recalled that 'when we were in college..., we learned from books about Chicago gangs and Russian immigrants in America, but we knew very little or nothing about the Chinese gentry in the town and the peasants in the village, because these were not in books' (1945a, p. viii). An anecdote in the history of the Lingnan University portrayed vividly how the American way of life was transplanted to China (Corbett, 1963, pp. 56–7):

> Athletic events were further enlivened by a brass brand [*sic*], organized in 1916 by Graybill and using instruments imported from America. Instruction was given by Ray E. Baber. His main interest was sociology, but he had played a band in his student days and succeeded in training the twenty members of the Lingnan band so that in a few months they could play in public looking very fine in their uniforms.

Some of the American sociologists in the Christian colleges were conscious of this weakness, and they sought to redress the balance by conducting research on Chinese social life. But the social surveys they championed came under heavy attack. The studies, according to the critics, were maimed by the lack of a systematic, theoretical framework. The picture of reality they produced tended to be static and disjointed. And as these surveys were mostly used as tools in the advocacy of reforms, they were subject to the further charge that their conclusions often preceded their investigations and that 'the purpose of social surveys was for propaganda' rather than for the discovery of scientific explanations of social phenomena (Chao Ch'eng-hsin, 1936, p. 162). But these shortcomings did not prevent this American missionary variety from stimulating the growth of Chinese sociology. Though it might not have directly aroused interest in sociology among Chinese students, it had to a considerable extent satisfied and encouraged their enthusiasm for the social sciences. Concerned with the plight of China, many of the patriotic students took up studies in the social sciences in order to prepare themselves for the day when they would guide their country. Their first contact with sociology almost invariably took place in the Christian colleges. As for research, the surveys were instrumental in promoting and popularizing empirical field studies. According to one estimate, between 1927 and 1935, surveys were so much in vogue that some 9,000 projects were completed in various parts of China, averaging about 1,000 surveys a year (*ibid.*, p. 157). In the process, a large amount of social information was collected and several valuable studies were made, such as John Lossing Buck's statistical reports on agricultural land utilization (1937) and Li Ching-han's comprehensive analysis of Ting Hsien (1933). The value of surveys was gradually accepted by Chinese officials, and government ministries began to incorporate social investigations as part of their functions. In 1930, following the path-breaking works of the Christian colleges, the Ministry of Commerce and Industry undertook surveys on the family budgets of workers in thirty-two cities (H. C. Yen, 1936, pp. 67–9).

During this period, seeds of change were already sprouting that were to give Chinese sociology a more native appearance as well as a more combative temperament. Chinese students began to go abroad for specialized training in sociology. Among the Chinese students in the USA of whom we have more detailed information, sociology was first taken up as a major subject by seven students in 1914, by nineteen in 1920–1 and by twenty-seven by 1927. In proportion, their percentage in the entire expatriate Chinese student population was small, fluctuating between 0.7 per cent and 2.2 per cent before 1930 (Y. C. Wang, 1966, p. 510). But the persevering ones among them returned to staff sociology departments in Chinese universities. T'ao Lü-kung (1887–1960), alias T'ao Meng-ho, was a representative case. He studied in Japan at Tokyo Normal College before going to England. As students in the London School of Economics, he and Y. K. Leong studied sociology under L. T. Hobhouse and E. A. Westermarck and co-authored the first book-length sociological analysis of Chinese society, *Village and Town Life in China* (1915). Back in China, T'ao taught sociology first at Peking Normal College, then at National Peking University

17

as professor and dean from 1914 to 1927. When the Institute of Social Research was opened in Peking, he became its director. He remained head after the Institute was amalgamated with the Institute of Social Sciences of the Academia Sinica in 1934. He pioneered studies on the Chinese family and standards of living (Union Research Service, Biographical Service, 1957, no. 149). Another conspicuous sociologist of this period was Hsu Te-heng, a famous student leader in the May Fourth Movement. A graduate in philosophy of the University of Peking, he studied sociology and economics at the universities of Paris and London. While in France, he was attracted by Durkheim's writings and translated *The Rules of Sociological Method* into Chinese (1925). He came back to China in the mid-1920s and taught at universities in Canton, Shanghai and Peking (see Klein and Clark, 1971, pp. 361–72; T. T. Chow, 1960, p. 95). Abandoning Durkheim for Marx, he later translated *The Poverty of Philosophy* and joined the radical intelligentsia then in formation. Hsu was an exception among the marxist intellectuals in that most of them were educated in Japan and few were specialists in sociology. A more typical personality among the marxist group was Li Ta (1890–1966). After a period of schooling in Hunan and Peking, Li obtained a scholarship in 1909 to study mining and metallurgy at Imperial University in Tokyo. He returned to China in 1920 and participated in organizing the Chinese Communist Party and worked as a journalist in Shanghai. After several years, he gave up journalism for sociological research and published a popular introduction to sociology. At one time, he was head of the sociology department of Chinan University at Shanghai, but he also taught in departments of law, economics and politics (Union Research Institute, 1970, pp. 398–9). This group of radical intellectuals translated many marxist classics in the 1920s, including Marx's *Capital, Wage-labour and Capital, Critique of Political Economy,* and *Eighteenth Brumaire;* Lenin's *The State and Revolution, Development of Capitalism in Russia, Peasants and Revolution, Historical Materialism and Empiric Criticism, The Proletarian Revolution and the Renegade Kautsky,* and *Revolution of 1917;* Engels's *Anti-Düring, Feuerbach, Revolution and Counterrevolution, Peasant War in Germany,* and *Origin of the Family, Private Property and the State;* and Bukharin's *Historical Materialism* (Wang Yü-ch'üan, 1938, pp. 356–7). Marxist sociology was emerging as a competing force, and its presence was beginning to be felt in the universities. Western-trained sociologists quickly dissociated themselves from this current, expressing abhorrence at the confusion of sociology with socialism. They complained about the practice of teaching 'socialism and radical economic principles' in the introductory courses of sociology in a few universities (L. S. Hsu, 1927b, p. 376).

TABLE 1.2   *Sociology in Chinese universities, 1934*

Type of university	No. of institutions	No. with sociology departments	No. of students majoring in sociology
National	13	4	239
Provincial	8	1	4
Private	20	12	240
Total	41	17	483

Source: Chiao-yü-pu t'ung-chi-shih (Statistical unit, Ministry of Education), 1936, pp. 48–9; 86–7.

Coming of age: towards sinification

If 1898 were taken as the year of adoption, then we might regard 1930 as marking the initiation of Chinese sociology which began to enter two decades of vigorous young adulthood. The sign of growing maturity was shown in the shift from imitation to sinification, that is, the development of an indigenous Chinese appearance and relevance, as well as a yearning for an independent intellectual existence.

In the universities, the quantitative expansion of teaching in sociology gathered momentum after 1930. From Table 1.2, we can see that by 1934, seventeen institutes of higher education had departments of sociology. It was a very popular subject and attracted 7 per cent of the entire university student population, a percentage only next to those of Chinese literature, western literature, history, and education (Chiao-yü-pu t'ung-chi-shih, 1936, pp. 86–7). The government-sponsored universities still lagged behind the private colleges in building separate departments for sociology. But the few which they had established were obviously much larger than those of private colleges since the total number of students enrolled in both types was about the same. There was another difference between the two in the way they classified sociology. In the national and provincial universities, sociology was regarded as a subject in the humanities. The departments were therefore put into the faculties of arts. During the early 1930s, in an attempt to end the extraterritoriality enjoyed by the Christian colleges, the Chinese government insisted that these colleges should follow suit by transferring sociology from the faculties of social sciences into arts. This administrative measure aroused considerable controversy and protest. Some colleges such as Yenching resisted passively by deferring the required reorganization.

In 1938, the Chinese government revised its position and

19

TABLE 1.3   *Sociology in Chinese universities, 1948*

Type of university	No. of institutions	No. with sociology department	No. with no department but offered courses	No. of teachers*
National and provincial	31	7	6	47
Private	18†	14	1	72
Total	49	21	7	119

*Including professors, assistant professors and lecturers.
†Among these, thirteen were Protestant colleges and three Roman Catholic colleges.
Sources: Chang Ch'i-yün, 1954; *She-hui-hsüeh hsün,* vol. 8, 1948, pp. 6–8; Lutz, 1971, pp. 531–4.

acknowledged sociology as part of the social sciences together with political science, economics and law (Sun Pen-wen, 1972, p. 50). By the end of this period, the number of universities offering instruction in sociology had increased to twenty-eight, staffed by 119 professors, assistant professors and lecturers (Table 1.3).

The private colleges continued to have a larger share in this area of academic endeavour, but a great change had occurred in the origin of the teachers. Among the 119 sociologists in the universities, all but five were Chinese. Permanent western teachers were replaced by visiting scholars who came to China to lecture and conduct research for relatively brief periods. Among these scholars were Eliot Smith, C. G. Seligman, Robert Ezra Park, Richard Henry Tawney, Wilhelm Schmidt, Alfred Reginald Radcliffe-Brown, Karl Wittfogel, Leslie White, B. W. Aginsky, and Reo Fortune. If it had not been for the Sino-Japanese War, Bronislaw K. Malinowski, Raymond Firth, and Edward Sapir would also have made their promised trips (F. L. K. Hsu, 1944, p. 13; M. H. Fried, 1958, p. 998).

As the number of sociologists began to grow, efforts were made to form professional associations. A short-lived attempt was launched in 1922, but not until 1928 did a group of professors in Shanghai and Nanking succeed in setting up a regional association called the Southeast Sociological Society. At the same time, the sociologists in Peking, represented by Leonard S. Hsu of Yenching University, proposed to organize a national association on the basis of the Southeast Sociological Society. This came into being in 1930 as the Chinese Sociological Society. In the next twenty years, nine annual meetings were held (Table 1.4) and six volumes of its

TABLE 1.4 *Annual meetings of the Chinese Sociological Society*

Meeting	Year	Place	Topic
1st	1930	Shanghai	Population problems of China
2nd	1932	Peking	Sociology of the family
3rd	1933	Nanking	(No information)
4th	1934	Peking	(No information)
5th	1935	Nanking	Social planning
6th	1937	Shanghai	Research reports
7th	1943	Chungking, Kunming and Chengtu	Social construction after the war
8th	1947	Nanking, Peking Canton and Chengtu	(No information)
9th	1948	Nanking, Peking Canton and Chengtu	Sociology in the past twenty years

official journal, *She-hui-hsüeh k'an (The Journal of Sociology)* were published.

The central figure of the Chinese Sociological Society was Sun Pen-wen. He was elected chairman on several occasions and also served as editor of the journal. Born in 1892 in Wu Kiang, Kiangsu, Sun graduated from the National University of Peking in 1918 after taking courses in sociology taught by Kang Pao-chung, 'the first native professor to teach sociology in Chinese universities' (Sun Pen-wen, 1949, p. 248). He then went to the USA and studied at the universities of Illinois, Columbia, and New York. He obtained his doctorate in sociology from New York University in 1925. A disciple of William F. Ogburn and William Isaac Thomas, he returned to China as an advocate of the 'American cultural school'. Appointed professor at Shanghai's Futan University in 1926, he was one of the founders of the Southeast Sociological Society. Moving to the National Central University in 1928 where he taught for the next twenty years, he became the most influential popularizer of sociology. Reviewing in 1948 the course traversed by the Chinese Sociological Society, he summed up its aim as 'furthering the development of Chinese sociology so that it can make contributions to the nation and secure a position in international academic circles' (1948, p. 2). The accomplishments of the Society included the drafting of a standard curriculum for sociology in the universities, the compilation of a comprehensive list of Chinese translations of sociological terms which was published by the Ministry of Education, and negotiating with the Chinese government over the expansion of sociology teaching.

21

Searching for an identity, the Chinese sociologists were dissatisfied with the western sociological transplants. They declared intellectual independence by insisting that sociological theories must be tested and modified in relation to Chinese reality. This new concern was voiced by social investigators of different theoretical persuasions. One advocate was Wu Wen-tsao, an able leader of the famous sociology department at Yenching. Born in 1901 in Kiangsu, Wu obtained his doctorate from Columbia University in 1928. Appointed around 1933 to head Yenching's department of sociology, he introduced the functional approach into China and steered the research efforts of the department away from social surveys and towards community studies. He initiated a series of sociological monographs in 1940 with the express purpose of sinification (*chung-kuo hua*). He believed that the only way for sociology to take root in China was to start field investigations guided by scientific hypotheses, so that 'theories will be in line with the facts, and the facts will in turn stimulate theory' (Ma-ling-no-ssu-chi, 1944, p. 1). A similar view was echoed in the works of Mao Tse-tung. Chiding the dogmatic theorists of his party and urging them to reform their method of study in 1941, Mao contrasted two opposite attitudes towards the relationship between marxist–leninist theory and Chinese reality (1965, pp. 20–2):

First, there is the subjective attitude.... With this attitude, a person studies Marxist–Leninist theory in the abstract and without any aim. He goes to Marx, Engels, Lenin and Stalin not to seek the stand, viewpoint and method with which to solve the theoretical and tactical problems of the Chinese revolution but to study theory purely for theory's sake.... Secondly, there is the Marxist-Leninist attitude. With this attitude, a person applies the theory and method of Marxism–Leninism to the systematic and thorough investigation and study of the environment.... It is not enough for him to know ancient Greece, he must know China; he must know the revolutionary history not only of foreign countries but also of China, not only the China of today but also the China of yesterday and of the day before yesterday.... Such an attitude is one of shooting the arrow at the target. The 'target' is the Chinese revolution, the 'arrow' is Marxism–Leninism.... To take such an attitude is to seek the truth from facts.

The sinification of sociology logically involved direct investigations and field work, and it was the flourish of original, empirical studies that characterized this period of maturation. Together with the stress on field work was an acceptance of the idea of the conscious direction of social change. There was a prevalent belief in the value of 'applied sociology', of using sociological knowledge for the formulation of social policy. This practical, problem-solving orientation was similar to that of the previous phase of missionary sociology except that the motivation was different. The sentiment of Christian charity and reformism was superseded by the feeling of patriotism, a sense of urgency and a feeling of responsibility in providing some cure for the deepening crisis engulfing China. Many sociologists forsook the so-called 'ivory tower' and rushed into the battlefield of 'national salvation'. Li An-che was an example. After graduation from Yenching, he took the conventional academic path. In an attempt to lay the intellectual foundation for a Chinese sociology, he wrote a sociological analysis of the Chinese classics, *I Li* and *Li Chi* (1931). He then went to the University of California around 1935. After preparing himself at the department of anthropology there, he did field work at Zuni in western New Mexico and wrote up his findings at the department of anthropology at Yale. His aim was to acquaint himself with a different culture so that he might understand his own better, and to learn the field technique of anthropology. But once back in China teaching at his *alma mater*, the national calamity he witnessed was such that he turned his back on 'academic' research which he condemned as worse than irrelevant (1938, p. 124):

> social scientists, if they are to prove themselves of any use at all at such a time must be dynamically oriented instead of being just 'academic'. To remain academic means death in such a crisis, but to be dynamically oriented means rebirth.

He justified the necessity for field research with the argument that 'first-hand knowledge will give rise to creative theories as well as to constructive social engineering' (*ibid.*, p. 125). The conviction of the utility of sociology was widely shared. According to a survey of books on sociology printed by the major Chinese publishers in 1930, about 67 per cent were about social problems and social policies. Only 13 per cent were 'pure sociology' and social thought (Sun Pen-wen, 1931, pp. 8–9). Among the better-known sociologists, performing services for the government became quite a common practice. Sun Pen-wen had been Minister of Education between 1930 and 1932. Leonard S. Hsu was given an extended leave of absence from Yenching in 1933. For five years he took up a variety of posts: member of the Rural Rehabilitation Commission of the Executive Yüan; adviser to the Ministry of Industry, and chairman of its Commission on Silver Values and Commodity Prices; member of two Commissions of the National Economic Council; member of the Treaty Commission of the Ministry of Foreign Affairs; member of the Economic Committee of the League of Nations; co-editor of the

Economic Year Book published by the government. Another member of staff from Yenching, H. C. Chang, became the director of the Department of Social Welfare of the Ministry of Social Welfare in Chungking, and later joined the United Nations' Department of Social Affairs (Edwards, 1959, pp. 291–2).

Though unified in the general direction towards sinification with an emphasis on original studies and social engineering, the activities of the Chinese sociologists took a diversified course with different methodologies. Besides the continually blooming social surveys which have already been discussed, four major types of research can be distinguished—general and translated works, historical sociology, community studies and macro-sociology. Underlying the diversity, two broad ideological currents were discernible, namely the marxist perspective advocating the thorough remoulding of society, and the pragmatic, liberal orientation aiming at gradual improvements. Before probing into the cleavage between these two orientations, let us first review the four types of studies in turn.

During this phase of sinification, the introduction of western sociological scholarship went on unabated. Many important Anglo-American monographs were promptly translated, including William Ogburn's *Social Change* (1936), Bronislaw Malinowski's *What is Culture* (1944), Raymond Firth's *Human Types* (1944), and Karl Mannheim's *Sociology of Knowledge* (1944). Sun Pen-wen remembered the principal scholars who had been known in China through translations (1949, pp. 247–8):

> the socio-psychological school is represented by the works of Giddings, Le Bon, Ellwood, MacDougall, Young, and Allport; the cultural school by those of Ogburn, Malinowski, Wissler, Radcliffe-Brown, and Firth; the anthropological school by Letourneau, Morgan, Lowie, Westermarck; the systematic school by Tönnies, Durkheim, Bouglé, Binder, Ginsberg, and Déat; the evolutional school by Spencer, Morgan, Letourneau, Müller-Lyer, Ellwood, and Haynes; the school of social thought by Bogardus, Sorokin, Cole, Barnes, Laidler, and Abel; the philosophical school by Mackenzie, Urwick, and Hobhouse; and the school of social pathology or social problems by Henry George, Lombroso, Binder, Fairchild, Blackmar, Gillin, and Thomson.

Sun himself was undoubtedly the most systematic and popular Chinese writer of general introductions to sociology. The various schools he listed above were treated in his *History of the Development of Contemporary Sociology* (1947) which showed him to be abreast of new trends of the West. His *She-hui-hsüeh yüan-li (Principles of*

24

Sociology) (1935) was adopted as the standard university textbook and went through eleven printings before 1949.

The second type, historical sociology, was mainly produced during a lengthy intellectual controversy over the nature of China's social history (*Chung-kuo she-hui shih lun-cheng*). This controversy, raging between 1928 and 1937, generated many analyses and studies on the character of Chinese society in terms of the marxist classification of historical stages. It originated in leftist intellectual circles after a serious setback to the Chinese communist movement in 1927 when a massacre of communists by the Nationalist government occurred, followed by ruthless suppression of radical thought. As a result of repressive measures, 'some scholars abandoned "dangerous thought"; others, connected with political and educational institutions, anxiously turned the attention of their students away from current problems, back to the past' (Wang Yü-ch'üan, 1938, p. 360). There was also a feeling among the marxist theoreticians that the setback they suffered was due to an insufficient understanding of Chinese society. Therefore they began to study the past of China in order to arrive at a correct theory to guide future political action. This concern was succinctly expressed by Wang Li-hsi, editor of a large collection of essays pertaining to the debate (quoted in Kwok, 1965, pp. 163–4, original emphases):

> The present is the time when blind and undirected revolutions have reached a blind alley, the time when the momentum of revolution can no longer be suppressed and therefore there is dire need of *correct* revolutionary theories to guide *correct* revolutions onto their new path. In the absence of revolutionary theory, there is no revolutionary action to speak of. . . .
>
> In order to search for the correct future revolution, we must first decide on the solution to a foremost problem: 'Upon what stage has Chinese society already embarked?'.

The polemics revolved around two major issues. The first concerned the problematic areas in the application of marxist theory to the Chinese case. What was the Asian mode of production, and had China passed through such a stage? Had there been a period of slave society in China, and was Chinese slave society similar to those of the Greek and Roman Empires? What were the characteristics of feudalism in China, and how did it emerge and disintegrate? (Ho Kang-ch'ih, 1937, p. 2). The second focus was on the nature of contemporary China, whether it was feudalistic or capitalistic, and how it was altered by the impact of western imperialism. The arguments surrounding this question prepared the ground for the later official Communist diagnosis that modern China was semi-feudal and semi-colonial. Participants in this debate were mostly

Chinese marxists, though writers of no clear political affiliations also took part (Schwartz, 1954, p. 145). The debaters' main forum was the journal *Tu-she tsa-chih (Reader's Miscellany)*,[10] and they were divided into two camps with Kuo Mo-jo and T'ao Hsi-sheng as their spokesman. Born in 1891, Kuo Mo-jo was a versatile literary writer who received a medical education in Japan. He translated the book *Social Organization and Social Revolution* by the Japanese marxist Kawakami Hajime in 1924, and in the same year announced his conversion to marxism–leninism. The Nationalist purge of communists in 1927 drove him from Shanghai to Japan where he remained for ten years, devoting himself to the study of ancient Chinese history. The first scholar to use oracle bones and ancient bronzes imaginatively as documents of Chinese antiquity, he published a controversial but highly-praised book called *Studies on Ancient Chinese Society* (1929). He divided Chinese history into the following periods: (1) primitive-communal, pre-Chou times; (2) slave society, Western Chou; (3) feudal, Eastern Chou and onwards; (4) capitalistic, the last hundred years. He noted the occurrence of three major social revolutions in Chinese history which established slavery, feudalism, and capitalism respectively by changing modes of production (Kwok, 1965, p. 167). The other prominent figure in the debate, T'ao Hsi-sheng, was born in 1899 and had a degree in law from the National University of Peking. He was a supporter and theoretician of the Kuomintang, well-versed in the literature of historical materialism. Important among his prolific writings were *Historical Analysis of Chinese Society* (1929) and *History of Chinese Feudal Society* (1930). He often revised his views and, in 1932, his conception of the historical development of Chinese society was that Western Chou belonged to the last tribal age; the period from the Warring States to Later Han was an economic stage based on slavery, a practice found in both the cities and the countryside; from the Three Kingdoms to the T'ang Dynasty was a fully-developed feudal and manorial epoch. During the Sung Dynasty, feudalism was said to be in dissolution, giving way to the urban handicraft economy of the cities, which T'ao termed pre-capitalistic. After 1840, China saw a period of semi-colonialism turning into industrial capitalism (Kwok, 1965, p. 166).

From the works of Kuo and T'ao, it was obvious that despite differences in the way they divided Chinese history, they shared common marxist premises as far as historical development of society was concerned. It was noteworthy that the debate was dominated by Chinese students educated in the Soviet Union and Japan (Cheng Hsüeh-chia, 1965, pp. 100–1), and most of them had not specialized in sociology. The conspicuous absence of Anglo-American-trained sociologists in the controversy was perhaps a reflection of their immunity to the marxist perspective as well as their intoxication with the present to the neglect of the past.

As it was concerned with the nature of the entirety of Chinese society in past ages, this form of historical sociology made no use of empirical field investigations. A different style of research, community studies, was promoted by a nucleus of western-educated sociologists. This type of study shared with the social surveys the common emphasis on first-hand observation of social reality, but it differed from the latter in that it abandoned the attempt at wide coverage and the use of questionnaires for data collection. The students of community had a 'self-conscious concern with the integrated institutionalized pattern within a clearly specified locality' (Fried, 1954, p. 17). The emphasis was on how various parts of a community were related rather than on the nature and content of any individual part. Under the rubric of community studies, several subjects conventionally regarded as separate in the West were amalgamated. We only have to call to witness Wu Wen-tsao, the key figure in Chinese community studies. The scope of community studies or 'comparative sociology', according to Wu, included rural and urban sociology, social and cultural anthropology, ethnography and ethnology (Ma-ling-no-ssu-chi, 1944, p. 2).

Ethnology, the study of alien cultures with anthropological techniques, had the non-Han peoples as its subject of study in China. Many of the later famous Chinese sociologists, such as Francis L. K. Hsu, Lin Yao-hua, Fei Hsiao-t'ung, Li An-che, and T'ien Ju-k'ang, had their intellectual initiation in the study of minority communities. Among the most influential personalities in this branch of studies was Serge M. Shirokogoroff (1887–1939). Born in the city of Suzdal, Russia, Shirokogoroff studied first at the University of Paris and the Ecole d'Anthropologie (1906–19), then in the Department of Science of the University of St Petersburg (1910–15). After two archaeological expeditions to northern Russia and the Caucasus, he did ethnographical and linguistic research among the peoples of Transbaikalia, the Jablonoi region, and Manchuria. In 1917, he was elected Anthropologist of the Russian Imperial Academy of Sciences. In October of the same year, he left Russia for China where he continued his anthropological investigations in Fukien, Kwangtung, Yunnan, Indo-China and Peking. He became famous for his studies on the social organization of the Manchus and the Tungus. He spent his last twenty years teaching at the National Tsinghua University and later at the Catholic University of Peking.[11] As a teacher, he exerted considerable influence on young, bright scholars such as Fei Hsiao-t'ung and Daniel H. Kulp II. As an ethnologist, his ideas of 'cultural complex' and 'ethnic areas' soon went out of fashion but his suggestions on the compilation of a map and a history of Chinese ethnography, and the establishment of a special Ethnographic Institute seemed to have anticipated later developments (Shirokogoroff, 1942, pp. 1–8). As ethnological research will be discussed in detail in Chapter 4, suffice it to note here that one of the spurs given to ethnology was practical necessity, especially after the Japanese invasion in 1937 when the Chinese government was compelled to move to the south-west and north-west where many non-Han groups resided. In order to consolidate the rear and to open up the border areas in preparation for war, research of minority groups was encouraged and ethnology was made a subject of study in colleges of Arts, Science, Law, and Education together with anthropology and frontier community studies in 1939 (Ho Lien-k'uei, 1955, p. 8).

Another branch of Chinese community studies bore the imprint of American rural sociology. The pioneering work in this tradition was a study of a Kwangtung village done by Daniel Harrison Kulp II (1925), an assistant professor of education from Columbia University who became professor and head of the sociology department at Shanghai College. Further impetus was provided by Robert E. Park of Chicago who visited Yenching University in 1931–2 and inspired many students to carry out community research.

In the search for a theory of community studies, the Chicago school of social ecology had attracted some Chinese adherents. But it was the functional school of British social anthropology that apparently won the day. Wu Wen-tsao was responsible for the adoption of the functional approach associated with the names of Malinowski and Radcliffe-Brown in Chinese community studies. Armed with newly-acquired functionalism, Yenching University grew to become a centre of community studies. Before being forced to evacuate by the Japanese invasion, the efforts of the Yenching group produced works such as Yang Ch'ing-k'un's study of *A North China Local Market Economy* (1933, published in English in 1944), Lin Yao-hua's 'A Clan Village in Fukien' (1934) which was later re-written as *The Golden Wing: A Family Chronicle* (1944), Huang Ti's 'Ching-ho: A Town Village Community' in *Sociological World* (1937), Cheng An-lan's 'Emigrant Community in Fukien' in *Social Research Weekly* (1938), and Fei Hsiao-t'ung's *Peasant Life in China* (1939). With the onset of the war with Japan, the centre of research shifted to Yunnan to become the Yenching–Yunnan Station for Sociological Research. Braving wartime hardship and difficulties this core of sociologists from Yenching continued to carry out investigations resulting in publications such as Fei's *Land System in Luts'un* (1940), Chang Chih-i's *Rural Industry in Yits'un* (1941) and *Land and Capital in Yuts'un* (1943) which was translated as the well-known *Earthbound China* (1945). Francis L. K. Hsu also wrote his *Under the Ancestor's Shadow* in this period. Other significant studies done by scholars outside of this core included Ch'en Ta's *Emmigrant Communities in South China* (1939), C. P. Fitzgerald's *The Tower of Five Glories* (1941), and Martin C. Yang's *A Chinese Village: Taitou, Shantung Province* (1945).

These community studies using a functionalist approach marked a definite advance in a deeper understanding of Chinese society. In able hands such as those of Fei Hsiao-t'ung, rural living in individual Chinese villages vividly came to life. These studies also signified a new departure from traditional Anglo-American social anthropology as they 'pushed the frontiers of anthropology outwards from savagery to civilization' (M. Freedman, 1963, p. 1). This transfer of the functional method perfected in simple non-literate societies to complex, literate ones such as China, had certain theoretical and political implications. Functionalism, at least in its Chinese adaptation, had as one of its basic tenets the belief that culture was a 'tool' and not something sacrosanct and immutable. This entailed a justification for change. But, coupled with a second tenet of the interrelationship among constituent parts, functionalism tended to counsel cautious and gradual modifications instead of drastic overhauls. By asking the question of how institutions were related instead of how they originated and evolved, the study of history was often neglected. The village studies of Fei Hsiao-t'ung for instance, made very little use of the wealth of historical information available in the form of genealogies and local gazetteers. A third tenet of functionalism was a concern with totalities. This concern raised the problem of the suitable unit of study when the anthropological technique was applied to complex Chinese society. In an attempt to tailor social reality to fit the instrument of investigation, Radcliffe-Brown put forth the view that in China 'the most suitable unit of study was the village, both because most Chinese lived in villages and because it was possible for one or two field workers to make a fairly detailed study in a year or so' (quoted in *ibid.*, p. 3). It was confidently believed by Malinowski, Radcliffe-Brown, and their Chinese disciples that a picture of the social structure of China would emerge from induction based on the detailed knowledge of individual villages. But in theory, it was not clear how the leap from the microscopic to the macroscopic level of analysis could be effected. In practice, such an approach restricted geographical coverage and contributed partly to the fact that most of the community studies were scattered along the coastal areas from Shantung to Yunnan where research could be conveniently carried out. When the researcher ventured to suggest action based on his knowledge of a small social unit, his vision might be so narrow that he failed to realize that the prescription for the village of Kaisenkung was not necessarily the cure for thousands of other villages, and what was meat for the Chinese coast was perhaps poison for the interior.

To point out the limitations of the functional approach is not to dismiss its importance in opening up a fruitful line of social inquiry in China. It was undeniably an improvement on the earlier fact-finding surveys. It also posed an effective theoretical counterweight to the marxist approach. Wu Wen-tsao made a conscious attempt to seek an alternative to what he regarded as doctrinaire marxism. In a review he wrote in 1932 on an adaptation of Leopold von Wiese's work, he revealed the motivation behind his subsequent effort to introduce the functional school into China (1932, pp. 336–7, original emphases):

> The reviewer believes that one of the reasons why marxian sociology has been so popular with the Chinese youth in recent years is this: In their eagerness for the study of western social thought, the Chinese students are seeking some sort of cogent system of social philosophy which will give them a conceptual frame of reference. The Chinese followers of Marx and Lenin propose that the dialectic method and the theory of economic determinism or historical materialism supply such a demand among the young people: the former gives them a convenient tool of investigation and the latter, a principle supposed to be universally applicable to social causation. A great danger of the one-sided theory of explanation and the over-simplified method of analysis is that they tend to encourage *wishful* thinking instead of *realistic* thinking. Professor Von Wiese's realist-systematic way of attacking the social problem is a proper corrective to this trend of thought in contemporary Chinese sociology.

Within the marxist school, the mistakes of mechanistic application of marxian theory were acknowledged by some of the leaders. One of the mistakes was the insistence that China must pass through the phase of bourgeois revolution on her way to communism, with the logical implication that co-operation with the Kuomintang was desirable. Another mistake was the belief that only the proletariat was the agent of change, resulting in a preoccupation with labour movements and a neglect of the peasantry. Mao Tse-tung was the arch-critic of these tendencies, and the main corrective he proposed was a type of social investigations akin to community studies. His famous 'Report on an Investigation into the Peasant Movement in Hunan' (1927), a prototype of marxist social analysis, was mainly a survey of peasant movements in five counties. His later rural studies, though lesser known, were much more intensive analyses of selected locations. His 'Hsing-kuo Survey' (1931) might be taken as representative. Investigating a district with about eight thousand residents, Mao began with detailed observations on eight families, then proceeded to analyse the previous system of land-ownership in the district and the various types of economic exploitation. He weighed the political attitude of various classes—the landlords, rich peasants, middle peasants, poor peasants, handicraftsmen, merchants etc. Then he reviewed the situation of land distribution after (the communist land reform policy, local administration and the militarization of the rural area (1970–2, pp. 185–252). This was a lengthy and comprehensive study conducted with Mao's conviction that policies must be founded on a first-hand understanding of the situation. Another notable researcher operating within a marxist framework was Ch'en Han-seng. Born in 1897 a native of Wusih, Kiangsu Province, we know little about his education except that he had studied in the USA and Great Britain. He began his academic career as a historian in the National University of Peking. Towards the end of the 1920s, according to *Pacific Affairs* ('Notes on contributors,' vol. 9, no. 3, 1936), he chose to specialize in agrarian research 'in an effort to understand Chinese history more thoroughly'. He attained fame as an agrarian sociologist and economist, being the head of the sociological section of the National Institute of Social Sciences, Academia Sinica, and an active member of the research committee of the China Institute of Pacific Relations before the Second World War. His first major publication was *Landlord and Peasant in China* (1936), a study of peasant communities in Kwangtung with special emphases on the system of 'land monopoly' and the process of 'rural proletarization'. This was followed by *Industrial Capital and Chinese Peasants* (1939) which was based on a combination of extensive investigations covering 127 villages in three provinces and in-depth analyses of 429 families in six representative locations. The subjects were Chinese tobacco cultivators, and Ch'en asked 'whether or not modern industrialization under semi-colonial circumstances . . . operates favourably on the livelihood of its peasants' (1939, p. iii). During the Anti-Japanese War, Ch'en was also forced to evacuate to south-western China. Like other sociologists, his attention was drawn to the minority communities and he completed two field studies on the Pai Yi people of Yunnan and Kamba people of Sikang. But unlike most of them, he retained his interest in agrarian problems and used explicit marxist categories for his analysis (1949, p.v):

> Although this study is limited to the agrarian systems of the Pai Yi and the Kamba in Sikang, it is intended to illustrate how

31

the agrarian problem is interwoven with national and colonial questions, or how agrarian changes are at once complicated by an alien administration and by problems pertaining to nationality.... Imperialistic penetration tends to preserve temporarily the traditional feudal relations.... Similarly, feudalistic penetration hinders the transformation of tribal land tenure as well as any pre-feudal social structure. In both cases alien domination retards rather than liberates forces that are necessary for the progress of society and its national culture. Indeed, agrarian problems today are intricately bound to international relations....

Inasmuch as the Chinese feudalistic administration has super-imposed itself upon the Pai Yi society and the Kamba society and hinder free development and progress there, the pre-feudal or primitive forms of land tenure of these two societies have been preserved for an abnormally long time.

As we have indicated, detailed community studies by themselves cannot yield an understanding of the entire society. This limitation was apparently recognized by a few investigators who attempted to ask larger questions about the characteristics of Chinese social structure. They produced the last type of research that we are going to consider—the macroscopic studies. Mao Tse-tung's 'Analysis of the Classes in Chinese Society' (1926) stood as a classic of the marxist endeavour in this genre. There were also efforts undertaken by non-marxist scholars. Fei Hsiao-t'ung's 'Peasantry and Gentry: An Interpretation of Chinese Social Structure and its Changes' (1946) was one of the studies well-known in the West. On the eve of the communist victory, Fei made a more ambitious attempt with his Chinese work *Hsiang-tu Chung-kuo (Rural China)* (1948a). From this diagnosis of the nature of Chinese society, he set out his policy recommendations in *Hsiang-tu ch'ung-chien (To Rebuild Rural China)* (1948b).

A comparison between the analyses of Mao Tse-tung and Fei Hsiao-t'ung may furnish some interesting insights into the key intellectual cleavage on the pre-Liberation sociological scene: the differences between marxist and non-marxist sociology. Both sides were in conscious competition with each other. The non-marxist attitude was exemplified by the statement of Wu Wen-tsao quoted earlier. The marxists, for their part, proposed the notion of a 'new sociology' as distinct from 'bourgeois sociology' which they regarded as at best a pseudo-science. The scientific study of society, according to them, began with Marx. But one may be tempted to overstate the differences. They were by no means irreconcilable. Internal variations and conflicts in approach and method existed within each school. As was common in situations of competition, intellectual exchange and borrowing occurred to some extent. In the works of professional sociologists, we may easily detect the assimilation of the ideas of class, means and relations of production etc. The marxists, on the other hand, tried to instruct themselves on the methods of social research (Li Jen, 1944, pp. 14–21). They acknowledged that some of the 'bourgeois' scholars such as Fei Hsiao-t'ung did possess a scientific spirit, and something of value might be learned from them.[12] As a result, both marxist and non-marxist studies shared many similarities in content as well as in method. What divided them appeared to centre around two questions: who were the historical actors moving China forward? And forward towards what kind of a future? Fei's study of the social structure of China differed from Mao's not in the absence of class analysis, but in that he saw the peasantry as a homogeneous mass. He differentiated various groups among the Chinese gentry, but not among the peasants. This flowed from his belief that the enlightened elements among the gentry formed the hope for the future. The belief that 'it is quite possible that a second generation of the old gentry and of the compradors may form a new responsible class on a professional basis, working for the modernization of China' (Fei Hsiao-t'ung, 1946, p. 16) influenced the questions he posed and thus his analysis. Mao Tse-tung, convinced that the peasants constituted a significant revolutionary force, identified several sub-categories among them. The categories were further refined, notably by Ch'en Han-seng who distinguished among landlords, rich peasants, middle peasants, poor peasants, and agricultural labourers (1936). Such a classification was later adopted by the Chinese Communist Party as the basic analytical principle for their land reform programme (P. C. C. Huang, 1975, p. 139). As for the vision of the future, the professional sociologists appeared to hold that the future could not be known. Because of this, they preferred a political system of checks and balances which could ensure gradual improvement. They were sceptical of grand designs of the future achieved through drastic transformations and a powerful government. In Fei's translation of Shih Kuo-heng's book on Chinese industrial workers, the preference for cautious change was clearly stated: 'A speedy cultural change always means the danger of disruption, and disruption brings with it social chaos and personal sufferings. Slow and sure progress is safer than speed. It also gives us time to test our methods as we go' (K. H. Shih, 1944, p. 98). But the marxists had a definite vision of a communist future towards which they strove. Their credo was change through revolution, and they had little patience with gradual reforms. The purpose of Mao's class analysis was to assess the attitude and potentials of various groups towards revolution. Ch'en Han-seng was equally firm in his conviction that '[the] essence of the agrarian problem and of the agrarian crisis in China, is how a national liberation movement can be successfully conducted to abolish the basis of all colonial and feudalistic exploitations' (1936, p. xvii). He believed that had Chinese scholars understood the national situation correctly, they would realize that they could 'no longer entertain any reformist moonshine for China' (*ibid.*, p. xvi).

Was it their 'bourgeois' background that led the professional sociologists to embrace liberal, reformist values? Their social origins did seem to colour their political attitude. For example, Fei Hsiao-t'ung, who was born into a local gentry family of Wuchiang, Kiangsu, confessed his emotional attachment to the social stratum he came from (1948b, p. 98):

> Though I regard myself as one of the 'sunken landlords' or those who have already renounced their position as landlords, I still feel I have a duty to ponder for the future of this stratum which can neither advance nor retreat, which is under fire from all sides. It is a fact that this social stratum still exists. It is a product of history, caught in an impasse in the great transformation of the epoch. I don't want to ponder for them in order to maintain their privileges as landlords, but I do want to find a reasonable way out for the people of this stratum.

But the outlook of the non-marxist sociologists seemed to be moulded more by their educational experience. Of course, this was related to their social origins in that their families must have been sufficiently well-to-do to be able to provide them with an education abroad, especially when no scholarship was offered by the Chinese government for specialization in sociology. Most of the sociologists who made their names before 1949 had studied either in the USA or in Great Britain. Those who held American doctoral degrees included Wu Wen-tsao, Ch'en Ta, P'an Kuang-tan (Columbia); Sun Pen-wen (New York); Chao Ch'eng-hsin, C. K. Yang (Michigan); Lin Yao-hua (Harvard); and Wu Ching-ch'ao (Chicago). Fei Hsiao-t'ung, Francis L. K. Hsu, and T'ien Ju-k'ang (London School of Economics) were trained in England. Most of them were impressed by the American and British social systems they observed, and they acquired western liberalism and Fabian socialism during their sojourns abroad. Upon their return, their political stance was reinforced as they tended to teach in American missionary colleges, and their research was mostly supported by western foundations such as the Rockefeller Foundation or the Institute of Pacific Relations. Thus their cosmopolitan orientation and favourable attitude towards co-operation with the West should not be surprising. Their attachment to a western democratic ideal led them to be disillusioned with the Kuomintang and apprehensive of the communists at the same time. Their feeling of being caught and squeezed between the two conflicting parties was well expressed by Wang Cheng who lamented that (1936, p. 100):

The fervour of political conviction is basically incompatible with the scientific spirit of social research. Therefore during intense partisan conflicts, social science naturally incurs the displeasure of both sides. Those who believe in the illegal ideology regard it as an obstacle hindering their effort to incite the youths, while those who defend the ruling ideology are afraid that it will be manipulated by their enemies. As a result, only a handful of naive fools remain to face poverty and want, and to study social problems as if they really matter.

The personal cost of holding an independent point of view and thus risking the disfavour of both the Nationalist and Communist Parties could be very high. Life was grim for Fei Hsiao-t'ung as Robert Redfield recalled. 'While in Yunnan he had been threatened with arrest by the Nationalist government and was fired upon in a public meeting where he had spoken unfavourably of Chiang's regime; on the other hand, communist voices in the North had attacked him bitterly for certain articles he had published.' (Fei Hsiao-tung, 1953, p. 3).

Civil war broke out after 1945, and the political situation approached complete chaos. Disenchantment with the Kuomintang government was such that intellectuals and students alike seemed unanimous in the belief that things could not be any worse. Some of the progressive intellectuals began to organize themselves and formed democratic parties. The most significant party was the Chinese Democratic League of which P'an Kuang-tan and Fei Hsiao-t'ung were members. But these sociologists were ambivalent in their political involvement. They regarded themselves essentially as academics, the custodians of moral and intellectual truth. Their approach to politics was elitist and half-hearted. Therefore the Democratic League was never an effective political force (N. T. Kennedy Jr, 1957). But even so, the League was not tolerated by the Kuomintang which declared it to be an illegal organization. Most intellectuals, noted a foreign scholar teaching in Nanking at that time, 'convinced that the Kuomintang could offer no solution and could tolerate no "third force", waited for liberation by the only other power that existed in China'. (O. B. van der Sprenkel, 1950, p. 70). When the communist victory was imminent, hope outweighed apprehension. Some sociologists such as Fei still held firm to their democratic principles and believed that they could become part of a 'royal opposition' to the Communist Government and would continue to criticize where criticisms were due.[13]

Reviewing the state of Chinese sociology prior to Liberation, we note that it was a period of vigorous growth, a time of 'the contention of a thousand schools'. With the intellectual monopoly of confucianism in decline, various currents of sociological thought formed and flowed. Competition necessitated their learning from one another, refining their conceptual and methodological tools to probe into various aspects of Chinese society. The fruits of their labour were so impressive that Maurice Freedman wrote in retrospect: 'It could be argued that before the Second World War, outside North America and Western Europe, China was the seat of the most flourishing sociology in the world, at least in respect of its intellectual quality' (1962). Addressed directly to urgent social and political issues, sociology was popular with Chinese students. Not only did marxism capture the imagination of the young, many professional sociologists also became influential writers who moulded public opinion. Academically, marxist sociologists were largely banished from the universities as a result of government suppression. But professional sociology of a non-marxist persuasion made enormous strides in gaining respectability and securing academic status within the short span of a few decades. But with the victory of the Communist Revolution, a new era was inaugurated. As with other aspects of life in China, sociology entered a new phase.

2 Sociology under socialism

Few sociologists fled the country upon Liberation. The majority appeared to have decided to stay in order to contribute to the building of a new China. Wu Wen-tsao, who was stationed in Tokyo as a member of China's Allied Council for Japan at the time, declined an invitation to teach in the Yale University and returned home in 1951. Meanwhile, the Communist Party began to unify and transform the nation. Externally, the most significant policies of the People's Republic of China were the emulation of the Soviet model of nation-building and strategy of economic development, and the attack on western capitalism and imperialism. The Korean War of 1950 confirmed and intensified these policies, and the government of the USA was identified as the arch-enemy. Internally, the intellectual scene started to change. Marxist social theory which had been kept out of the formal institutes of higher education by the Nationalist regime was no longer just a school of thought among many. It became *the* guiding thought of the country. Its validity seemed to have been vindicated by the success of the Revolution. Political economy, dialectical materialism, and the history of the Chinese revolutionary movement were made required courses for first- and second-year students in all universities (Sprenkel, 1950, p. 60). A process of re-education was initiated for non-marxist intellectuals. They had to learn marxist social theory and were made to realize how their past efforts had been mistaken because they had not embraced scientific marxism. A confession of past errors by Fei Hsiao-t'ung was illustrative. He admitted that 1949 was a 'year of learning' for him and everything humbled him (1950a, p. 7):

> Without an active participation in the Revolution, intellectuals such as myself were unfamiliar with the latent, vital forces of life. As a result, I lacked faith in the development of history and

37

the transformation of the people. Because of this difference in departure, my estimation of the world situation was mistaken.

Fei attributed this lack of confidence among the intellectuals to the timidity and impotence of the Chinese bourgeoisie.

The re-education of the intellectuals also found institutional expression in the reorganization and reform of higher education which affected the status of sociology. Once the reform began, the existence of sociology as an academic discipline in the universities was in doubt. After the Conference on Higher Education in 1949, a curricula reform act was published. It contained only general directives on sociology without departmental listings and specific instructions. This led to speculations that sociology departments may be abolished. The threat of extinction was two-fold: there was the accusation that sociology was closely related to capitalism; and even if this charge could be dismissed, there was the argument that marxism had made academic sociology superfluous.

As the survival of the discipline was in danger, a group of sociologists tried to defend its status by emphasizing its importance and 'making very ambitious plans for their science' (G. W. Skinner, 1951, p. 368). The professors of sociology in Tsinghua, Yenching, and Fujen Universities held a discussion in 1950 and put forth their opinion concerning the role of sociology in higher education (Fei Hsiao-t'ung, 1950b, p. 21):

We unanimously agreed that from now on the basis of social sciences will be marxism-leninism. Therefore no matter whether it is political science, economics, history or philosophy, all should have a common basis from which special foci can be developed to form separate disciplines. From now on, there should be more interchange among departments to work towards the establishment of an Institute of Social Sciences, and each department will be a special focus in the Institute. At that time, the major courses of the sociology department will become the basic courses of the Institute, and the more vocational courses of sociology will constitute one of the special foci of the Institute.

At present, conditions are not yet ripe for the amalgamation of the Faculties of Law and part of the Faculty of Arts. When other departments of the social sciences still exist independently, there is no need for the early abolition of the departments of sociology. Actually, departments of sociology can be employed as the basis for strengthening the teaching of fundamental theoretical courses of marxism-leninism, and preparing for the future Institute of Social Sciences.

Thus the sociologists accepted marxism–leninism as the theoretical foundation of their discipline. They resisted the suspension of sociology by asserting its useful role in providing basic knowledge for other social science subjects, as well as specialized training in areas left unattended by other departments.[1]

This group of sociologists also put forth a proposal on the curriculum of sociology. The proposed curriculum included three types of courses:

1　Theoretical courses on marxism–leninism;
2　Cultural, instrumental courses including native language training, reading ability in foreign languages, statistical techniques, social research methods, Chinese and world history;
3　Vocational courses, with urban and rural sociology, minority studies as suggested areas of specialization.

This proposal on the academic status of sociology was published in anticipation of the Conference on Higher Education held in Peking in June 1950. It represented an attempt by the sociologists to plead their case and to justify their profession. Though their suggestions were not adopted *in toto*, the status of the sociology departments was assured by the Conference and their role was defined as follows (quoted in Skinner, 1951, p. 369):

> To learn to use Marxism–Leninism and the thought of Mao Tse-tung to analyse concretely practical social situations; to give professional and technical knowledge to those who will do important work in government and related agencies (such as the Ministries of Interior and Labor and the Commission of Tribal Affairs); and to train teachers . . . .

According to Skinner, the curricula of the departments of sociology recommended by the Conference consisted of eight courses:

1　Materialist sociology concerning the dynamics of the development of social phenomena, the forces and relations of production in society, and the superstructure which is derived from them, namely the legal, political, familial, religious, and philosophical systems;
2　Methods of sociological research;
3　Social statistics;
4　Modern world history;
5　The condition of Chinese society which will deal with the practice of new democracy in various segments of society, and with the characteristics of and the interrelationship between various social classes;
6　Anthropology, on 'how it is that labour created mankind', on

'ancient societies, including the economic reasons why primitive peoples change from one stage to another', and 'the development of the social history of human society, the purpose being to prove the regularities of social development';

7   Government policy and law;
8   Selected readings in marxism–leninism.

In addition to these required courses, four specializations would be provided by the departments:

1   Theory;
2   Ethnology;
3   Internal affairs;
4   Labour.

The recommended curricula revealed two characteristic features of sociology in the universities at the time. First, it was to conform to marxist–leninist theory, and many courses were concerned with elaborating and demonstrating the validity of this social and historical theory. Second, the emphasis was on practical utility, with the training of administrators and government officers in accordance with social need as one of its aims. Although there were modifications in the nature of sociology being taught, academic sociology was allowed to exist for the time being.

In the course of this transitional period, what types of sociological works were produced? A rough classification of the books, articles and discussion items concerning sociology published in the periodicals *Hsüeh-hsi* (*Study*) from 1949 to 1951, and *Hsin chien-she* (*New Construction*) in 1951 might give us some idea (Table 2.1). A listing of some of the characteristic titles might indicate the nature

TABLE 2.1 *Sociological writings published in* Study, *1949–51, and* New Construction, *1951*

	Books	Articles	Discussion items
Marxist social theory	1	17	20
Studies on marxist classics	2	4	1
On Chinese society	0	6	15
On social policies	0	3	1
Critiques of capitalist theory and society	0	2	0
Total	3	32	37

of works in the various categories. Under marxist social theory, I have included works that sought to elaborate or popularize marxism. A book by Hu Sheng *et al.* on *Fundamental Knowledge of the Social Sciences*, was serialized in *Study*. Its chapter headings were 'The fundamental viewpoint of historical materialism', 'The developmental process of society', 'Our time', and 'The Communist Party—the leader of the struggle for liberation of the labouring people'. There were also articles with titles such as 'Concerning the productive forces of society', 'What is the fundamental law of societal development?', 'Concerning the institution of kinship and paternalism'; and discussion items such as 'What is the moving force of the development of communist society?', 'When did human labour begin?', 'Why is it that the rebellion of the slaves could not end exploitation and why is it that the slaves could not create a new mode of production?'; and explanations of concepts such as 'class', 'endogamy and exogamy', and 'group marriage'.

Among the marxian classics I include studies of the works of Marx, Engels, Lenin and Stalin. Two books were serialized: *Introducing the Communist Manifesto,* and *Explanation of Lenin's 'Imperialism'.* There were also articles on *From Ape to Man, Family, Private Property and the Origin of the State*, and Lenin's *On the State.*

Articles classified under Chinese society include titles such as 'Slave society in China', 'The causes of the long continuation of feudalism in China', 'The problem of land in Chinese society', 'Peasant wars in China's past', and 'The colonial, semi-colonial, and semi-feudal society of Old China'.

A few articles dealt expressly with contemporary policies such as 'The principle and criteria for the classification of social classes' and 'Concerning the present urban–rural relations'.

Direct critiques of capitalist society and theories were few in number. Only two could be identified, one dealing with the 'Pauperisation of the labouring peoples of various capitalist countries', and the other on 'How did the Malthusian theory of population serve imperialism'.

An analysis of the works produced in this period tends to confirm the characteristic thrust of sociology as observed in the departmental reform proposals. Judging from the kinds of work being produced, it seems that the preoccupation at this time was the dissemination and popularization of marxist–leninist theory, and the reinterpretation of Chinese history to accord with this perspective. Marxist theory was treated as a scientific truth and there were no critical examinations of it, as shown in the phrasing of the questions. Most of the questions were posed in the form of 'What is meant by...' and 'How is it that...' instead of 'Is it true that...' such and such is the case.

41

Limited field work and community studies were still being carried out by some sociologists and their students. During this period, C. K. Yang and a group of his students managed to continue their field study in Nanching, a village in the vicinity of Canton, until 1951. They had recorded the early changes brought about by Liberation in that village. The study was later published in the USA by C. K. Yang as *A Chinese Village in Early Communist Transition* (1959). Since the written records of the field investigation could not be brought out of China, the information contained in the book was reproduced from memory by C. K. Yang in 1952. In spite of this, it remained one of the few valuable documents on the social changes created by land reform and collectivization in a Chinese village community during the early years of the People's Republic. And it was one of the very few community studies done by Chinese sociologists in the post-1949 period.

As for the situation of the Chinese sociologists, some of them, such as C. K. Yang, Francis Hsu, left the mainland and migrated to the USA. Of those who remained in the People's Republic, many stayed in the universities. Some of the well-known and more anthropologically oriented ones, such as Wu Wen-tsao, Fei Hsiao-t'ung, Lin Yao-hua, were transferred to the newly established Central Institute for Nationalities to teach or to do research on national minorities in China. In general, few of the Chinese sociologists published works related to sociology during this period. I have been able to find only two articles of a sociological nature written by a professional sociologist. They were both authored by P'an Kuang-tan. One of them was an examination using Chinese historical data of Engels's thesis that at the early stage of paternal society, the relation between maternal uncle and nephew was more intimate than that between father and son (P'an Kuang-tan, 1950). Another article was a study of the institution of *i-t'ien* (communal land) and its relation to feudalism in the villages of southern Kiangsu using historical data drawn from village records as well as data collected through field research[2] (P'an Kuang-tan and Ch'üan Wei-tien, 1951).

Abolition of sociology

After an initial period of political consolidation and reorganization, China launched the first Five Year Plan which was modelled after the Soviet Union's. The main concerns of this period, as indicated by Chou En-lai, were to 'further strengthen and develop the People's Democratic Dictatorship' and to speed up the national plan of economic development (1956).

In the academic field, the effects of emulating the Russian model were felt. During the 1951 Conference on Higher Education in Peking, though the academic status of sociology was temporarily assured, it was overshadowed by the reported remark of a Russian expert in education that sociology had no place in the university organization and curricula of the Soviet Union at that time. Then in 1952, the worst fear of the sociologists was confirmed. Departments of sociology were suddenly abolished. The decision appeared to be an administrative measure not open to public debate or challenge. It was only in 1957 when a milder political climate prevailed that some former sociologists openly aired their dissent and demanded that the Minister of Higher Education explain the elimination of subjects such as labour studies (*JMJP*, 30 August 1957; trans. in *SCMP*, no. 1613, September 1957, p. 23).

Why was sociology denied an academic existence? The reasons can only be inferred. An obvious factor was the influence of the Russian educational model, as revealed in the criticisms made by Professor Wang Kan-yu of Nankai University against the measure in 1957 (quoted in R. MacFarquhar, 1960, p. 26):

After the liberation, people who had in the past studied social sciences suffered a certain mental blow, because some of the social sciences were abolished and some lost their independence. Much of the curricula of the past was abolished simply because there were no such curricula in the Soviet Union.... Take sociology for example. This is a study which is very broad in scope. When this department was abandoned, many specialized fields—such as demography, ethnology, and social thought— were ignored and no one studied them....

Related to this Soviet influence was the emphasis on technical and industrial training resulting from the priorities of the First Five Year Plan. Engineering and the natural sciences were given top priority because they were believed to be central to economic development. This tendency was evident in the distribution of the 1953 new admissions to institutes of higher education throughout the nation. Only 8 per cent of total intake were assigned to the field of the humanities, finance and economics, and politics and law (Table 2.2).

The neglect of social science was also shown in the organization of the Chinese Academy of Sciences established in 1955. Among its four divisions, only one was devoted to social science and philosophy. And in the ten foci of work for the Academy as outlined in its first five year plan by Kuo Mo-jo, President of the Academy, the only focus bearing some relation to social science was 'research in the fundamental theoretical problems in our national construction in this transitional period' (*HCS*, no. 7, 1955, p. 64). There were reported to be 172 members in the natural science division of the

TABLE 2.2 *Distribution of new students in institutes of higher education by fields of study, 1953*

Subject	%
Engineering	43
Education	26
Health	10
Science	6
Forestry	5
Humanities	4
Finance and economics	3
Physical education	1
Politics and law	1
Art	1
Total	100

Source: Ma Hsü-lun, 1953, pp. 13–14.

Academy in 1956, half of whom were active in research. The social science division had fifty-one members among whom only a few could devote most of their time to research (Chou En-lai, 1956). Besides considerations of utility and the capacity to produce tangible benefits to development, sociology seemed to be regarded as a doubtful pursuit by the Communist Party because of the political threat it posed. The academic and political activities of the non-marxist sociologists before the communist victory furnished some ground for the suspicion that social studies could train people in 'political leadership potentially capable of offering an alternative to the regime' (E. Snow, 1971, p. 391).

As sociology ceased to be an academic discipline, teaching stopped and no new sociologists were trained. What happened to those who had already made their careers in sociology? According to Fei Hsiao-t'ung, who had surveyed the problem of intellectuals in 1956 and 1957, they could be grouped into three categories (1957a, p. 2). The first included those who were employed in a new vocation closely related to sociology. In this category Fei included himself, Wu Wen-tsao, P'an Kuang-tan, and Lin Yao-hua who were engaged in minority affairs. Among the second were those who had switched to new jobs. A few of them attained high positions in the new government. Hsu Te-heng became a member of the Political and

Legal Affairs Committee under the Government Administration Council. He was also appointed a vice-chairman of the Law Commission, and delivered a major report in 1951 on the 'provisional regulations governing the organization of people's courts'. In 1956, he assumed the post of Minister of Aquatic Products in the government (Klein and Clark, 1971, p. 362). Ch'en Han-seng became the deputy director of the Research Institute of International Relations of the Chinese Academy of Sciences, and served as vice-chairman of the editorial board of the English-language magazine, *China Reconstructs*, from 1952 to 1966. But many of them, according to Fei, though performing competently in their new jobs, would have liked to resume their roles as sociologists if given the chance. Much less fortunate were those in the third category who had remained unsettled after the educational reform. Some had quit teaching to learn Russian in order to do translation work. Others were attached to government consultative bureaux with little else to do except to study marxism-leninism on their own and to re-educate themselves.

The arrested careers of Ch'en Ta and Li Ching-han were illustrative. Ch'en Ta, who obtained his doctorate in Columbia University in 1923 and had since taught at Tsinghua University for twenty-nine years until 1951, was an expert in population and labour problems. In an interview published in 1957, he indicated his hope that after Liberation, his work on population and on labour movements might be of some use to the country (*KMJP*, 14 January 1957; trans. in *China News Analysis*, no. 168, February 1957, p. 6). But he was not consulted in the preparation for and the execution of the 1953 census. After being transferred from Tsinghua University and made the deputy director of the Peking Labour Cadres' School of the Ministry of Labour, he stopped teaching and spent most of his time in research though he had no assistants. He studied the Chinese labour movement during the Japanese War (1937–45) for several years, and his manuscript was reported to be near completion in 1957. But it did not appear in print.

Li Ching-han, famous for his Ting Hsien survey, was the head of the department of sociology at Fujen University before Liberation. When the departments were abolished, he was assigned together with many professors in sociology to the labour studies unit of the Central Institute of Finance and Economics. There he worked as an assistant first to a teacher in mechanics, then to an instructor in textiles. After one year, he was moved again to the People's University to serve as a deputy to a teacher in 'labour insurance'. He prepared lectures for three courses on labour problems over the years without ever getting a chance to deliver any of them (*JMJP*, 16 May 1957).

Thus the careers of many of the former sociologists were suspended. They were either under-employed or engaged in jobs unrelated to their training. The situation of the Chinese sociologists became the subject of a minor international controversy. The protagonists were Fei Hsiao-t'ung and Karl A. Wittfogel, who reviewed Fei's book *China's Gentry*. The book under review, consisting of translations of several of Fei's pre-1949 writings, was prepared and published in the USA in 1953 by Margaret Park Redfield on Fei's behalf but without his prior knowledge. In a review which appeared in the January 1955 issue of *Encounter*, Wittfogel expressed his doubts on whether Fei was satisfied with his lot. The main thrust was in Wittfogel's concluding remarks (1955, p. 80):

> Fei stopped writing to his friends immediately after the
> Communists seized power; and his statements since that time
> do not necessarily express his innermost feelings. But having
> known him personally, I consider it more than likely that in the
> depth of his heart he comprehends fully the tragedy which has
> overwhelmed him and his country.

Several of Fei's friends in Britain immediately sprang to his defence, and Fei himself wrote a letter to *Encounter* and later published an article in *People's China* to counter Wittfogel's assertions and to give a picture of his life and frame of mind under the new government.

The *Encounter* incident reflected the cold war climate of the 1950s. The fate of the Chinese sociologists should be seen in context. As a result of international tension between the capitalist and communist camps, sociologists on both sides who were committed to the ideal of cultural understanding suffered. The McCarthy purge had ruined the careers of many American students of Chinese society, such as those related to the Institute of Pacific Relations (J. N. Thomas, 1974). Accusations against the Chinese sociologists as 'cultural compradors' of western powers had been replicated in reverse in the USA. Mutual suspicion between the two governments had virtually blocked the communication between Chinese and western sociologists. Foreign social researchers, once so active on Chinese soil, became unwelcome guests. Only a few investigators sympathetic to the new government had the chance to record the momentous changes that were taking place at first hand (e.g. S. J. Burki, 1965; D. Crook and I. Crook, 1966; W. R. Geddes, 1963; J. Myrdal, 1965; B. M. Richman, 1969).

Although Wittfogel's speculation on Fei's 'innermost feelings' was unwarranted, some of his comments could not be simply dismissed as anti-communist and trite. He said that Fei 'was kept out of the villages, which in the past he had studied so intensely', and that 'his position is high, his voice low' (*op. cit.*, p. 80). These remarks Fei did not directly refute. He had been given a high post as deputy director of the Central Institute of Nationalities, and was elected a representative to the People's Congress. In his reply, he admitted that for four or five years after Liberation, administrative work had taken up most of his time so that he was not able to do research (1956, p. 15).

Thus for several years the field of sociology lay fallow. Few of the former sociologists appeared in print for two main reasons. First, they were neglected; second, they were apprehensive. Chou En-lai's 1956 report on the intellectuals was revealing. According to Chou, the predominant attitude of the party cadres towards intellectuals was one of distrust and neglect, thus the expertise of the intellectuals was often wasted. Reasonable working conditions and remuneration were not often provided. Apart from the cadres' distrust, the programme of re-education had an inhibitive effect on academic activities. From the criticisms levelled against the Communist Party in 1957, we learn that many intellectuals felt that they had been left out of the scene, that they could not participate actively in national affairs. Rules and norms of academic conduct they used to uphold were criticized as erroneous and self-serving, and they had had to re-educate themselves and accept the teachings of marxist theory. Thought reform was backed by social sanctions with very practical consequences on prospects for remuneration and promotion, on the chances of further studies, and even on matters of love and marriage. In addition to these sanctions, many of the intellectuals found the teachings of marxism–leninism ambiguous. For example many of them were bewildered by the distinction between the 'materialistic' and 'idealistic' mode of thought which purportedly differentiated correct and incorrect points of view. Under such conditions, many intellectuals resorted to rote learning, repeating theories verbally in spite of disagreement, avoiding mentioning theories that were different from those in the textbooks, or attacking and criticizing books and theories in accordance with authoritative opinion without consulting the originals (see Fei Hsiao-t'ung, 1957b; *Hsüeh-hsi*, no. 11, 1957, p. 10). These behaviour patterns appeared to be a form of compliance, on the part of at least some intellectuals, with the official effort to establish marxism-leninism as the only valid paradigm for understanding and interpreting the social world.

The inactivity and low productivity of the former sociologists was reflected in the paucity of publications. Among the few books and articles published, those with a theoretical bent were primarily of two kinds. The first included the introductions to marxist theory of social development. Two books on this theme are known to me: Chieh-fang-she (ed.) *A Brief History of Social Development*, Peking, People's Press, 1952; and Chang Yung, *Talks on the Laws of Social Development*, Shantung, People's Press, 1957. The former was published with the express aim of providing general knowledge of social development to people new to social science. It was the revised edition of a work originally published in 1948 as a designated text for party cadres. It dealt with the morphology of societies, from primitive communism, the system of slavery, feudalism, capitalism, the transitional stage between capitalism and communism, to communism itself. The latter book was similar in nature. The Russian influence and marxist perspective were apparent in its citations: of a total of forty-nine quotations, eleven were from the *History of the Russian Bolshevik Party*, eleven from Marx and Engels, ten from works of Stalin, and ten from Mao Tse-tung. These works were mainly continuations of the effort to popularize the marxist theory of social development. The other kind of theoretical works were articles criticizing the theory of rural construction proposed by Liang Sou-ming prior to Liberation. Such criticisms might be taken as a reflection of the continuing influence of Liang's social thought among the intellectual community.[3]

Reassertion of sociology

When the year began in 1956, the political climate changed unexpectedly for the milder. A thaw was in the air, promising 'soft rain and gentle breeze' in what the *People's Daily* was to recall as 'the unusual spring'. For a time, it appeared that the intellectuals would be offered a new deal, and the frozen subject of sociology might be given a new lease of life.

This brief period of liberalization was brought about by a combination of domestic and international factors. In the latter half of 1955, according to Mao Tse-tung, 'the situation in China underwent a fundamental change' (1977, p. 239). By this Mao meant primarily the collectivization of agriculture which had achieved results beyond his expectation. Within a few months of his setting a new target for collectivization, over 60 per cent of the peasant households in China had joined the Agricultural Producers' Co-operatives. It seemed probable that this form of 'semi-socialist' collectivization could be implemented throughout the country in 1956. At the same time, the movement to eliminate 'anti-revolutionaries' and the attempt to socialize Chinese industry by forming joint state-private enterprises met with similar success. It looked likely that the First Five Year Plan would be completed ahead of schedule. 'All these momentous and encouraging achievements', declared Chou En-lai (1956), 'were unimaginable a year ago.' With the transition to complete socialism in sight, leaders such as Mao and Chou believed that they should abandon the original blueprint of development which appeared to be too conservative (Mao Tse-tung, *op. cit.*, p. 239). In order to quicken the pace of industrialization, they assigned top priority to economic production. They reckoned that they had to enlist the support of all sectors of the population for the task. In this respect, the intellectuals were particularly valuable. Therefore, a large conference was convened in January 1956 by the Central Committee of the Chinese Communist Party (CCP) to discuss the question of intellectuals. Chou En-lai gave the main speech in which he emphasized that party officials should regard the intellectuals as an asset to economic development. He knew that genuine marxists were still in the minority among the intellectuals, but he believed that the majority had basically been reformed and could be relied on to give general support to the CCP's work. After the conference, working conditions for the intellectuals were improved. They were provided with better housing, better library and research facilities. Their salaries were revised with increased promotion prospects. The conferment of degrees and academic titles were restored. Political and administrative duties were reduced to ensure that they could devote most of their time to professional work. Jobs were found for the unemployed or misemployed intellectuals to accord with their skills. Two bodies were set up by the State Council to co-ordinate intellectual affairs. One was the Scientific Planning Committee which guided the drafting of a twelve-year plan for the promotion of education, culture and scientific research. Emphases were placed primarily on the natural and applied sciences, but the social sciences were not entirely left out. Several fields in the social sciences were chosen for special attention, including 'the application of Marxism–Leninism to the socialist construction and practical problems of China, research on Chinese history, the struggle against bourgeois ideology and idealism etc.' (T. H. E. Chen, 1960, p. 116). The other body was the Experts Bureau (Chou En-lai, *op. cit.*, p. 107). The chief of this bureau was reported to be Fei Hsiao-t'ung (H. L. Boorman and R. C. Boorman, 1967–71, vol. 2, p. 18).

Just as China was about to embark on this accelerated programme of industrialization, several political bombshells exploded within the communist bloc. At the Twentieth Congress of the Communist Party of the Soviet Union held in January 1956, Khrushchev delivered the 'secret speech' denouncing Stalin. The immediate effect of de-stalinization was that the legitimacy of a personality cult for Mao Tse-tung was undermined. In the new Chinese constitution passed later in the year, the important role of the 'Thought of Mao Tse-tung' was not mentioned. But the attack on

Stalin raised more fundamental questions for the Chinese leaders. What should be the relationship between the Communist Party and the people it led? In view of Stalin's mistakes, should China adhere to the Soviet model of development? Addressing himself to these questions, Mao Tse-tung presented the speech 'On the ten major relationships' on 25 April in which he argued for an independent path of industrialization, and began to grapple with the problem of how to handle 'contradictions' among the people under socialism. He discussed in particular the relationship between party and non-party people, and the question of whether China should have a one-party or a multi-party system. He came to the conclusion that it was better to have 'long-term co-existence and mutual supervision' of the Communist Party and the other minor democratic parties (Mao Tse-tung, 1977, pp. 284–307; R. MacFarquhar, 1974, pp. 48–9). A week later, he made the speech of 'Let a hundred flowers bloom, let a hundred schools contend' to a closed session of the Supreme State Conference (MacFarquhar, op. cit., p. 51). He urged for liberalization in the intellectual and cultural spheres, apparently in the belief that it was beneficial to allow critical opinions to be expressed rather than subdued. He sought to launch a rectification movement. Outside groups would be allowed to criticize the mistakes of his Party members so as to forestall disturbances such as the Polish revolt. But Mao's attempt to relax ideological control was opposed by a significant portion of the Party members as well as several top leaders such as Liu Shao-ch'i and P'eng Chen. They insisted that rectification should be an intra-Party affair and that members should not be exposed to attack from the outside (R. H. Solomon, 1971, pp. 288–96; MacFarquhar, op. cit., pp. 110–21). It was the Hungarian revolt in the autumn of 1956 that ultimately strengthened Mao's hand in persuading his Party to launch the 'Hundred Flowers Movement' in earnest.

The intellectuals, for their part, were cautious in their initial response. They had reservations about the sincerity of the CCP in permitting free speech. Fei Hsiao-t'ung, who had canvassed the opinion of the intellectuals from the winter of 1955 to early 1957 by extensive travels to Nanking, Soochow, Hangchow, Kunming and other cities in southwestern China (A. R. Sanchez and S. L. Wong, 1974, p. 787), summed up his impressions in an influential article published in the *People's Daily* (1957b). Most intellectuals, he wrote, were impressed by Chou En-lai's report. Some even considered it to signal their 're-liberation'. But, said Fei metaphorically, the 'early spring weather' was unpredictable. It could suddenly turn frosty and chill the early blossoms. He expressed the prevalent doubt among the intelligentsia that the 'Hundred Flowers Movement' might be a trap to lure them to reveal their true political colours.

Therefore they were hesitant to respond. But in the first few months of 1957, the top leadership of the CCP gave repeated assurances and encouragements to the intellectuals to speak their minds without fear of retaliation. The intellectuals finally broke their reserve. For five weeks of unchecked criticisms from 1 May to 7 June, they poured out their grievances against the CCP.

One of the issues raised in the Hundred Flowers Movement was the value of sociology and the place it should have in socialist China. Articles appeared in newspapers and magazines arguing for the need to rebuild the sociological enterprise. These arguments gained temporary ascendency. In the 1957 annual index of the periodical *New Construction*, some articles were grouped under a new category called 'sociology'.

Those who advocated the re-establishment of sociology were all former practitioners of the discipline. The initial spark for this reassertion was provided by the participation of Russian scholars in the Third World Congress of Sociology and the resumption of sociological research and teaching in the USSR (Wu Ching-ch'ao, 1957a, p. 61). This event undermined an important rationale for the abolition of sociology in China. The Soviet Union, whose educational practices China imitated, had changed her course. But, possibly out of political caution, the Russian example was not invoked in the subsequent arguments for the re-establishment of the discipline. Instead, the former sociologists adopted the strategy of emphasizing the utility of the research methods and the importance of sociological studies in gathering information for policy formulation. They stressed the instrumental and technical aspects of sociology, without directly challenging the role of marxism–leninism as the theoretical paradigm of social research. Indeed they actually stated that they were merely trying to build a sociology based on marxism–leninism. According to them, such a sociology was necessary because during socialist construction, new social relations and problems would emerge which demanded concrete investigations and empirical studies for correct diagnoses. The areas of research proposed by these advocators included the following: problems of population; the re-education of intellectuals and their employment; the problem of work and labour; political relations among the people in a socialist society, such as the relation between party and non-party members; the nature of political institutions such as the People's Congress etc.; relations within the family such as those between the sexes and among generations; rural and urban sociology, and criminology (*ibid.*; Fei Hsiao-t'ung, 1957a; *Hsin chien-she*, no. 7, pp. 40–8). Sociology was useful, it was argued, in providing solutions to these problems. For instance, Fei wrote (1957a):

I don't mean to list a large number of problems here. I only want to point out that problems like these will continually arise in the process of social development, and it will not be all peace and quiet. It is better for us to investigate and study these problems with scientific methods than to close our eyes and pretend that everything is fine.

Another line of the argument was to justify the study of western sociology. It was asserted that not all of western academic sociology was ideological. There were portions, particularly the research methods, which could be incorporated and absorbed into marxism-leninism. The ideological elements of 'bourgeois' sociology should be rejected. But the content and development of western sociology must first be clearly understood before substantial and valid criticisms could be made.

The question of the status of sociology took on political overtones when the issue was taken up by the Chinese Democratic League. This League was one of the eight minor political parties existing in China. The People's Republic adhered to a policy of 'United Front' and a form of multi-party system, though all the minor parties had to accept the leadership of the Communist Party and its interpretation of the basic tenets of marxism–leninism. Organizationally, 'United Front' policy was embodied in the Chinese People's Political Consultative Conference (CPPCC) which was convened in 1949 to declare the establishment of the People's Republic of China in the absence of a national election. Since then, the CPPCC had been superseded by the National People's Congress as the supreme source of governmental authority, but it had been convened occasionally to reaffirm national solidarity. In terms of seats in the People's Congress and the CPPCC, the Chinese Democratic League was the largest of the minor parties (Wen Shih, 1963, pp. 157–64; L. P. Van Slyke, 1967, pp. 209–11). Its members were mostly intellectuals and professionals, and the sociologists Fei Hsiao-t'ung and P'an Kuang-tan were its delegates to the CPPCC.

Early in 1957, the League set up a committee to investigate problems concerning the scientific enterprise. After collecting opinions from the scientists within the League, a proposal concerning scientific institutions in China was put forth (*KMJP*, 9 June 1957). The proposal contained a section on the social sciences which was later said to be the brain-child of Fei Hsiao-t'ung, P'an Kuang-tan and Ch'en Ta. In this section on the social sciences, three fundamental questions were raised. First, what should be the status of sociology? It was noted that after Liberation, the natural sciences were given top priority owing to the need for industrialization. This relative emphasis was acknowledged to be correct given

China's circumstances at that time. But it was asserted that the social sciences were also important and should not be neglected.

Second, what should be the attitude towards the social sciences? In order to develop social science, it was argued, the attitude towards the 'old' social sciences should be altered. It was alleged that the existing attitude was to regard the social sciences in capitalist societies as unscientific with nothing that was worth inheriting or absorbing. Therefore the action taken towards the social sciences was negation rather than transformation. Some disciplines, such as sociology, political science, and legal studies were abolished or denied an independent existence. Such action was considered to be inappropriate. Sociology should be transformed and not abolished, and it was agrued that certain disciplines should be revived.

Third, what role should the social sciences play in the formulation of social policies? The government was criticized for the tendency to regard its policies as identical with objective laws, e.g. after government officials had made reports on important policy issues, scholars could only do some propaganda or explanatory work. This state of affairs was regarded as regrettable because government policies, though basically correct, were not free from mistakes. It was suggested that social scientific investigations should be encouraged so that proposals and suggestions could be made to improve government policies. Government departments were urged to provide relevant information and suitable research conditions for the social scientists. Only then, it was argued, could theoretical works catch up with practical needs.

These suggestions for reform amounted to an explicit criticism of past government policies and attitudes toward the social sciences. The main thrust of the proposal was to argue for the participation of social scientists in the process of political decision-making and the recognition that the social sciences had a distinct and useful role in providing data and ideas for policy formulation and implementation. The plan for the development of social sciences appeared to be part of the Chinese Democratic League's effort to obtain a share of political power and to assume the role of an effective opposition party.

Many former sociologists were active in organizing themselves to work for the revival of their discipline. In the vanguard was Fei Hsiao-t'ung who championed the cause of the displaced intellectuals and a forsaken sociology. As if smarting under Wittfogel's implied charge that he had lost his moral fibre, and to prove to his old friend Robert Redfield that he was true to his word and would criticize where criticisms were due, he fired one of the most resounding shots of the Hundred Flowers Movement with his article 'The early spring weather for the intellectuals'. Besides Fei, Ch'en Ta and

Wu Ch'ing-ch'ao were also energetic advocates of sociology. On 7 March 1957 they jointly tabled a motion before the CPPCC National Committee urging for the establishment of a research unit on population and the inclusion of a course on demography in the curricula of the universities. As their advocacies encountered no official displeasure, they might have been led to believe that they had the blessing of the political leaders. It had been reported that their ideas and demands 'have received the attention and support of the Party and the Government' (*Che-hsüeh yen-chiu*, no. 3, 1957, p. 148). On 23 April 1957 a forum was convened by the Philosophy and Social Sciences Division of the Chinese Academy of Sciences to discuss arrangements for sociological research. A preparatory committee was elected consisting of Fei Hsiao-t'ung, Wu Ching-ch'ao, Li Ching-han and five others to set up a 'social problems research committee' in the Academy. Members of the preparatory committee subsequently met on 9 June and drew up a plan. If they had had their way, sociology would have been reborn. The name of the 'social problems research committee' was changed to 'sociological work committee' with Ch'en Ta elected as its chairman. A list of all the Chinese sociologists both on the mainland and abroad was prepared in order to renew domestic and international academic ties. The creation of a Society of Chinese Sociologists was suggested. Wu Wen-tsao, P'an Kuang-tan and others were chosen to draft plans for reinstating departments of sociology in the universities in Peking, Shanghai, Canton, Chengtu and other places. The main centres of sociological research were to be the Central Institute of Nationalities, People's University, and the Labour Cadres' School. It was planned that Fei Hsiao-t'ung was to be in charge of studies on minorities in the Central Institute of Nationalities and to gather researchers for a study of world ethnology; Li Ching-han and Wu Ch'ing-ch'ao were to initiate urban sociological surveys in the People's University; and Ch'en Ta was to introduce studies on population and labour in the Labour Cadres' School. They also proposed to set up a social survey unit in the Academy of Sciences, and a field headquarters in a prefecture near Peking (with a population of about 300,000 people) where surveys might be carried out regularly (*JMJP*, 30 August 1957; M. Kaneko, 1958, pp. 107–8).

Some sociologists had also resumed empirical research, and two significant studies were published in the early half of 1957. One was Li Ching-han's 'The past and present of family life in the villages on the outskirt of Peking' (*JMJP*, 1–3 January 1957), and the other was Fei Hsiao-t'ung's 'Chiang Ts'un revisited' (1957c). Both were attempts to assess social changes in the Chinese villages brought about by the Revolution by re-studying the villages they had investigated before 1949. And both were field investigations which might be classified as community studies.

In 1926, Li Ching-han had studied the villages on the outskirts of Peking. He had published several books on family life in these villages. In the autumn of 1956, at the request of the editors of the *People's Daily*, he made a re-study of these villages. He published his report in early 1957. Using an average household with five members as a unit of measurement, he attempted to compare the differences in household expenditure and standard of living in these villages between 1926 and 1956. He assessed the average consumption in food, clothing, housing, fuel, medical care, wine and cigarettes, cultural recreation, education, as well as the qualitative aspects of family relations. He demonstrated quantitatively that the standard of living, especially that of the poor peasants, had much improved. The average family income in 1966 had increased by 40 per cent as compared with that of 1926. On the whole, he concluded, life in these villages had improved and a solid foundation for better living in the villages had been laid. But he also revealed the existence of certain discontents among the villagers. The shortages and difficulties created by rationing were major complaints. The perceived difference between their own livelihood as farmers and those of the factory workers was another, and Li reported comments such as 'Even the girls here will first try to find their marriage partners among the workers.' Then there was the reported feeling of 'lack of freedom', e.g. to engage in sideline occupations in the family; time for attending to personal affairs was lacking; extra money was often mobilized to be 'voluntarily invested'. Thus, in his article, while confirming the post-Liberation achievements on the whole, Li had directed attention to certain problems created by central planning and the rural co-operative movement, as well as to the discrepancy in the standards of living between workers and peasants.

The other study by Fei Hsiao-t'ung was a revisit to Kaisenkung, the village he had investigated in 1936 and described in his book *Peasant Life in China*. With several research assistants, he spent twenty days there in 1957 to re-study the livelihood of the peasants. He tried to assess changes in the standard of living in this village quantitatively. He found that the gross income of individual peasants had not increased appreciably in 1956 as compared to 1936 (in 1936, the gross income of an individual farmer was 800 catties of grain; in 1956, it was 850 catties) in spite of the fact that agricultural production in the whole village had increased by some 60 per cent. He identified the cause in the decline of sideline occupations which had been important subsidiary sources of income. Sideline occupations such as the rearing of silk worms and marketing by agent boats were either prohibited or made impossible by inefficient allocation of resources in the process of central planning and allocation. On the basis of these findings, he revived his idea of a diversified small-scale industry in the countryside and urged that it be reconsidered as a strategy of economic development. He thought that such a strategy would increase income and thus savings in the villages, and rural industries could help to train skilled factory workers for the nation. Then he analysed another phenomenon he had observed—the change toward relaxation in the pattern of low consumption and frugality among the villagers. He listed three factors contributing to the relaxation of frugality. First, as Liberation brought about stability and improvement, the peasants began to spend more on necessities which hitherto they could not afford. Termination of past hardships led to compensatory consumption. Second, socialist construction had created a state of euphoria and optimism, and many people thought that the co-operative movement could solve all their problems. Cadres also tried to stimulate mass enthusiasm with promises. There seemed to be no need to restrain consumption since everything would be rosy. Third, since land had come under the ownership of agricultural co-operatives, peasants tended to rely on the cadres to solve problems. Individuals refrained from solving problems independently because most of their familiar methods and ways of doing things were said to be inappropriate. It seemed that since everything was managed from 'above', when problems emerged, they were expected to be solved from 'above' as well. From the factors listed by Fei, it could be inferred that several tendencies such as rising expectations, unrealistic optimism and a pattern of dependence had been created by the rural co-operative movement. Fei had dwelt on these ominous tendencies at considerable length on the grounds that these pitfalls on the path of socialist construction should be identified and avoided.

The studies by Li and Fei, though positive on the general achievements of the government in improving the livelihood of the farmers, were critical of certain mistakes and revealed the existence of some serious problems. They had provided a valuable and rare glimpse into rural living in contemporary China of the time.

The early months of 1957 were heady months for the former sociologists. Their attempt to rebuild their profession appeared to be progressing smoothly. Success seemed to be at hand. Just at this point, frosty weather set in and killed their sprouts of hope.

Why the sudden change? Was the Hundred Flowers Movement a trap after all? Judging from available evidence, the critical and outspoken intellectuals were apparently the victims of a shift in the balance of power within the Communist Party. At least at the beginning, some of the leaders seemed to be genuinely interested in encouraging criticisms against the mistakes of dogmatism and bureaucratism among their ranks. There were indications that certain issues raised concerning sociology had the blessing of very high officials. During a meeting of the Supreme State Conference in March 1957, Chairman Mao had acknowledged the necessity of demographic research. He suggested that the government should establish a department or a committee on population affairs, and that non-governmental bodies should carry out research on the question of birth control (Mao Tse-tung, 1969, p. 97). But as the movement developed, the Communist Party leadership was shocked by the scope and intensity of the discontent expressed by the students and intellectuals. To the CCP, two trends were particularly alarming. One was the expansion in strength and ambition of the democratic parties. It has been estimated that from June to December 1956, the total membership of the democratic parties had nearly tripled to about 100,000. The Democratic League emerged as the largest minor party with a maximum membership of around 35,000 (Van Slyke, 1967, p. 242). Its rapid growth was clearly shown in its Shanghai branch alone, which was said to have increased from 956 members at the beginning of 1956 to 3384 by August 1957 (Wen Shih, 1963, p. 164). The other was the attempt to assess the standard of living of the peasants by investigators such as Fei Hsiao-t'ung and Li Ching-han. Their findings tend to show that the livelihood of the peasants had not improved significantly after Liberation, and that economic and social disparities existed between the peasants and the industrial workers. The 'worker–peasant alliance' which the CCP regarded as the basis of their power was directly called into question. The majority of the CCP members were evidently worried. They wanted to put a stop to the hostile attacks. One 'rightist' CCP member had reportedly said, 'Chairman Mao was under very great pressure. In this domestic crisis, telegrams [from Party officials in the provinces] flew like snowflakes, all demanding restriction [of free criticisms]' (*JMJP*, 22 July 1957, p. 2; quoted in Solomon, 1971, p. 316).

The counter-attack came in June 1957. The activists of the 'Hundred Flowers Movement' were labelled as 'rightists'. All the proposals concerning sociology were dismissed. The works of the former sociologists during the 'Hundred Flowers' as well as the pre-Liberation period came under close scrutiny. Suspicions were cast on their political motives and intellectual integrity.

The most important accusation directed against the effort to rebuild sociology was that it was a political plot. The logic of the critique was that sociology was a form of bourgeois ideology. On the level of theory, bourgeois sociology would obstruct the spread of marxism because it propagated idealist thought, encouraging reformism instead of revolution. It had allegedly been used to strengthen reactionary political rule by furnishing remedies to social problems in the form of social work and social administration (Sun Pen-wen, 1957b). On the level of practical action, bourgeois sociology would entail the resurrection of a capitalistic social order. Thus the plan for the social sciences as outlined by the Democratic League was denounced as a libel against marxism. Their suggestion that sociologists be permitted to evaluate government policies was accused of having been designed to capture the leadership of the country and to alter the direction of socialist construction (Kuo Mo-jo, 1957).

Besides the alleged attempt to compete for power, the social researches done by the sociologists during this period were said to be subversive propaganda on four counts. First, it was said that these researches had neglected the importance of class analysis. The use of averages in the measurement of household income in Fei's study was criticized for covering up differential rates of improvement in various classes. It was asserted that the average increase in income for the poor peasants should be 40 per cent and that for middle peasants 20 per cent. The gross average of 5 per cent increase arrived at by Fei was attacked as an erroneous computation. During the 'Anti-rightist' movement, Fei Hsiao-t'ung's research assistants admitted that the calculations were inaccurate, though they were not errors directly attributable to Fei (Chou Shu-lin *et al.*, 1957). According to Sun Pen-wen, who was obviously mobilized to condemn the 'rightists', the gross average of increase in income should have been 22 per cent (1957b). These corrections, however, were simply asserted. No details were given as to how they were calculated or what baseline was used for comparison to arrive at the percentages. These criticisms do not seem convincing as academic arguments for they lack solid evidence. They appear to me to have been mainly attempts to discredit research findings by attributing political motives to the researchers.

Second, the studies were accused of underplaying great post-Liberation achievements. It was said that Fei should not have compared the income of the peasants in 1957 with that of 1936, because the income of the peasants in 1936 was the highest during the pre-1949 period. The choice of 1936 as the baseline of comparison was seen to have been deliberate in order to degrade achievements under socialism.

Third, the investigations were charged with having opposed and raised doubts about the leadership of the Party and the merits of socialism. The problems and discontents revealed in Fei and Li's studies were attacked as distortions of reality that sought to incite dissatisfaction among the peasants against the government and against the workers. They were described as acts of 'setting fire' and sowing dissension in the villages in order to undermine the agricultural co-operative movement and to challenge the correctness of the Party leadership. The ultimate aim of the researches, it was alleged, were to create a 'Hungarian incident' to topple the socialist government. Thus, 'if Chinese society today really needs analyses and investigations, these are better left to be done by the Party and the State, and by people who are loyal to socialism' (Sun Ting-kuo, 1957, p. 4).

Fourth, the studies were accused of being in the service of imperialist countries. Fei had allegedly signed a contract with a British publisher to release his research findings in the United Kingdom. This was criticized as an attempt to provide anti-Party and anti-socialist materials to imperialist countries injurious to the interests of the nation.

There were few discussions about the facts and on the validity of the findings in these criticisms. Whether the problems and conditions reported by Fei and Li existed or not was not settled with scientific evidence. The tenor of the 'Anti-rightist' campaign was that sociological activities were in competition with a marxist interpretation of reality and were thus regarded as subversive. It is an article of faith among sociologists that the very nature of their discipline impels them to unmask official versions of social reality. Such a position proved to be intolerable to the established authority in the People's Republic, resulting in an open conflict which was resolved politically. The voices of the advocators were silenced with mass criticism. The sociologists had to admit their 'crimes' to the people (Fei Hsiao-t'ung, 1957d).

For sociology, this had been a period of frantic activity. For several eventful months, we are witnesses first to the struggle for sociology's rebirth, second to the agony of its still-birth, and finally to the caustic obituaries on the death of professional sociology that concluded the episode.

Sociology in oblivion

Following the unsuccessful attempt to rebuild sociology, the public activities of the former sociologists subsided. Very few articles written by them appeared. The labels of 'rightist' were removed from people like Fei and P'an Kuang-tan after about two years, and they resumed their positions in the Central Institute of Nationalities. We learn about an encounter between Chairman Mao and Fei Hsiao-t'ung during the Anti-rightist campaign from a speech given by the Chairman to the Supreme State Conference in October 1957. Chairman Mao referred to Fei (1969, p. 136):

I had a talk with him, and I said, 'Can you possibly change your ways?' (laughter). He had adopted our method of 'establishing roots and forging ties' developed during the land reform movement. He had over two hundred high-level intellectuals as his friends who were scattered all over Peking, Chengtu, Wuhan, Shanghai, and Wuhsi. He said that's his trouble. He could not extricate himself from that circle. Not only did he fail to extricate himself, he consciously organized them, and represented them in blooming and contending. I told him, 'You can give up those two hundred, and find another two hundred among the workers and peasants'. He said he did not know whether we still want to have him. I said, 'Have you not been talking about investigations? You can investigate again, and if you investigate from the standpoint of the workers, who will get rid of you?'

We do not know whether Fei took the Chairman's advice. In any case, he disappeared from the public view for a long time. He re-emerged again in 1972 and has received foreign visitors on several occasions.

Some theoretical articles related to sociology could be found after 1957, though they were few and sporadic. A number of them were extensions of the critique against the bourgeois nature of the pre-Liberation writings of the Chinese sociologists. The popular and influential textbook by Sun Pen-wen, *The Principles of Sociology*, was subject to its author's own criticisms and the adverse evaluation of others (Sun Pen-wen, 1958). Sun Pen-wen summarized his mistakes in seven points—the book leaned towards theoretical compromise in that it tried to combine three different bourgeois sociological theories; it neglected the determining effect of the mode of production on social structure and development; it slighted the role of the masses in history; it over-emphasized the importance of technological discoveries; it propagated reformist thought of the Fabian socialist variety; it popularized the reactionary Malthusian theory of population growth; it paid too much attention to the importance of culture at the expense of the economic substructure. Sun concluded that 'since my *Principles of Sociology* had adopted the standpoint, perspective and method of the bourgeoisie, it was completely mistaken and useless'.

The remaining articles were nearly all related to the polemical debate against Russian 'revisionism' following the open ideological split with the Soviet Union in the early 1960s. One article titled 'Idealistic sociology under the banner of Marxism' criticized the social philosophy of a Russian-educated social theorist, Fung Ting, for 'exalting individual welfare as the highest aim of socialism' and for implying a theory of 'technical determinism' which assigned a central role to technology in economic development. Both of these mistakes were perceived to be the key doctrines of Russian revisionism which deviated from marxist theory (Kuo Lo-chi, 1965). Another article, by Chuang Fu-ling, was a critique of the theory of class and class conflict, often referred to as social stratification in western sociological literature (Chuang Fu-ling, 1963). In this article, western theories were criticized as anti-marxist. According to Chuang, western theorists had not directly denied the existence of class and class conflict in society. Instead they had tried to confuse the issue on the question of the classification and demarcation of social classes. One attempt was the 'distribution theory' placing prime emphasis on the difference of distribution in society and using income differentials as the criterion for class division. Another was what Chuang called the 'organizational theory' which stressed occupational differences in the social organization of production as indicators of class. Differences in education and cultural standards were also used. On the question of class conflict, western theories such as the theory of technocratization and the rise of 'managerial' society, the theory of social mobility, the theory of the emergence of the middle class etc., were criticized as a camouflage disguising acute class conflicts in capitalist societies. These theories were seen to be theoretical justifications for class co-operation, substituting class conflict with improvement in economic distribution as the means of social improvement. It appears that the implicit target of the article was the Soviet Union's strategy of development. The interesting point about this article was that, despite the usual reasoning deducing from marxist premises such phenomena as the polarization of classes, its analysis was sophisticated. It showed knowledge of recent developments in the western theories of social stratification, including the Davis and Moore hypothesis, indicating that at least some current western works on sociology were available in China.

In recent years, as the People's Republic of China has broken out of a long period of diplomatic isolation, cultural relationships with the United States and other western nations have been resumed. We have had more opportunities to hear of people like Fei Hsiao-t'ung, Wu Wen-tsao, and Lin Yao-hua. Fei and his colleagues have told a group of American visitors that they have already discarded their sociological selves (G. Cooper, 1973, p. 482):

> We realize that you are concerned about us of the old society who have studied anthropology in the West and about the work we have done and are doing....
>
> As for your calling us 'anthropologist', we can only accept it as a title of the past. We are the ones who have studied

61

anthropology. This point we will not and cannot deny. It is a historical fact.

They also told their visitors that no new sociologists have been trained. Their break with their past seems to be complete for Fei confessed that he regarded his books as completely worthless: 'I cannot even read the works I've written on the Chinese peasant in the past...' (*ibid.*, p. 481). Though Chinese sociologists are apparently 'very much a dead species', the need to study sociology is not denied. On one occasion, Fei said that, with critical evaluation, western sociology can be used in the understanding of the current state and nature of capitalism (*Hsin wan-pao* [Hong Kong], 31 May 1975, p. 1). In October 1971, C. K. Yang, who has been teaching at the University of Pittsburgh, visited China. He met his teacher Wu Wen-tsao and asked about Wu's academic work. Wu said he wanted to write some critiques of Max Weber's theories. He had the main writings by Weber, and Yang promised to send him the more recent publications from the USA (Yang Ch'ing-k'un, 1972, p. 56). But we still have to wait for these promised reviews and critiques of western sociology to appear. Meanwhile, some visitors returning from the People's Republic observed that the library holdings on the social sciences in the universities are quite outdated. Most of the books in English are pre-Liberation editions (see, for example, J. S. Prybyla, 1975).

3 Social investigation and research

The philosophers have only interpreted the world in different
ways; the point is to change it.

> —Karl Marx, 1845
> (T. B. Bottomore, and
> M. Rubel, 1963, p. 84)

In order to change the world, one must understand it
correctly. The way to achieve correct understanding is to carry
out investigation and research.

> —Hsia Ying, 1961
> (*JMJP*, 30 March 1961)

... there exists a fundamental difference between the things that
anthropologists do, both in theory and practice, and our
revolutionary work in China.

> —Fei Hsiao-t'ung, Wu
> Wen-tsao, and Lin Yao-
> hua, 1973 (G. Cooper,
> 1973, p. 482)

If the Chinese communists are dedicated to change Chinese society
in terms of a socialist vision, they do not always handle this task in
the same manner. We have been told time and time again by the
communist leaders themselves that tendencies of 'subjectivism' and
dogmatism exist in the Party. Some party funtionaries are fond of
translating their wishes into policies, and others are energetic in
applying the textbook marxist–leninist tenets mechanically. In the
eyes of Mao Tse-tung, these are grave mistakes. The antidote he

prescribes is contained in a capsule: 'No investigations, no right to speak.' He practises what he preaches. While he was still in the political wilderness, he attempted an analysis of the class structure of Chinese society (1926). Prior to an important debate on Party policy, he returned to his native province, Hunan, to explore the question of peasant movements. He wrote an influential report on the subject (1927) which redirected the revolutionary strategy of the Chinese Communist Party. He emphasized the significance of the peasants and defied the Comintern's orthodoxy of placing exclusive stress on the urban proletariat. To collect material for his report, he approached the poor peasants and succeeded in establishing rapport with them. Some forty years later, he recalled how he cultivated one of his informants (1969, p. 553):

> I sought out a farmer to have a game of domino, and then I invited him to a meal. Before, during, and after the meal, we talked and I understood how violent were the class struggles in the villages. He was willing to talk to me because firstly I treated him as a human being, secondly he enjoyed a free meal, and thirdly he could win some money. I was a perpetual loser. I lost one or two dollars to him, and he was satisfied.

Mao had no illusions as to the painstaking nature of social inquiry. He did not think he had fully grasped the class situation in the countryside until he had spent ten years there carrying out more than eight investigations. It was on such a foundation of knowledge that he drafted the 1933 land reform proposals that won his Party's widespread support (ibid., p. 474).

During the Anti-Japanese War when he led his Party from strength to strength, he advised his followers that good leadership could only result from an intimate knowledge of actual social conditions, and the only way to know the situation was 'to make social investigations, to investigate the conditions of each social class' in real life (1965, vol. 3, p. 11). He lamented the lack of social scientific information about China, a sad state of affairs which he attributed to the weakness of the Chinese bourgeoisie, and which he thought must be rectified by his comrades (ibid., p. 13):

> Speaking generally, the infant bourgeoisie of China has not been able, and never will be able, to provide relatively comprehensive or even rudimentary material on social conditions, as the bourgeoisie in Europe, America and Japan has done; we have therefore no alternative but to collect it ourselves. Speaking specifically, people engaged in practical work must at all times keep abreast of changing conditions, and this is something for which no Communist Party in any country can

depend on others. Therefore, everyone engaged in practical work must investigate conditions at the lower levels.

His exhoration on the importance of social inquiry had been formalized as a policy in August, 1941. 'The Resolution of the Central Committee of the Communist Party on Investigation and Research' stipulated that bureaux be established in central and regional party organs to carry out 'systematic and comprehensive social surveys as the basis for decision-making'. Several methods of data-collection were suggested: to use documentary sources such as newspapers, periodicals, books, local gazetteers, and genealogies; to organize fact-finding meetings composed of informants and experienced cadres; to conduct individual interviews; and to gather biographical material on important personalities in each locality (Chieh-fang-she, 1950, pp. 57–60). Research and investigation became one of the five fields of study in the professional education of cadres (J. W. Lewis, 1963, p. 147).

Such a realistic approach of assessing actual social conditions to formulate revolutionary strategies and tactics brought the Communist Party to victory in 1949. What has happened to social inquiries since then? Chairman Mao addressed this topic again in 1961, probably after some reflection on the excesses and mistakes committed during the Great Leap Forward. Though sporadic efforts had been made since Liberation, he complained at the Ninth Plenum of the Eighth Central Committee, cadres had generally neglected investigation and research. Though nobody opposed his injunction on investigations, he said, few supported it with enthusiasm and actually acted on it. Therefore he suggested that 1961 be made 'a year of investigation and research' (1967, pp. 262–4). This call from Mao resulted in numerous articles in the official press instructing cadres on this matter. A book of quotations drawn from Mao's writings concerning this topic was published (Chung-kuo jen-min ta-hsüeh, 1961).

The significance of social inquiry has been appreciated not only by the communist leaders, but also by non-marxist Chinese scholars who learned the techniques of social analysis from the West before Liberation. Unlike the philosophers criticized by Marx, these scholars were not content with just interpreting the world. They stressed the close relationship between social scientific knowledge and political action. They sought to make their academic efforts useful. As the young Fei Hsiao-t'ung, who might well speak for his generation of Chinese sociologists, noted (1939, p. 4):

An adequate definition of the situation, if it is to organize successful action and attain the desired end, must be reached through a careful analysis of the functions of the social

65

institutions, in relation to the need that they purport to satisfy and in relation to other institutions on which their working depends. This is the work of a social scientist. Social sciences therefore should play an important role in directing cultural change.

It is apparent that, at least prior to 1949, both the communists including Mao and the sociologists including Fei were equally emphatic on the importance and usefulness of social research. But the communists have maintained all along that their social investigations differ from the practice of the sociologists. They used to employ the notion of the 'two sociologies' to mark the difference. There is, according to marxist theoreticians, an old sociology which is 'bourgeois' and erroneous, and a new sociology which stands for the true social theory of 'historical materialism' (Shen Chih-yüan, 1947, p. 47). Later, even the term 'sociology' is abandoned for its 'bourgeois' connotation. In a recent interview, the reformed Fei Hsiao-t'ung, Wu Wen-tsao, and Lin Yao-hua spoke of their 'revolutionary work' as distinct from sociology and social anthropology. But what are these fundamental differences in theory and in practice to which they refer? To seek an answer, we have to examine the nature of so-called 'investigation and research' (*tiao-ch'a yen-chiu*) in some detail, probing first into their basic assumptions, and then into the practical steps by which they are conducted.

When we turn the sociological perspective back upon the subject of sociology itself, it is obvious that its form and its development are shaped by the social and political contexts in which it is embedded. To paraphrase a familiar dictum, a society gets the sociology it deserves. If so, western sociology probably owes its being to a particular form of social organization. We shall return to this question in more detail later. It would suffice to note here that the social system of contemporary China differs quite radically from the social systems of Western Europe and North America. Consequently, we would not expect the values and assumptions governing social analysis in these countries to be the same. There are, I believe, five major points of divergence.

1 On the existence of social laws

The Chinese communists assert that laws on the formation and transformation of society exist, and that the main outlines have already been discovered by Karl Marx. Accordingly, marxism is the only valid and scientific theory of society. With this belief, it is logical that there should be one monolithic theoretical framework.

This is in stark contrast with the multifarious schools of thought in western sociology nurtured by the attitude that human knowledge is necessarily imperfect. Objective social laws, even if they exist, are thought to be beyond human comprehension. With this consciousness of the unknowable, opinions are often held tentatively. Divergent theoretical positions are tolerated and accepted in principle.

2 The partisan principle

Knowledge about the social world is held to be inherently partisan. Social science is defined as part of the superstructure (e.g. Hua Kang, 1952, p. 3). Social knowledge is held to be affected by the class position of the investigator. Therefore there can be no disinterested, 'objective' knowledge which transcends class interests. The partisan principle is vividly expressed in the Chinese critique of western sociology. 'Bourgeois' sociology is thought to emerge as a response of the ruling elites in capitalist societies to the threat posed by marxism. 'The bourgeoisie desperately needed a new theory to resist the revolutionary theory of the proletariat in order to justify its existence as a class. To fulfil this need, a sociology which attempted to integrate all bourgeois social sciences emerged' (Chou Yang, 1963, p. 3). The claim of sociologists to remain neutral and non-partisan, even with the best of intentions, is inevitably a myth and a form of false consciousness. Even though they may try to avoid the sin of commission by not acting as defenders of the capitalist order, sociologists nevertheless commit the sin of omission by not embracing marxism–leninism. Since not to oppose the corrupted *status quo* actively is to endorse it, it is argued, sociologists necessarily serve the interests of the bourgeoisie in effect if not in intent. To be partisan in itself is not thought to be invalidating or hindering to the pursuit of truth and knowledge. What is important is that one should serve the 'progressive force' in history. Sociologists err because they choose the wrong side and serve the wrong master. Implied in this argument is the assumption that certain social groups have privileged access to truth. In the People's Republic, this group is thought to be the proletariat. As the Communist Party represents the interests of the proletariat, social investigators must serve the Party if they are to achieve valid knowledge. Academic autonomy and detachment are thus meaningless because they are theoretically impossible. The counterpart of this partisan principle in practical affairs is the denial of the legitimacy of a liberalism that subscribes to the theory of political checks and balances. The centralized political framework cannot be challenged. This has been regarded as the touchstone that differentiates right from wrong, good from bad.

In his revised speech 'On the Correct Handling of Contradictions among the People', Mao Tse-tung has formulated six criteria to judge all scientific as well as artistic activities. Words and actions, he said, should not undermine the following phenomena: the unity of the various nationalities in the country; socialist transformation and socialist construction; the people's democratic dictatorship; democratic centralism; the leadership of the Communist Party; and international socialist unity. Of the six criteria, Mao regarded the socialist path and the leadership of the Party to be the most important (1977, p. 412).

3 The function of social inquiry

The technique of investigation and research is regarded as a democratic device. This view was succinctly expressed by a local cadre in Honan during his conversation with Michel Oksenberg. Replying to Oksenberg's question 'What do I have to understand in order to comprehend why you think China is a democracy?', the cadre said, 'Investigation work, you must understand investigation work' (Oksenberg, 1974, p. 28). One of the main structural problems of the People's Republic is the relation between the leaders and the led. In communist vocabulary, this is the contradiction between 'centralism and democracy'. The danger for the cadres, the vanguards of the socialist revolution, is the possibility of their becoming alienated from their followers. One of the correctives to excessive centralism is the mounting of social surveys that can monitor the condition and aspirations of ordinary people.

4 Advocacy and analysis

But investigation and research is not simply an instrument of opinion polling, and this leads to the fourth characteristic of advocacy and analysis. While the question of advocacy is still a controversial issue in western sociology, Chinese communists are unambiguous in emphasizing relevance and commitment. Since the cadres should lead and educate the masses instead of passively reflecting their wishes, social investigations should also be used for didactic purposes. The stress on advocacy is interconnected with the image of man and the idea of potentiality in Chinese marxism. According to D. Munro, man is regarded as malleable and perfectible by the Chinese communists (1971, pp. 609–40). The marxist maxim that it is social existence that determines social consciousness has apparently been stood on its head. Much importance has been attached to will power, to the correct worldview. This voluntaristic tendency in the ideology of Chinese marxism has been noticed by many scholars.

James Coleman, for instance, classifies the strategy of social change adopted in contemporary China as one that rests heavily on the transformation and enlightenment of the individual (1971, pp. 633–50). This strategy embodies a notion of 'potentiality' or 'potential consciousness'. Existent reality is less significant than the potential one that can be 'called forth' under certain conditions. Objective conditions and human response towards such conditions are also important, but with proper revolutionary leadership and education, it is believed, human responses may be improved and objective conditions are not ineluctable (see L. Goldman, 1969, p. 122; J. Gray, 1972). Therefore the criterion of truth is not simply the correspondence with existing reality, but the practical results which knowledge can bring about. Truth, then, lies in the effects. Herbert Marcuse has provided an insightful analysis of this logic in Soviet marxism which seems to fit the Chinese case as well (1958, pp. 86–7, original emphasis):

> The key propositions of Soviet Marxism have the function of announcing and commanding a definite practice, apt to create the facts which the propositions stipulate. They claim no truth-value of their own but proclaim a pre-established truth which is to be realized through a certain attitude and behaviour. They are pragmatic directives for action . . . . Within the context in which they appear their falsity does not invalidate them, for to Soviet Marxism their verification is not in the given facts, but in 'tendencies' in a historical process in which the commanded political practice will *bring about* the desired facts.

5 Specialist and generalist

The idea of potentiality is related to the last characteristic of a preference for the generalist, the non-professional, and an abhorrence of a compartmentalized form of social division of labour. Mao Tse-tung is critical of the intellectuals for possessing only book knowledge. In line with a strategy of mass mobilization as opposed to technocratic management, he appeals to the creativity and initiative of the ordinary people, and urges them to break away from a 'superstitious' reliance on the experts. To the specialists, Mao counsels a combination of 'redness' and 'expertness'. Applied to social research, this means the ideal investigator must attend to political orientations and consequences as well as to techniques and methods.

What are the practical implications of these basic assumptions in actual social inquiry? Let us now turn to the organization and execution of social investigations and research.

Research personnel

Investigative activities in contemporary China have been described by some observers as 'mass sociology' or 'the layman's social research' conducted by 'the masses of peasants and workers' (L. C. Young, 1974; C. C. Lau, 1974). These descriptions evoke the exciting picture of eight hundred million social analysts. It is a picture that may contain grains of truth if it means that a popularized form of 'sociological imagination' has become part of everyday culture. There are grounds for believing that through participation in 'study groups' and political meetings, the common people in China today tend to understand their individual life situations more and more in terms of social class as well as national and world history. It may well be, in C. W. Mill's phrases, that a link is being forged by individuals between their 'private troubles of milieu' and the 'public issues of social structure'. But it would be misleading to imply that social investigations are performed by men and women on the street. It appears to me that the tasks of investigation are mainly assigned to two categories of people: the cadres, and the teachers and students in the universities.

Cadres at all levels of government are urged to learn and to practise social inquiry so as to become what might be called administrators-cum-researchers. The ideal cadre appears to be a generalist who can merge several tasks into one role. Cadres carry out investigations for two main purposes. The first one is therapeutic and educational. The intention is to keep them in touch with their followers by periodical 'role reversals'. The *hsia-fang* (sending down or downward transfer) system which forces cadres out of their offices either to the shop-floor or to the countryside, the later system of *tun-tien* (squatting at a spot) which requires cadres to spend their stay in the countryside in a single production team instead of drifting from place to place, and the most recent May Seventh Cadres' School scheme in which cadres stay together in a school in rural areas to learn through physical labour, are all schemes meant to make those in leadership positions aware of actual situations by 'stepping into the shoes' of their followers.

Besides this educational intent, cadres also carry out investigations to solve specific problems. Such investigations are usually performed by research teams. It is recommended that the suitable size of a team consist of four to five cadres (Yang Po, 1959, no. 4, p. 40). If a research task cannot be handled by one team, several should be sent, and the leading cadre should co-ordinate the efforts. Oksenberg has reported an instance of how a research team is selected in his description of a survey carried out on the fishing industry in the coastal areas of Kwangtung (1974, p. 25):

The head of the Price Section in the General Office of the provincial Finance and Trade Development selected the section cadres who would go on this investigation. He chose specialists in fish prices and cadres who previously investigated conditions there. He was reluctant, however, to assign cadres to their native place or to a place where they have previously held a position, since strong personal ties might inhibit the investigation. Because the coastal areas are particularly sensitive areas from a public security stand-point, he also chose the politically more reliable cadres. The Price Section also notified other pertinent provincial agencies of the number of investigation cadres they were to send.

It is interesting to note that a rule of avoidance is observed; and that investigators are drawn from several government agencies.

As for university teachers and students acting as social researchers, this is a relatively recent development. Unity between theory and practice is a major theme of the Cultural Revolution in education. Students in the humanities and the social sciences are exhorted to treat the whole society as their laboratory. Teams of students and teachers often spend part of the year doing research outside the campus. For them, research also serves a dual purpose: to facilitate learning, and to provide reference materials for various government departments (see Wu-han ta-hsüeh, 1972).

Organization

Unlike the situation in most western societies, social research institutions are mainly attached not to the universities but to Party and Government organizations. The Party and the Government are the most important sponsors of social research. We have already referred to the 1941 resolution of the Communist Party which directed the higher organs of the Party to set up research bureaux. The persistence and extent to which this resolution has been put into effect is not very clear. But a sampling of the investigation reports published in *Red Flag* shows the existence of many research units formed by organizations such as the Ministry of Commerce, the Municipal Committee of Peking, the revolutionary committee of a county in Shansi etc. In a study of the research reports printed in the *People's Daily* and *Red Flag* between 1968 and 1970, it has been found that social research is sponsored at all administrative levels of the Government—the local level (at or below the people's commune), the regional level (at or below the province), and the national level. Organizations at the regional level have been found to be the most active sponsors (C. C. Lau, 1974, p. 15). As investigators operate within the administrative hierarchy, they tend to comply with its line of authority. The attention of investigation is directed downwards, that is, teams organized at the national level will study problems in the provinces, and regional teams will investigate matters at the local level.

Research problems

The choice of research problems does not rest with the investigators. Research workers are instructed to study 'what are being required, what are being tackled, and what need to be solved by the leadership of the Party and the Government' (Yang Po, 1959, no. 3, p. 24). For a concrete case, we may look at the 1971 student research project conducted by the Political Economy Department of the Wuhan University. The teachers first applied to the Ministry of Commerce which, in turn, suggested to them about twenty research problems. The teachers and students then selected several from among the twenty. Their primary concern was whether the topics were relevant to the struggle for production and whether they fit in with the work schedule of the administrative sections involved. While in the field, the research teams had to modify their research problems once again to suit the plans of the local administrative units (Wu-han ta-hsüeh, 1972, p. 50). Since research topics are defined by administrative organizations, most of the investigations are instrumental in nature and deal with specific questions such as the condition of the co-operative movement, education reform, or rural medical service in particular localities. Very few theoretical studies synthesizing scattered findings and grappling with macroscopic problems have been attempted. The rare ones that come to mind are nearly all works by Chairman Mao, such as his thesis on internal contradictions among the people, and his essay 'On the Ten Major Relationships'. As for the applied investigations and research, they may be conveniently classified into three categories—data-collection related to policy formulation, to policy implementation and to policy evaluation (see Hung Yen-lin, 1956). Without a systematic survey of all available research reports, it is my impression that a relationship exists between the hierarchial position of the investigator and the types of research that are carried out. It appears that research problems are ranked in an order of importance to be tackled by cadres at suitable administrative levels.

Studies that are theoretical in nature or intended for the formulation of major policies are done at the national level. Theoretical studies have already been discussed. Data gathering for the formulation of important policies is frequently carried out by leaders at the top echelon. The province of Hunan seems to be a favourite spot for their field trips. The prototype of this kind of study is of course Mao's 1927 investigation of the peasant movement there. In 1955, he returned to the same province and also travelled to Fukien. After sampling several localities and examining the development of agricultural co-operatives, he promulgated an important directive on the question of strengthening the leadership by poor peasants in the co-operatives (Hung Yen-lin, 1961). Another example of field trips by high officials is the one carried out in 1961 by Liu Shao-ch'i and his wife Wang Kuang-mei. They spent forty-four days investigating six production brigades of three communes in three counties of Hunan. On the basis of the material gathered, they formulated an influential report on agricultural policy. This policy was subsequently severely criticized during the Cultural Revolution, and Liu Shao-ch'i was accused of misusing the rubric 'investigation and research' (Ting Wang, 1967, p. 313).

Provincial research teams are mainly occupied with investigations to ensure the successful implementation of policies, as well as monitoring progress and results. It has been stressed that 'during the execution and planning of policies, frequent inspections and evaluations should be carried out. When the work is completed, there should be an overall evaluation' (Hung Yen-lin, 1961). Similar research tasks face local level organizations, but they are much less active. Among 443 sponsors noted by Lau in his survey of research reports published between 1968 and 1970, only about 5 per cent were local level agencies.

Research methods

The techniques employed in investigation and research may be divided into direct and indirect methods. The relative emphases that should be assigned to these methods has been a controversial issue which perhaps reveals a conflict between the demand for central planning and that for local initiative.

The indirect method includes the use of questionnaire surveys that rely on either complete enumeration or various forms of statistical sampling. Many professional statisticians and central planners have been the champions of this method. They have upheld the need for accurate and comprehensive data. Hsüeh Mu-ch'iao, Director of the State Statistical Bureau before its virtual disintegration during the Great Leap Forward, once stated that 'in socialist countries, the most important research method is complete coverage' owing to the need of data for the management of national industries (1957, p. 8). For some time, the direct method of 'model' research has been dismissed as crude and unscientific. Many statisticians have regarded this method of little use because it

73

cannot yield accurate estimates of the total phenomenon. It is thus unimportant for the purpose of central planning. During the Great Leap Forward, this attitude came under heavy fire. Those who held this view were criticized for discouraging cadres from carrying out research. Since then 'model' research has been given primacy, and most reports published in Chinese newspapers and magazines are of this genre.

The 'model' method employs first-hand observation. It has been compared graphically to 'the anatomy of a sparrow'. A model, or *tien-hsing*, does not mean the most common phenomenon or the statistical average. Rather, 'it shares some common basic characteristics with the totality, and possesses a definite representative nature among phenomena of the same type' (Yo Wei, 1965, p. 49). In this sense, it has some resemblance to Weber's notion of the 'ideal type' as an attempt to capture the typical. The difference is that a model is not a theoretical and heuristic construct. It carries the meaning of a 'specimen' and an 'exemplar' (Hung Yen-lin, 1956, p. 39). The procedure of selecting models for investigation is to classify the subjects to be studied into three types—the advanced, the average, and the backward in terms of the degree of success in policy implementation. If the researcher wants to derive some estimate of the existing situation, it is advised, attention should be paid to the average models. But if the investigator is interested in the way in which certain policies are being executed, he should examine the advanced models to see why they succeed, and the backward models to learn the lessons of their failings. But very often, it is the advanced or 'positive' models that command the attention of the investigating cadres and receive extensive publicity. Hung Yen-lin has given us an illustration of how a model should be chosen (*ibid.*, p. 41):

> If we want to find a model of a farming co-operative, we
> must carry out general investigations to have a general view of
> the characteristics of the local peasant economy and the
> development of the co-operative movement. Then from a village
> with more thorough mass mobilization and better foundation of
> co-operative movements, we select a co-operative which has
> considerable achievement and which has a better execution of
> the Party's rural class policy to be the model.

After the selection of models, tentative research outlines should be drafted. Then interviews can start in earnest. A favourite means used to solicit information is the fact-finding meeting. A discussion group consisting of knowledgeable informants will be organized. The opinions of these informants frequently appear as direct quotes in the investigation reports. The researchers also have to interview

74

other people. In order to establish confidence and trust, they are urged to become complete participants by 'eating, living, working and studying' with their respondents.

Such a procedure does not seem to differ radically from the techniques of participant observation and intensive case studies used in professional sociology. What is disquieting to a sociologist is the lack of precautions against subjective bias and unrepresentative sampling. But the value placed on accuracy and representativeness is relative to the aims of the research. Model investigation is conceived to be an instrument of social experimentation and engineering. According to Yang Po, this method has three advantages over complete coverage (1959, no. 2, pp. 36–7). First, it is convenient and economical, and can be carried out with little manpower in a short period. It can thus provide timely information. Second, it yields detailed and vivid material whereas survey data are necessarily abstract and simplified. It is useful in understanding the causes and processes of development of certain social phenomena. Third, and most importantly in relation to the problem of representativeness, model research is sensitive to the emergence of new trends. Since new phenomena are inevitably atypical and in the minority when they first emerge, they may not be noticed readily in complete enumerations because of their numerical insignificance. Large-scale surveys, in this view, have a conservative bent, ill-suited to depicting the dynamic aspect of social conditions (Yo Wei, 1965, p. 47):

> frequent model investigations so as to have a timely grasp of the budding of new phenomena which signify new trends in the process of development of the totality are very important in speeding up the metamorphosis of contradictions and the development of the revolution ... if the emphasis is on overall surveys and not model studies, we would be blind to the evolvement of new phenomena ....

The role of a model, in this case, is to serve as a trendsetter embodying the ideal state of affairs as seen by the leadership. It serves as an example that should be emulated. This function of the model investigation may be compared to that of the hero figures in Chinese revolutionary literature which embody social ideals. Used in this fashion, the question of whether the model is representative becomes quite irrelevant.

Presentation of results

The presentation of research results is affected by the social function of investigation and research to promote social experimentation.

Since mass mobilization is in fact the dominant strategy of development, the key audience of the published reports is the general public rather than the professional circle as is the case in academic sociology. Because of this difference, such conventions as detailed footnotes and references are abandoned. The virtues of plain language and brevity are extolled. To illustrate, let us look at two exemplary reports which received the praise of the editor of the *People's Daily* in 1972. In an introductory note to these two pieces of work, the editor wrote (reprinted in *Hung-ch'i*, no. 8, 1972, p. 43):

> These two research reports are short and clear. Such a style should be encouraged.
>
> Many articles in our newspapers are too lengthy. Who would read them? This should be corrected.
>
> Thirty years ago, Chairman Mao criticized long essays which are devoid of content in his 'Oppose the Party's "Eight-legged" Essays'. He indicated that 'we should reflect on how to make our writings shorter and more concise'. This exhortation is still meaningful today. We hope to solve this problem together with our comrades to make our essays shorter, and shorter still.

The two investigations were conducted by the Ministry of Commerce, and they dealt with the question of supplementing forestry with sheep-rearing in a production brigade in Honan, and the pig-rearing enterprise in another brigade in Chekiang. The topics were concerned with problems of the livelihood of the common people, and this was the orientation common to most other investigations. The reports followed a nearly standard format, and we can take the report on the brigade in Honan as an example (*ibid.,* p. 43–4). The first part described the location and setting. Quantitative details were provided. This particular brigade was situated in a hilly region. It consisted of sixteen production teams with 236 households, 1,221 persons, and 1,725 *mou* of agricultural land. Owing to the infertile soil, production was low, and any drought or floods would endanger self-sufficiency in food. Since 1965, the brigade had followed Chairman Mao's instruction to diversify and began rearing sheep. In 1965, the number of sheep was 240, and by 1971, it had grown to 1,300. Following the presentation of background information, the next section outlined two conflicts in the organization of production. The first conflict concerned whether the sheep should be reared by individual households or by the collectivity. The reports demonstrated that both extremes were harmful as shown in the decline in output. The correct solution was given as a compromise, and the positive results were furnished in figures. The second conflict was over the correct allotment of land to be devoted to forestry and sheep-rearing. A suitable balance was indicated in the plan worked out by this brigade. Innovations in the organization of production were suggested to other brigades in similar situations. In the concluding section, the merits of these innovations were shown in the increases in public accumulation and investments in the construction of water-works and small factories in that locality.

From this example we can see that only materials that are considered to be immediately useful and relevant to the specific problem at hand are provided. This feature, coupled with the tendency toward selective publication of the ideal case, render these research reports unenlightening as to actual social conditions. They are rather examples for affirming and illustrating current policies. As such, they may be useful in providing hints on trends in official thinking about the ways in which certain social issues ought to be handled.

4 Ethnology and the minority nationalities

If the marriage between sociology and anthropology came early in China, as Maurice Freedman has observed, then separation occurred soon after 1949. While professional sociology was banished from the academic arena, research and teaching in anthropology persisted. Western anthropology includes both the physical and cultural branches. It is the latter, also known as ethnology, which has been so entwined with sociology in China. Two fields closely related to ethnology—anthropological archaeology and linguistics—have made much progress in the People's Republic (see F. L. K. Hsu, 1961), but they are peripheral to our present concern. The attention of post-Liberation ethnology has mainly focused upon the social organization and cultural life of non-Han peoples who are mostly non-literate. For a short time, research interest also rested on the emigrant communities in south-eastern China from which most of the overseas Chinese originated.

Ethnological studies of the minority peoples appeared soon after the social sciences were introduced into China. Interest was aroused partly for reasons of national security. The significance of the non-Han peoples lay not in their numbers but in their locations. Comprising not more than 6 per cent of the entire Chinese population according to the 1953 census, they occupied more than half of the total area of the country. The land they inhabited stretched along frontier regions such as Inner Mongolia, Sinkiang, Tibet, Yunnan and Kwangsi (Wu Wen-tsao, 1955). Therefore the security of the borders had to depend on their allegiance to the central government. On their own, the minorities were also capable of creating internal political turmoil. Historically, some groups such as the Mongols and the Manchus succeeded in capturing the throne and ruling the Han majority. In more recent times, improved means of communication as well as forced migrations created by war have led to increased contacts between the Han and the minorities. The need for knowledge and understanding, combined with a rather paternalistic ideal of enlightenment on the part of some Han researchers, furnished the impetus for an ethnological enterprise.

One of the important pioneers in the field was Ts'ai Yuan-p'ei who first used the term *min-tsu-hsüeh* in 1926 as a translation of ethnology (Hsu I-t'ang, 1944, p. 27). Ts'ai studied ethnology in Leipzig, Germany at the turn of this century. Field survey began in earnest after he had created an ethnological unit within the Academia Sinica in 1927. Within the next decade, research was carried out in north-east, south-east and south-west China, with only the north-west relatively untouched (Ho Lien-k'uei, 1955, pp. 19–20).

Anthropology and ethnology first appeared in the curriculum of higher education when the Ch'ing government published its 1903 'College Institution and Curriculum'. In the early years of Republican China, courses on ethnology were offered only in Peking University where Ts'ai Yuan-p'ei was the Chancellor. Though teaching in this subject subsequently spread to other universities, academic respectability was not readily achieved. Very often ethnology failed to attain status as a discipline in its own right, as Fei Hsiao-t'ung testified in his reminiscence about his pre-Liberation career (1957a, p. 2):

As a student and as a teacher, I always had some relations with sociology. In fact, some friends and I had smuggled in something else under the name of sociology. How to call these we were not sure. They included investigations of minority groups, rural villages, towns and factories. In the eyes of orthodox American and British sociologists, such studies would normally be regarded as outside their discipline. If we must insist on an academic label, they were similar to what was known in America and Britain as social anthropology, or what we now call ethnology. But at that time, anthropology and ethnology were not regarded as respectable academic labels, so very often they had to take shelter in the departments of sociology.

Though for many Chinese students of society, sociology and anthropology were inextricably enmeshed, some preferred to regard themselves as ethnological specialists and a Chinese Ethnological Association was established in 1934 (Hsu I-t'ang, 1944, p. 28). These ethnologists found their intellectual mentors in famous western anthropologists such as A. Bastian of Germany, L. H. Morgan of the USA, and E. B. Taylor of Great Britain. Among the Chinese ethnologists who had made their names during this period were Ho Lien-k'uei, Ling Shun-sheng, Hsu I-t'ang, Ruey Yih-fu and

Li An-che. A number of foreign researchers also contributed to the field, notably the Russian expatriate S. M. Shirokogoroff, the British scholar H. R. Davies, the French missionary F. Schram, and the Danish researcher Jacobsen (Ho Lien-k'uei, 1955, pp. 12–13).

The efforts of the ethnologists bore some fruit before 1949. Research projects were mostly initiated on an individual basis. With the lack of planning and co-ordination, studies were necessarily sporadic. The richest harvest was in ethnographies, or the collection of descriptive materials on different minorities, but the quality of scholarship varied. In the field of theory, there were few outstanding attempts at creation or synthesis.

Communist interest in the question of minorities was first stimulated by the exigencies the movement faced in the course of its history. The massacre of 1927 forced many communists to flee to southern China where they came to live with non-Han peoples. Later, the Long March to the North which traversed many minority-inhabited territories, and the experience of the Anti-Japanese War, led the communists to realize the importance of securing the support of the minorities. A comprehensive nationalities policy gradually evolved. The overthrow of traditional minority leaders was urged, local autonomy promised, and the preservation and further development of minority cultures and languages pledged (H. G. Schwarz, 1973, pp. 197–9).

In order to enlist the minority peoples as revolutionary allies, political activists were required. The Yenan Nationalities College was, as a consequence, founded in 1941. Besides the primary target of teaching and training cadres from various nationalities, another aim was to conduct research into various aspects of ethnic groups. The College had three sections—education, research, and general services. Probably because of limited resources, research was not given high priority. An administrative reform in 1942 reduced the research department to a research room attached to the education division. According to the recollection of one of its members, the subjects taught to students of the 'research' and ordinary classes in this College included marxism-leninism, political economy, the national question, history, problems of the Chinese revolution, and current events and politics (Tsung Ch'ün, 1961).

The general outline of the nationalities policy was retained after 1949. But as a party in power, the leadership had to reconcile communist ideals with practical realities. The political status of the minorities was a knotty problem. Equality of nationalities was regarded by the Party as a fundamental internationalist tenet of communism, and national self-determination was a Leninist principle. But the interest of national unity and solidarity dictated restraints on strong local nationalism. In a policy statement, a Chinese official sought a theoretical compromise (trans. in G. Moseley, 1966, p. 71):

> In sum, the principal aim of Materialists in insisting on the necessity of recognizing the right of national self-determination is that of opposing imperialism by seeking to make allies of the oppressed nationalities in the socialist revolution of the international proletariat; it is clearly not their aim to advocate indiscriminately the separation of each nation nor to urge the establishment of a great number of small nation-states.

The other sensitive area was economic reform. The goal of the Communist Party was to build a socialist economy and to remove the disparities in living standards among the various ethnic groups. But such reforms would require some changes in the customs and traditions of the minorities. Fierce resistance might be aroused if the minorities perceived such measures as encroachments on their identity. Thus the Chinese leaders declared that they opposed a policy of forced assimilation, and stressed that reforms would be tailored to suit special ethnic characteristics so that the nationalities could be 'induced to cast off their backwardness' (*ibid.*, p. 37). If these policies were to be implemented successfully without causing disaffection, the characteristics of the various ethnic groups had to be thoroughly understood. Such information and knowledge could only be obtained through investigations.

During the first seven years of the People's Republic, instruction and research in ethnology were taken out of the universities and confined to the newly-created institutes of nationalities. The primary aim of these institutes was to train more political functionaries of minority nationalities. The first to be established was the Northwest Nationalities Institute (1950). Then the Kweichow Nationalities Institute and the Central Nationalities Institute were set up in 1951. Regional branches subsequently proliferated, and by 1961 there were nine nationalities institutes (*SCMM*, no. 287, 13 November 1961, pp. 22–4).

The academic activities of the Central Institute of Nationalities in Peking are better known. A Norwegian anthropologist, Gutorm Gjessing, visited this institute in 1954 and found that it was then the only place where 'academical tuition in anthropology' was given. Teaching, being in the trial stage, was conducted in the form of seminars in which further studies were planned (Gjessing, 1957, p. 59). By 1956, according to a press report, two five-year courses on the study of nationalities and on their histories were offered. The course on nationalities covered 'the development of individual traits in the culture and life of nationalities in China and the rest of the world, the origin and distribution of nationalities and their relations'. The other course would cover 'historical data on nationalities preserved in China' (*NCNA*, 18 May 1956; trans. in *SCMP*, no. 1296, 25 May 1956, p. 12). Besides teachers, Gjessing found a research staff of fifty persons. Fifteen of them were on the professorial level, including historians, linguists and anthropologists. Gjessing told us that field work was then in a preparatory stage. Surveys were undertaken by research teams. 'Every year such teams are being sent out in the field to study a particular ethnic group for some three months stressing mainly on social systems and the living history of the people concerned' (1957, p. 60).

In these early years, political representation of the minorities was an important issue. As political equality was promised, various groups emerged and claimed independent identities for themselves. Several hundred names of nationalities had been put forward during the general elections of the National People's Congress (Fei Hsiao-t'ung and Lin Yao-hua, 1956a). How to ascertain the status of these groups became the foremost task of researchers. There were groups with different names which shared either residential proximity or linguistic affinity. There were others which bore the same name but had dispersed over different areas. Still others had migrated as a consequence of war and had come to settle in the midst of the Han Chinese without being fully accepted. Should they be regarded as independent ethnic units, or just parts of other nationalities? A different problem was created by the Han Chinese who had resettled in minority areas: were they part of the Han nationality? Some of these earlier settlers had grown so different that they demanded to be treated as minorities, whereas the later Han migrants were unsure of their origin. Such questions of identification were reported to be the centre of attention at the First Scientific Discussion Session sponsored by the Central Institute of Nationalities in July 1956 (*NCNA*, 6 July 1956; trans. in *SCMP*, no. 132, 19 July 1956, p. 6). The prevailing view of the scholars was perhaps reflected in an article jointly authored by Fei Hsiao-t'ung and Lin Yao-hua. They proposed to identify a nationality by four characteristics—the sharing of a common language despite variations in dialect, a common territory in which the group had resided permanently, the evolution of close economic ties, and the possession of similar psychological traits or national 'characters' (1956a, pp. 14–16). Fei and Lin asserted the usefulness of research in 'bringing up data and analysis... to help those groups which have already brought forward names of nationalities so that through consultation they may themselves consider whether they are minority nationalities, or constitute an independent nationality' (*ibid.*, p. 17).

By this time, Chinese investigators had distinguished forty-five minority nationalities and recorded their characteristics. The findings had been summarized and presented in Chinese publications. The materials on the ten largest minorities may give the flavour of their work (Table 4.1).

By 1956, however, the focus of attention began to shift and ethnological research entered a new phase. The problem of distinguishing nationalities gave way to more detailed inquiries into their social organization and histories. With directives from the Party leadership, an ambitious long-term and large-scale project hailed as 'the first of its kind in the nationalities work and in the scientific research of our country' was launched (*NCNA*, 7 July 1956; trans. in *SCMP*, no. 1332, 19 July 1956, p. 6). Besides the Central Institute of Nationalities, new co-ordinating bodies were called into being. The Nationalities Committee of the National People's Congress planned the first stage which began in 1956 and was scheduled to be completed in four to seven years. Eight research teams were sent to study minorities in Szechwan, Yunnan, the north-west region, Kweichow and Hunan provinces, Tibet, Kwangsi and Kwangtung provinces, Inner Mongolia, and the north-east region (*ibid.*, p. 5). Two years later, new units were established in the Scientific Planning Committee of the State Council, and the Chinese Academy of Sciences, the Central Institute of Nationalities and other universities. More than one thousand people were said to have participated in various stages (*ibid.*, p. 32; *KMJP*, 21 May 1963).

Why this ambitious project? The fact that ethnology was accorded a place in the Russian scientific scheme undoubtedly had some influence. The presence of a Soviet expert in the 1958 inaugural meeting of the Nationality Research Institute of the Chinese Academy of Sciences had been specially noted in the Chinese press (*NCNA*, 24 June 1958; trans. in *SCMP*, no. 1804, 3 July 1958, p. 21). But more important, the nationalities question was a sensitive political issue which must be handled with care. After several years of preparation, democratic and socialist reforms of the minority areas were initiated in 1956. Administratively, autonomous areas which recognized the national minority characters of the regions were set up at the provincial, intermediate, and county levels. The autonomous areas were given the right to political representation in congresses and governments, as well as some control over finance and public security. But these rights were subordinated to national laws and regulations so that, in the opinion of Franz Schurmann, these autonomous areas were 'for all practical purposes provinces' or counties (1970, p. 149). Culturally, attempts were made to change the customs and practices of the minorities which might hinder

TABLE 4.1 *The characteristics of the ten largest minority nationalities in China, 1956*

Nationality	Population	Area of distribution	Economic situation	Language and religion
Chuang	6,610,000	Living principally in the western part of Kwangsi	Principally agricultural economy	No written language; believe in polytheism
Uighur	3,640,000	Living principally in southern parts of Sinkiang	Principally agricultural economy, some handicrafts and small commerce	Uighur language used; believe in Islam
Hui	3,550,000	Living in larger communities in Kansu, but also found in all parts of country	Principally agricultural economy, with some small commercial activity	Use Han language; believe in Islam
Yi	3,250,000	Living principally in the Liang-shan areas on the borders of Szechwan and Yunnan	Principally agricultural economy	Newly created Yi language being promoted; believe in polytheism
Tibetan	2,770,000	Living principally in Tibet region, and Chamdo area	Agricultural and pastoral economy	Tibetan language used; believe in Lamaism

Miao	2,510,000	Living principally in southern part of Kweichow and western part of Hunan	Principally agricultural economy	In some areas Miao language, but not universal; believe in polytheism
Manchu	2,410,000	Distributed over Liaoning, Kirin, Heilungkiang, Inner Mongolia and Peking	Economic situation same as that of Han nationality	At present Han language universally used
Mongol	1,460,000	Living principally in Inner Mongolia Autonomous Region, and the provinces of Kansu, Liaoning, Kirin and Heilungkiang	Principally agricultural economy, with consider-able activity in animal husbandry	Mongol language generally used; believe in Lamaism
Puyi	1,240,000	Living principally in the Pankiang basin in the southwestern part of Kweichow	Principally agricultural economy	No written language; believe in polytheism
Korean	1,120,000	Living principally in Yenpien area in Kirin	Principally agricultural economy	Korean language used; mostly Buddhists, some Christians

Source: *Shih-shih shou-ts'e*, no. 17, 17 September, 1956, translated in *CB*, no. 430, 10 December, 1956, pp. 6–7.

economic development. These reforms, to be effective, had to be based on valid understanding. Another political function of the investigations was to publicize the 'tremendous successes' and achievements of the Party's nationalities policy and to educate the minority peoples in 'socialism and patriotism'. According to an official in nationalities affairs, the minority peoples were leading happy lives after Liberation. 'But some local nationalists do not remember the wretched days of the past. They have forgotten that it is the Communist Party that has brought about the good times they now enjoy' (Chung-kuo k'o-hsüeh yüan, min-tsu yen-chiu so, 1958, pp. 27–8). The investigations were to impress this fact upon them. Besides these political aims, one of the academic goals was to 'rescue' the data that was going to be irretrievably lost during rapid social changes. '[If] we do not put on record in time the conditions of the minority peoples', wrote Fei Hsiao-t'ung and Lin Yao-hua, 'we shall soon lose the chance of direct observation since they are being or will very soon be subject to socialist transformation' (1956b, p. 18). A further academic justification was that the investigations would yield significant historical data not only for ancient Chinese history, but for the general marxist theory of social development as well. This was based on the theoretical assumption that the social organization of many of the minorities corresponded to certain marxian historical stages—primitive communism, slave society, and feudal society. With the material on the minorities, it had been argued, Chinese sequels to Engels's *The Origins of Family, Private Ownership, and State* and Morgan's *Ancient Society* could be written. Here the academic reasons shaded into the political. Inquiries into the minorities could substantiate the marxist theory of social development and add an aura of historical inevitability to the Communist Revolution. The foremost Party theoretician of the day, Ch'en Po-ta, wrote: 'Such research will not fail to lead people on to the conclusion that the people of all nationalities in the nation must struggle for the socialist cause' (Su K'o-ch'in, 1961, p. 32). It appears that the 1930s controversy on social history and the fight to fit China into the marxian scheme of universal history had found a new battleground in minorities research in the 1950s.

The tasks of the investigators had been defined by directives from the Communist Party: 'First, to investigate the forces of production, systems of ownership, and class structures of the nationalities; then, to collect as far as possible data on historical development and special customs and habits so as to arrive at systematic studies of their histories' (Chung-kuo k'o-hsüeh yüan, min-tsu yen-chiu so, 1958, p. 34). On the basis of such inquiries, books were to be written on three topics—short records of the nationalities, their short histories, and the conditions in nationalities autonomous areas. In a series of articles published in the official press, Fei Hsiao-t'ung and Lin Yao-hua had outlined a more detailed programme. Social morphology was obviously an important area, and they gave illustrations of minorities that displayed characteristics of primitive society, slave society, and different types of feudal society. But they were apparently not comfortable in the theoretical straitjacket and warned against doctrinaire application of the marxist scheme. They were critical of those who 'instead of making penetrating investigation, ... quoted some sentences from classical writings and were satisfied with picking out some odd cases to substantiate the correctness of general rules' (1956b, p. 24). They warned against hastiness and advised comprehensive collection of ethnographic materials and repeated inquiries to ensure validity of the data obtained. The social formations of minority societies were complex, they asserted. Characteristics of the slave as well as the feudal stages might be found in the same minority society. Even though some nationalities might be classified into the same historical stage, they usually possessed individual pecularities. Furthermore, the course of a minority's development might not follow the theoretical sequence of stages. But the most interesting line of research, it appears to me, was their brief discussion on the question of the transition to socialism. The Communist Party had assisted many minority peoples in skipping several stages of development, but often the socialist and the traditional forms of economic distribution clashed. For example, the Oulunch'un are a hunting people living in the forests of the Hingan Mountain Range in north-east China. In the past, they worked collectively and divided their catch in equal shares. During the process of transition to socialism, they were organized into production co-operatives. This form of organization coincided with their traditional practice of collective labour, therefore implementation was smooth. But difficulties arose over the new system of distribution based on the socialist principle of 'to each according to his labour' which entailed unequal sharing. The majority of the Oulunch'un resisted this reform measure. The new system, according to Lin Yao-hua, had to be modified before it was accepted (Joint Publications Research Service, 1962, p. 31):

> The hunting catch of the Oulunch'un was distributed, as before, on the basis of equality, but a certain percentage of that catch, approximately 20–30 per cent, was given in addition to the share of the best hunters. This preferential distribution stimulated hunt productivity and, at the same time, was based on respect for the centuries-old traditions of the Oulunch'un. Therefore, they accepted this application easily.

It would be fascinating to know more about the impact of such changes on the social structure of the minority communities. But usually this question only received cursory treatment in investigation reports. It appears that this line of research, though promising from an academic point of view, was not actively encouraged.

Another area in Fei and Lin's design for ethnological studies was the cultures and ways of life of ethnic minorities. Material culture including the means, the knowledge and techniques of production was the first subject on their list. Then followed special customs and possible class variations in such habits among individual nationalities. The third aspect of culture they emphasized was art and literature. They urged investigators to relate both the contents as well as the forms and styles of minority art to their historical and social contexts (1956c, pp. 26–30).

Fei and Lin wrote these programmatic essays at a time when the political atmosphere was more relaxed. When a more frosty climate set in, many ethnologists were criticized as 'bourgeois' scholars. More stringent restraints were imposed on minority studies. Party leadership was re-asserted, and all investigation teams were required to work under the supervision of central as well as local party organs. Topics for research were chosen to accord with Party policies. As a result, certain subjects and conclusions became taboo. Researchers who suggested that there existed no clear class differentiation in a minority group were denounced as heretical. They were urged to pay more attention to the study of economic structure and class relationship so that they would not draw such mistaken conclusions. Minority nationalism and separatist movements were forbidden topics. The only acceptable explanation of these phenomena was that they were the disguised expression of the class interests of the conservative ruling strata of the nationalities. Finally, the study of 'backward customs' and 'traditional remnants' were frowned upon. Interest in the exotic and outlandish were regarded as morally distasteful and politically devious. Efforts should better be devoted to 'progressive' phenomena, it was advised (Chung-kuo k'o-hsüeh yüan, min-tsu yen-chiu so, 1958, pp. 14–22). Some of these criticisms were of course justified to a certain degree. For example, ethnological studies could degenerate into academic voyeurism and could become fixated on the exotic for its own sake. But once these political and moral values were propounded as guidelines for research, the academic 'voyeur' and the 'reactionary' might be thrown out together with many a theoretical creator and explorer.

Operating within these limits, minority studies displayed some features that were different from ordinary western ethnological works. In terms of theoretical perspective, obviously it could not be other than marxist. Morgan's *Ancient Society* was virtually the only western anthropological treatise available in translation. In terms of research methods, there were several characteristics. First, team work and not individual inquiry was the rule. The collection of information, preparation of the preliminary drafts, discussions, and then revisions for selective publication were all conducted collectively. The 'red' and the 'expert', or the politically conscious and the technically proficient, were combined in the same team if not in the same individual. The merit, according to Su K'o-chin, was that such team efforts 'strengthened the training and education of their young members and promoted the ideological transformation of their old members'. Second, historical research formed an inseparable part of these studies. Attention was paid to the collection and utilization of old books, documents, and archives. Third, participation in the everyday routine of the minority peoples was urged. Investigators should live, eat and work with those they study partly because this was the mass line, and partly because they might thus establish 'close relations' with the masses and increase their 'perceptual knowledge' (Su K'o-chin, 1961, pp. 32–4).

By 1963, seven years after it was initiated, this large-scale investigation project was declared to be successfully completed. Quantitatively, the yield was quite impressive. Two hundred and sixty-eight reports were said to have been compiled which amounted to over two million words. Scientific documentary films had reportedly been made and historical relics collected (*KMJP*, 21 May 1963). Five research reports by several groups had been released in 1958 as an interim summation and review (Chung-kuo k'o-hsüeh yüan, min-tsu yen-chiu so, 1958). We are also told that a voluminous *Collection of Annals of the National Minorities of China* had been compiled in 1962 by the Central Institute of Nationalities (*NCNA*, 11 March 1962; trans. in *SCMP*, no. 3007, 26 June 1963, p. 7).

The majority of the research reports belonged to the category of ethnography or descriptive studies. I have not come across any significant theoretical work that aimed at comparison and synthesis. As ethnographies, some of them were detailed and comprehensive. The range of topics covered may be shown through the content of a 1962 monograph of the Owenk people of Inner Mongolia, acclaimed in the Chinese press. The first chapter dealt with the mode of production including the kinds of instruments used, methods of hunting and fishing, the division of labour between the sexes, the system of public ownership and equal distribution, the improvement in the forces of production and emergence of private ownership, the forms of commercial exchange and their socio-economic effects, and the changes in the system of distribution. The second chapter dwelt upon their kinship-based social organization. The nature of their clans with related phenomena of adoption and blood feuds, the structure of individual families, the system of marriage, and terminology of kinship were described. The third chapter bore the heading of 'spiritual culture' and discussed topics such as 'empirical knowledge', religious beliefs including the worship of nature, totems and ancestors, and literature and art. The final chapter was on 'the transition from primitive communism to socialism' and touched upon 'the causes for the slow pace of social development prior to Liberation' and the subsequent 'great transformations' (Chiu Po et al., 1962).

How far these ethnographic materials were used by the cadres and informed their efforts in minority affairs is unclear. But most Chinese commentators acknowledged vaguely that they provided valuable data for the socialist transformation in nationality areas. Academically, new courses were offered in the Central Institute of Nationalities on the basis of these findings. Researchers in the social sciences were also said to have utilized such data in their work. No matter how successful these seven years' investigations had proved to be, they constituted no more than a good start. But as nationalities affairs apparently ceased to be one of the foremost concerns of the Party leadership after the initial phase of socialist transformations, ethnological studies of the minorities have since declined and await the stimulus of a second 'leap forward'.

Another group in the Chinese population to which some research efforts were directed was the overseas Chinese in Southeast Asia and their dependants residing in the Chinese mainland. Methods similar to those of the minority studies were employed except that the major centre of investigation was confined to the Institute of Southeast Asian Studies of Amoy University which produced a crop of articles in 1957. The leader of the group appeared to be the British-trained social anthropologist T'ien Ju-k'ang who had studied the Chinese in Sarawak before his return to China.

The Chinese in Southeast Asia had mostly emigrated from the two southern Chinese provinces of Kwangtung and Fukien. Many of them maintained contact with their dependants at home who formed a marginal group in that their livelihood depended upon remittances, and they displayed a distinct style of life. After Liberation, they posed a thorny problem to the new Government. Many cadres regarded the overseas Chinese and their dependants as bourgeois elements beyond socialist redemption. But overseas Chinese remittances constituted a significant source of foreign exchange valuable to economic development. Thus on the eve of the national co-operative and collectivization movement, assessment of this marginal group became necessary. Historical researches on the overseas Chinese were carried out. One of these was a project on a district in Fukien. A team of researchers utilized a variety of sources including historical relics, genealogical records, interviews, folk songs, and archival documents to explore several aspects of the history of Chinese overseas emigration—the time and place of embarkation; the reasons, the routes, and the magnitude of emigration; the livelihood of these settlers in Southeast Asia; and their subsequent relationship with China (Chuang Wei-chi *et al.*, 1958). Besides historical research, surveys on the rural economy of the emigrant communities were also conducted (Chang Chen-chien *et al.*, 1957). To discover their special social and economic characteristics, so that the process of collectivization might be suitably adjusted, was one of the aims. The other was to stress the finding that only a tiny minority of the overseas Chinese dependants might be classified as bourgeois; the majority of them actually came from the peasantry. The data were meant to settle the qualms of the cadres and justify special treatment being accorded to this sector of the population.

After this overview of the investigations into the minority nationalities and the Chinese emigrant communities, we cannot fail to observe that these were virtually the only areas relatively open to inquiry by the former practitioners of sociology and anthropology. Why? I would suggest the reasons are twofold. First, these groups are characterized by a measure of 'marginality' and 'foreignness'. Knowledge based on familiarity cannot be readily assumed by the administrators, and this renders conventional anthropological techniques useful to some extent. Immediately after Liberation, a Chinese official wrote (P'an Ch'i, 1951, pp. 10–11):

> We should admit that the work concerning minority nationalities appears as a completely new problem to our cadres. We lack experience in this area. We need to learn, beginning from the first lesson. It is not easy for Han cadres in particular to understand the sufferings, the feelings, the characteristics, and the demands of the minority peoples. They are not good at shaping their work in accordance with the special conditions of the nationalities. Consciously or unconsciously, they display the erroneous attitude of Han chauvinism. They tend to oversimplify the nationalities problem. Sometimes they even adopt an arbitrary and rash approach.... We should promote investigations and researches on minority communities, so that our work can be based on an understanding of the history as well as the social, political and economic conditions of our brother nationalities.

In recent years, the relation between anthropology and colonialism has been passionately debated among the more radical researchers in the West. As the minority nationalities have been part of China for a considerable period of time, it is inappropriate to describe the attempt to study and integrate them as a form of colonial activity.

Whether we interpret these studies as constituting an arm of ethnic domination depends on our judgment of the nature of the minority policy of the People's Republic. In any case, the existence of this area of research does suggest the usefulness, or even necessity, of some kind of anthropology to a political authority whose administration extends over diverse ethnic groups.

Second, these areas are quite safe politically in that the investigations would not be too threatening to those in power. Unlike Fei Hsiao-t'ung's revisit to the village in the Yangtze delta which might enable the researcher to wield political influence by identifying and advocating on behalf of his subjects, the predominantly Han investigators engaged in minority studies most probably have had to remain perennial strangers because of their different ethnic origin. Their political prospects are further reduced when they are dispatched as members of government-sponsored research teams.

5 The four histories

The compilation of *ssu shih*, or the 'four histories', has been described by two Chinese writers as 'a large scale social survey of the masses' (Chao Yu-fu and Li Hai, 1965, p. 5). Echoing this assessment, an observer outside China wrote somewhat hyperbolically that 'the four histories movement... is the world's biggest social investigation effort' (Shih Ch'eng-chih, 1972).

There can be little doubt about the immensity of the research effort. The yield in terms of quantity is impressive. Within a year of its initiation in 1963, it was estimated that nationally nearly two hundred studies had been compiled and published in book form, and more than a thousand articles on the four histories had been printed in various newspapers and periodicals. But these were just the tip of the iceberg. In Peking alone, over ten thousand pieces of work had been written which amounted to nearly seventy million words. Among these, only a very small portion has been published. The ratio of published to unpublished material was reported to be 1:230 (*KMJP*, 6 October 1965, p. 4; Chao Yu-fu and Li Hai, 1965, p. 1). The compilation of a collection of family histories called *The People of Taihang* (Shan-hsi sheng Chin-tung-nan ch'ü ssu-shih pien-chi wei-yüan hui, 1964; trans. in S. L. Greenblatt, 1976) illustrates the process of selection of material for publication. According to the publisher, the preparation of the anthology has gone through four steps. The first step was the mobilization of a large number of 'intellectual youths' in the south-east Chin district of Shansi to interview local residents and record the stories of their lives. This produced over seventy thousand pieces of family history. The second step was initial picking and editing. From the large number of drafts, ninety-six 'models' were chosen. The criteria for selection were not given by the publisher. The third step was refinement. Individual pieces were rewritten by 'comrades of higher ideological levels and literary skills'. In the fourth and final step, the revised drafts were checked for accuracy and then circulated to Party branches, *hsien* committees, and the Southeast District Committee for approval. The end-product was an anthology consisting of seventeen family histories (Chung-kuo ch'ing-nien ch'u-pan she, 1965; Greenblatt, 1976, p. xx).

The four histories compilation activity was apparently nationwide in its coverage. Because of the incomplete collection of these works outside China, it is not clear whether there are regional concentrations of effort. The high-tide of the four histories was between 1963 and 1965. After that it ebbed like most publishing and research activities with the onset of the Cultural Revolution. Signs of its revival appeared in 1972 with the establishment of special units at commune or county levels to take charge of the writing of four histories. By the end of 1976, at least five book-length studies had been published—the history of the first commune set up on the outskirts of the city of Shanghai (Shang-hai Ch'i-i jen-min kung-she shih pien-hsieh tsu, 1974); the development of the Kiangnan Shipbuilding Factory from 1865 to 1949 (Chiang-nan tsao-ch'uan-ch'ang shih pien-hsieh tsu, 1975); the history of the Shanghai harbour docks (Shang-hai kang ma-t'ou ti pien-ch'ien pien-hsieh tsu, 1975); the chronicle of a former squatter area (Chao-chia peng ti pien-ch'ien pien-hsieh tsu, 1976); and the history of the Nanking Road in Shanghai (Shang-hai shih Huang-p'u ch'ü ko-ming wei-yüan hui hsieh-tso tsu, 1976). It is interesting to note that all of these studies originated from the Shanghai area. This may reflect a concentration of effort related to the ideological concern for 'class education' on the part of the 'Gang of Four' who controlled Shanghai during this period. Or, it may simply be the result of the greater productivity and efficiency of the Shanghai publishers.

The magnitude of the four histories compilation effort is easier to determine than its nature. How far is the label 'social investigation' an appropriate one? If it is, are the four histories no more than one variety of investigation and research? There are grounds for assuming that this is the case if investigation and research is taken to be simply a method of inquiry. The repertoire of tools employed to obtain information is virtually the same. One of the major means is direct interview. Through this means, the vicissitudes of individual lives are recorded and reconstructed to form the bulk of the family histories. The familiar form of fact-finding meetings are also frequently held. Nearly all of the informants are of considerable age—'old workers, old poor peasants, old cadres, old soldiers' (*KMJP*, *op. cit.*)—which is natural as they have a lifetime of experience to retell. Other sources of data include documentary materials such as land sale documents, judicial records, genealogies, pre-Liberation newspapers, and relevant historical relics such as measuring rods, the torture instruments used by the landlords, the clothes and beggars' bowls of the poor peasants, as well as the wills and other objects left by revolutionary martyrs. Besides the methods used, the characteristics of the investigators also resemble those engaged in *tiao-ch'a yen-chiu*. They are nearly all non-professional social researchers. The only difference appears to be the wider spectrum of people involved. We can identify several categories of four histories investigators. There are the cadres of the Party, of the Government, and of various scientific institutions, as well as university teachers and students. Then there are those who possess specialized skills, mainly historians, literary writers, journalists and editors. In contrast to these are people with little or no training in writing. For instance, it was reported that a poor peasant, after having overcome the obstacle of illiteracy with the help of a dictionary and a primary school teacher, completed by himself the history of his family in about a thousand words so that he might pass it on to his offspring (Chao Yu-fu and Li Hai, 1965, p. 5). But these diverse elements do not act in a spontaneous and *laissez-faire* fashion. All these activities are under the direction of the local administrations. More concerted efforts gradually evolved with the formation of organized and integrated research teams. The compilation unit of the history of the Kiangnan Ship-building Factory, for example, is a 'triple alliance' consisting of workers, cadres, and economic historians.

But if *tiao-ch'a yen-chiu* is taken to mean applied policy research, then the four histories should be regarded as a different entity. The subject matter of the four histories is more focalized, as its name implies. 'Four' refers to four 'basic' social institutions that are the bread and butter of professional sociologists—the family, the village, the commune, and the factory or the mine. Aside from these central concerns, other topical studies have also been carried out, such as the history of a garrison, a militia, a peasant association, a squatter area, or a group of road construction workers. As for the term 'history', it indicates that the studies are more comprehensive in scope and more continuous in temporal coverage than those of investigation and research. Instead of concentrating on a specific aspect relevant for a certain policy, these studies aspire to the 'systematic understanding and analysis of the changes in a village or a locality, embracing the transformations in ecology, class structure, economic culture, customs and ways of life etc.' (Chao Yu-fu and Li Hai, 1965, p. 5). If *tiao-ch'a yen-chiao* are snapshots, the four histories are chronicles of social change.

But a more fundamental difference lies in the aims of the two types of inquiry. The function of the four histories is expected to be didactic rather than instrumental. Instead of specific practical issues, it is to the broad realm of outlook, of political consciousness, or in more fashionable sociological terms, of the 'cognitive map of society' that the four histories are orientated. Four histories activity originates not as an academic exercise, but as an integral part of a political campaign started in the winter of 1962—the Socialist Education Movement.[1] The slogan of the campaign was Mao Tse-tung's warning to the Party and the nation: 'Never forget class struggle.' The warning was a response to the perennial problem faced by successful revolutionaries—how to prevent the revolution from losing its momentum, and how to avoid the stifling routinization of the revolutionary spirit. Mao was worried that the socialist revolution might gradually degenerate with the resurgence of capitalist elements and the 'embourgeoisement' of the working class. In order to rekindle revolutionary passion and to revive a correct political vision, Mao insisted that class struggle still exists under socialism, and that the subject of class conflict 'should be discussed every year, every month, [and] every day'. He attached great import-ance to the Socialist Education Movement, referring to it as the most comprehensive and gigantic political movement launched since the land reform campaign in the early 1950s (Mao Tse-tung, 1969, p. 437). Knowledge about class and class struggle, according to Mao, could not be effectively acquired through abstract theoretical teaching. Direct experience of oppression and exploitation was essential for the creation of class consciousness. If the opportunity for obtaining such direct experience was no longer available, one should at least relive the experience either through recall or through empathetic identification. The task of instilling vicarious experience of class conflict was assigned to the four histories (Chao Yu-fu and Li Hai, 1965, p. 2):

> Without an understanding of the 'old society', a revolutionary
> cannot really comprehend the proletarian revolution.
> Consequently he will not become a dedicated revolutionary who
> would carry the socialist revolution to the end. But the old
> society has gone forever. Direct knowledge of that phase of
> class struggle can no longer be obtained through painful
> personal experience. To fill this gap in our knowledge, the only
> practical method is to use the 'four histories'. Thus, class
> education is the basis of socialist education, and the 'four
> histories' education is in turn the core of class education.

The editors of the Peking series of four histories gave various examples to demonstrate the therapeutic effect of 'four histories' writing (*ibid.*, p. 3–4). The main target was the younger generation born and reared 'under the red flag'. Many young intellectuals, the editors asserted, could not grasp the meaning of class and class conflict because they could not relate these ideas to their daily lives. They tended to believe that the landlords depicted in the revolutionary literature were pure fiction. Hence they did not appreciate what had been achieved since Liberation. Failing to compare their present livelihood with that of the past, they were often agitated with discontent. The editors recorded the case of a young female secondary school graduate of poor peasant origin who was assigned to her native village for agricultural work. She disliked the hard life there and felt her abilities wasted. Participating in four histories activity and listening to her own mother recounting past sufferings, the girl reportedly realized that she should be grateful for the fact that she had been educated and adequately fed and clothed. Since then, she participated more actively in the work and social life of the production brigade.

Another group of youths who have benefited from the four histories activity, according to the editors, was the offspring of former exploiters. Many of them accepted the notion of class conflict in theory but remained emotionally identified with their families. A young lecturer in the Peoples' University was cited as an example. He was convinced that his father was a 'kind landlord' whose success was built on frugality and diligence. He could not bring himself to hate his family's past. But through investigating the family history of another landlord, he was said to have realized the real nature of exploitation by the landlords and the hypocrisy of their professed charity. He wrote an article to declare his hatred and his determination to break with his class of origin, and stated his determination to devote himself to the socialist revolution.

It was not only the younger generation that was politically revitalized. Those who had suffered in the old society, the editors wrote, also needed frequent 'recalling of past bitterness' so that their commitment to socialism would not be eroded with the passage of time. The illustrating case for this category of people was an old night-soil collector who was interviewed for his life history. At first, he saw no point in dredging up the memory of past suffering which he blamed on fate. Then gradually he opened up to the interviewers who persisted in working with him. Once he started, he went on for days. When his family history was completed, he was said to have worked harder and he constantly told his story to the youngsters in the village.

Despite this major ideological goal of class education, four histories activity was by no means devoid of academic intentions. A secondary aim was to contribute to the understanding of modern Chinese history. The four histories were expected to accumulate materials and data for the writing of both national as well as local histories such as provincial and county gazetteers (Yang Li-wen, 1965, p. 25; Mao Tse-tung, 1969, p. 27). The academic value of the four histories has been elaborated by Chao Yu-fu and Li Hai (1965, p. 7):

> A well-written village history can be said to be a microcosm of Chinese rural society. The pre-Liberation section of the village history truthfully reflects the conditions of rural class division and land ownership, the landlords' methods of economic exploitation and political oppression, various types of spontaneous peasant rebellions, and different social customs and habits. A bitter peasant family history shows concretely the process of bankruptcy and the amount of suffering which the Chinese peasants had undergone. A landlord's exploiting and criminal family history realistically reveals the process of land concentration, of collaboration with bureaucratic capitalism and imperialism, and of mad profiteering at the expense of the peasants. A factory history vividly records historical materials on the development of capitalism in China. The detailed description of the heroic anti-imperialistic struggle of the working class since the May Fourth Movement provide a large quantity of new data for the study of workers' movements in China.

This brings us to another question. How far should the four histories be regarded as historical rather than sociological works? To pose this question is to assume the existence of well-defined boundaries between history and sociology. To me, the distinction between the two disciplines is mostly a matter of convention. Of course, the subject matter of the four histories is treated diachronically. But there are several characteristics which would place it in the grey area of social history or historical writing infused with a sociological perspective. In terms of the treatment of time, the focus is not on the remote but on the immediate past that shades into the present. The guideline for the writing of village history is that the suitable starting-point is the Anti-Japanese War and that post-Liberation development should be a main emphasis (Yang Li-wen, 1965, p. 27). The history of the commune deals with an even more recent period as its subject matter is a novel social phenomenon. A 1974 publication of this genre describes the complete process of the evolvement of a commune, analysing the rationale, the process of implementation, and the obstacles encountered in various stages of development from land reform, the formation of mutual aid groups and high-level co-operatives, the establishment of the commune system, the re-emergence of private plots and free markets, the 'ssu-ch'ing' or 'Four Clean-up Campaign', up to the Cultural Revolution

(Shang-hai Ch'i-i jen-min kung-she shih pien-hsieh tsu, *op. cit.*). The term 'contemporary history' has been used to describe these local histories (Yang Li-wen, 1965, p. 27), a term which some professional sociologists would probably adopt to designate their endeavours.

In addition, these studies are seldom strict narratives. Either implicitly or explicitly, they employ a comparative framework of a 'before and after' nature to assess and demonstrate the effect of the Communist Revolution, as revealed by the catchphrase 'recall past bitterness and appreciate present bliss'. Consider the study of squatter areas in Shanghai (Shang-hai she-hui k'o-hsüeh yüan, ching-chi yen-chiu so, 1965). Three out of five chapters of the book are devoted to an analysis of various facets of the squatters' lives in the pre-Liberation era: why such urban squalor came into existence in the most 'prosperous' city in modern China, why squatters were distributed along the borders of foreign settlements, the living conditions and the pervasive control by secret societies, as well as the causes of the poverty of the inhabitants. These features are then contrasted with the post-1949 abolition of the squatters and the improvement in the employment status and the housing condition of the inhabitants. The change substantiates the thesis of the investigators that urban squatters are chronic problems of a capitalistic form of social structure that can only be solved by a new social arrangement. What is unique about the framework employed is that no comparative attempt has apparently been made synchronically, that is, comparing one factory with another factory, one commune with another commune, or one village in China with a village in another country. The reason for this constraint is probably related to the social function of these studies in setting up a 'legitimate' baseline for measuring improvement and success. If a cross-regional or cross-national framework is used, it is likely to result in a tendency towards rising expectations. The peasants in Shantung may become dissatisfied when they are compared to their counterparts in Kwangtung who are more affluent. A locally confined 'before and after' comparison can keep such a tendency in check by focusing attention on the improvements upon the past.

As we have already indicated, most of the topics covered and the categories used for analysis are familiar to sociologists. Writers of village histories have been urged to pay special attention to problems of class and class conflict. 'Internal contradictions' among the people that constitute obstacles to social change should also be tackled. These obstacles include the opposition of rich farmers to socialism, as well as the inertia of middle and poor peasants in switching to collective agricultural labour. The process for overcoming these should be depicted (Yang Li-wen, 1965, p. 24).

Histories of the factory, such as the study of the Kiangnan Ship-building Factory, have presented data on wage levels, residential patterns, the impoverishment of the workers, and the organization of trade unions and industrial actions by the workers and communist activists during the revolutionary period. The approach to the four histories departs from conventional Chinese historiography in that the limelight is directed to non-elites, the hitherto neglected social strata of Chinese society. Dock workers, road construction labourers, miners, farmers, women etc., are elevated to the centre of the historical stage. The sentiment underlying such an approach has much in common with that of the sociologists. Former Chinese sociologists, such as Fei Hsiao-t'ung, have conceived of their role as 'plaintiffs' of the poor and the inarticulate; whereas many western sociologists would agree that the nature of their inquiries would impel them to provide 'a platform for those who would not otherwise be heard' (M. Albrow, 1970, p. 1).

The four histories also differ from conventional historical studies in that they tap a greater variety of sources. Relying heavily on interviews, much of the product may be called oral history. Despite many possible methodological objections to oral sources, it can hardly be disputed that they are valuable in filling in the gaps of knowledge and correcting the biases contained in the documentary records.

Apparently, then, the four histories are relevant to sociology. But how scientific and reliable are the findings? Are they really of much value in contributing to an understanding of the recent development of Chinese society? A western historian answers emphatically in the negative (S. Uhalley Jr, 1966, p. 9):

> It is a loss to history that the great amount of energy and organization being invested in this programme could not have been more soundly motivated and more objectively directed, so that materials of genuine value might be collected and preserved. The results could be of immeasurable help to those trying to gain an understanding of China's recent past. The peasants and workers of this transitional generation would, indeed, have much to tell—if objective, apolitical questions could be put to them. Instead, to the degree that the movement is politically successful it will serve only to obscure history.

At least some historians in China also had a low opinion of the 'four histories' for their 'lack of scientific value'. The existence of such an attitude was indicated by the appearance of numerous articles in the Chinese press persuading them to believe the contrary. Are these negative evaluations justified? I think they tend to be too sweeping and indiscriminate. Several considerations ought to be taken into account when we assess the value of the four histories.

First, they do not form a homogeneous entity. Their subject matter varies. They may be about villages, individual families, communes, factories, mines, or dockyards. They are also uneven in standard and quality, a natural consequence of the multitude of writers involved. The quality may range from the short auto-biography of a farmer composed with limited vocabulary to the lengthy and meticulously compiled history of the Nanyang Tobacco Company (Chung-kuo k'o-hsüeh yuan, 1960). The form of presentation is also far from uniform. The village histories alone adopt several formats. There are chronological histories recording events by the year, or collections of episodes selected for their importance, or fictionalized narratives that stress popular interest, or editions of biographies of significant personalities (Yang Li-wen, 1965, p. 28).

Second, related to the question of heterogeneity, it is necessary to have a comprehensive inventory as well as a proper classification of all four histories which have been published. In want of such an inventory at the moment, assessment of their value is made difficult.[2]

Third, it is problematic as to what criterion is appropriate for measuring their worth. The studies are intended for popular consumption. As a historian of the People's University has pointed out, the four histories are the 'histories of the masses, for the masses' (Hsia Hsiang, 1965). They are not addressed to an audience of fellow professionals. In terms of their own aims, even the presentation of a family history in the form of a pictorial series is acceptable—which renders the criterion of academic significance quite irrelevant.

Finally, one objection against the four histories is that they are distortions of reality. There are two possible meanings of distortion. One is that the standard of accuracy is lax. It has been observed in relation to the compilation of family histories that 'no efforts were made to assure authenticity, much less provide for replicability' (Greenblatt, 1972, p. 171). The reliability of the verbatim conversations frequently used in the family histories is particularly doubtful. In this respect, the four histories are similar to traditional chronicles and unofficial histories (*i-shih*) or historical romances (*yeh-shih*). As H. L. Kahn has noted about the latter: 'The characteristics of this literature seem to be those of all historical fiction: thematic truth encrusted with imaginative, often fabulous details' (1965, p. 236). But it is necessary to make the distinction between the norms that are upheld and their actual realization in practice. There is no doubt that by embellishing the narratives with

101

dramatic details, a considerable number of the four histories fall short of the ideals of accuracy and reliability. But their failings have not gone uncriticized (*KMJP*, 6 October 1965). It is insisted by Chinese authors themselves that the four histories can only be effective by being accurate and truthful. Writers are urged to exercise judgment and care in establishing the validity of their data through cross-checking. Many compilers have obviously neglected the importance of standardizing units of measurement and monetary values, thus diminishing the value of their data. This has duly been pointed out by other Chinese writers as matter for improvement. Simple enumeration of isolated facts is another defect. In response, the need to seek relationships among various phenomena is emphasized. Reviewing the progress in 1965, Li Hai has expressed the following opinion (*ibid.*):

> To write the history of a village, it is necessary to describe not only how the poor peasants had been exploited and oppressed by the landlords, but also the economic conditions (such as the state and changes in the ownership of land, houses, livestock, transport, vehicles, agricultural implements) and political conditions (such as changes in the power structure) of that village.

Since then, there are signs that subsequent studies have been more rigorous in their approach, and their reliability has apparently been improved. But there is another meaning of distortion. Social reality can be distorted through selective emphases and deliberate omissions. Such practices are approved in the compilation of the four histories, as shown in the explicit guidelines which have been laid down. Materials must be interpreted in terms of class struggle. According to the editors of the Chinese Youth Publishing House, four histories should stress the following themes (Chung-kuo ch'ing-nien ch'u-pan she, 1965):

> First, to publicize the superiority of the socialist road. Second, to expose the ugly features of the bourgeoisie and the doom of the capitalist road. Third, to expose the crimes of aggression against China committed by the imperialists, especially the US imperialists. Fourth, to continue to expose the evil of feudalism.

In order to highlight these themes, urged the editors, descriptions of the 'internal contradictions among the labouring people' unrelated to class struggle should be muted. These 'internal contradictions' include the conflicts between mothers-in-law and daughters-in-law, between masters and apprentices, and among different sisters-in-law. Besides, ideas incompatible with socialism,

102

such as the yearning to get rich, the hope for a happy family and a secure livelihood, the belief in fatalism, should not be described even though they may exist (*ibid.*).

After taking the above considerations into account, my tentative assessment is that the sociological value of the four histories may be twofold. They are useful to sociologists either as a variety of sociological work, or as a research source. In their approach, the four histories are similar to the branch of sociological research that utilizes self-portraits, life-histories, or case studies to present the participants' definition of social reality. The historical accuracy of the information may be quite immaterial compared with the insights that can be gained into the subjective perceptions, experiences, and attitudes of significant actors. In this connection, it is interesting to note the close resemblance between the four histories and the rare studies conducted by western scholars based on direct investigations in the People's Repulic. Jan Myrdal's *Report from a Chinese Village* (1965) is particularly striking in that it is virtually a 'village history'. Through intensive interviews, Myrdal collected detailed life-histories of the residents of the Shensi village of Liu Ling. With these self-portraits, he weaved an impressive tapestry of the Communist Revolution at the grass-roots level. Apparently, Myrdal was not aware of the indigenous researches on the four histories which had just been initiated when he carried out his study between 1962 and 1963. The similarity may either be the result of coincidence, or more probably, selective permission granted to outside scholars whose approach happened to agree in spirit with the four histories. In any case, Myrdal operated basically within the guidelines laid down by the Chinese authorities for four histories writing, and his study showed what can be achieved for this variety of work with good craftsmanship.

As a research source, the four histories have obvious shortcomings in terms of the factual information they contain. The deliberate omission of materials on the 'internal contradictions' is a serious loss to the sociologists and anthropologists. We can only hope that these data may be contained in the vast number of unpublished drafts, and that these drafts would be kept and preserved in governmental files or archives. But fortunately, there are other aspects of social life that receive fuller treatment in the published works. These include systems of land tenure, forms of employment of agricultural and industrial workers, methods of factory management, techniques of industrial action and mobilization, and various customs and folkways of the poorer sectors of the population. Careful analysis and comparison of individual studies may give a picture of regional variations in these social institutions in China.

Besides the factual information they contain, the four histories are significant as documents on social morality. They are explicitly didactic, and tend to produce idealized depictions of the past with parades of positive heroes interspersed with a few gangs of irredeemable villains. In this respect, they are comparable to the traditional literary devices of moral approval and censure. Traditional works of this genre include the taoist morality tales such as the *T'ai-Shang kan-ying p'ien (The Treatise of the Exalted One on Response and Retribution)* (Greenblatt, 1976, pp. xxxiv-xl); the genealogies (J. M. Meskill, 1970, pp. 146–7); and popular confucian books such as *Hsiao ching (Book of Filial Piety), Lieh-nü ch'uan (Biographies of Heroic Women),* and *Chung-i chi-wen lu (Records of the Loyal and the Upright)* (Ch'en Chien-ts'ung, 1882). In fact, Mao Tse-tung and other contemporary Chinese writers have drawn attention to these parallels by referring to the four histories as 'genealogies of the proletariat' (Mao Tse-tung, 1969, p. 444; Chao Yu-fu and Li Hai, 1965, p. 2). Certainly, differences exist between the four histories and traditional genealogies as they are the products of dissimilar social and political conditions. In the family histories, as Greenblatt has pointed out (1976, p. xxiv):

> clan members once deemed too low in status to be accorded recognition in the clan and family records are given genealogical records of their own; and this change is accompanied by a replacement of what were formerly positive with negative status-honors. Thus if civil service honors, the birth of male heir, the birth-day of an aged head of the household, auspicious signs and ceremonies, and newly acquired property contributed to the destiny of the family in the traditional family history, the loss of jobs, death, sale and abandonment of children, death in advance of old age (resulting from frustration and mistreatment) and ignominious burial for the heads of households, inauspicious signs and ceremonies, the loss of property, and the accumulation of debts decree a family's destiny in the new family history.

But these substantive differences should not obscure their basic similarities in function and format. In the same vein as the popular moral literature of the past, the four histories employ allegedly historical incidents as concrete embodiments of abstract ethical principles. For example, in the anthology of *The People of Taihang,* there is the family history of 'Revolutionary Mother Pao Lien-tzu'. Mother Pao contributes her effort to the Communist Revolution by carefully nursing the wounded soldiers of the People's Liberation Army. She put the welfare of the soldiers before that of her children, using the children's quilts and blankets to protect a wounded guerrilla from cold weather. With such actions, she exemplifies proletarian virtues and comradely love. A ready parallel can be found in the *Biographies of Heroic Women* compiled during the Ch'ing Dynasty which recorded the life of a filial woman, Madam T'an (Wang K'eng, 1779, section 7, pp. 41–2). The husband of Madam T'an died soon after their marriage when she was just eighteen. Within a few years, her mother-in-law and all of her brothers-in-law also passed away. Because of poverty, they could not be properly buried. Madam T'an spun cotton day and night for ten years and accumulated enough money to bury all of the eight members of her husband's family who had died. Her deeds were finally known to the emperor and she was decorated as a filial woman. Although the moral standards have changed drastically from an emphasis on filial piety to 'class love', both Madam T'an and Mother Pao personify the prevailing norms of their times. They are intended to serve the same aim of moral education. Therefore, the spirit of Meskill's remarks on the nature of the genealogies may be equally applicable to the four histories (1970, p. 159):

> The Chinese genealogy is the product of a particular ideological environment. It reflects to a larger extent than the social reality of Chinese kinship the standards and aspirations of the Confucian tradition during its last centuries. Although genealogies cannot wholly obscure the ways the real world of families and lineages departs from the Confucian canon, they tend to record primarily what agrees with accepted standards and is relevant to them. In the process, genealogies make the reality look more uniform and conventional than it ever was. Despite these limitations, the social scientist and the social historian can benefit from the study of genealogies.

6 Reflections—sociology and society

At the end of our survey, several questions remain. Why is sociology regarded as a problematic pursuit in contemporary China? What are the forces that shaped the present state of social inquiry? What can be learned about the nature of sociology as well as Chinese society? What are the future trends likely to be?

There is a widely-held notion, at least among sociologists, that their discipline is wedded to freedom of expression and tolerance of dissent. The view of Alex Inkeles is a good example. Concluding a guided tour of the sociological landscape, he remarks, 'Sociology can thrive only under freedom . . . only a nation which provides the conditions for free inquiry may with reason hope for the development of social science knowledge which permits ever deeper understanding of man in society' (1965, p. 117).

He arrives at this generalization after observing, with a shudder, the situation of Chinese sociologists under socialism. The indictment is clear: sociology has withered in contemporary China because it is not a free society. But the converse of the argument is strange: sociology bloomed in pre-Liberation China because freedom was to be had? Inkeles may well be affirming his personal faith and political ideals, but as a sociological generalization, his statement is unsatisfactory on several counts. First, it is tautological. After declaring that sociology can thrive only under freedom, he asserts in the next breath: 'Indeed, the extent to which sociologists may pursue their interests, fully publish their results, and freely state their conclusions is one important *index* of the degree to which a nation qualifies as a free and open society' (*ibid.*, emphasis added).

Second, the generalization, being sweeping, takes the phenomenon to be explained—sociology—as a homogeneous entity rather than a conglomerate with multifarious facets. Surely it would be more fruitful to assume that the impetus for the development of different kinds of sociological endeavour may not be the same. One possible typology is to classify sociological work by its nature, the institutional setting, and the role specifications for practitioners. We may then have the following broad categories forming two ideal types:

Ideal type A		Ideal type Z
Theoretical, critical	/	Instrumental, applied
Autonomous, institutionalized	/	Dependent, diffused
Specialized	/	Amateur
Individualistic	/	Collective

Sociological enterprises in North America and Western Europe resemble ideal type A whereas the case of China approximates ideal type Z. Rearrangement of the variables can yield several intermediary types. What Inkeles is defending appears to be sociology of the type A variety.

Third, being abstract and fluid, the concept 'freedom' is hardly enlightening without translating it in terms of political organization and values. David Apter has constructed two main models of political structure—the sacred–collectivity and the secular–libertarian—which he names the mobilization system and the reconciliatory system respectively. The reconciliatory system, Apter asserts, is analogous to the market-place. It rests on individuals with the capacities to reason and to know their self-interest, and the political authority provides the framework to accommodate plural interests and free play of ideas. Its principle of legitimacy is equity. The mobilization system, on the other hand, may be likened to a 'corporation'. It stresses the unity rather than the diversity of its members. The political authority exists to educate and improve the community. 'It depends less on the free flow of ideas than on the disciplined concentration upon certain political and economic objectives.' Potentiality is its basis of legitimacy (Apter, 1965, pp. 22–33). These two types appear to correspond to Zygmunt Bauman's distinction between a decentralized and centralized mode of decision-making (1971, pp. 21–31). With such classifications, we may reformulate Inkeles's generalization as follows: sociology of the type A variety can flourish only in a pluralistic, reconciliatory political system.

This leads us to our final point. Granted the reformulation, we have to explain why it is so. It has often been observed that a link exists between the scientific perspective, to which sociology is committed, and a certain political stance. It is thought that the scientific outlook with an empirical approach to reality is entwined with liberalism. Such an interconnection has been suggested by Bertrand Russell (1968, pp. 21–2, original emphases):

The essence of the Liberal outlook lies not in *what* opinions are held, but in *how* they are held: instead of being held dogmatically, they are held tentatively, and with a consciousness that new evidence may at any moment lead to their abandonment. This is the way in which opinions are held in science; as opposed to the way in which they are held in theology . . . . Science is empirical, tentative and undogmatic; all immutable dogma is unscientific. The scientific outlook, accordingly, is the intellectual counterpart of what is, in the practical sphere, the outlook of Liberalism.

Such a view has also been championed by Karl Popper who argues for an affinity between scientific empiricism and the political doctrine of piecemeal and patchwork reform. The compatibility results from a similar temper of mind with the awareness that human knowledge is imperfect and that ideas, be they scientific or political, may be mistaken (Popper, 1969). Because of this political affinity, it appears, the scientific perspective would be unwelcome in a centralized mobilization system as it engenders dissent and opposition. But this argument would apply to all scientific subjects. Why then the special treatment often accorded to sociology in particular? A possible answer is that while all scientific efforts are liberal, sociology is more liberal than others. Studies on academic attitudes in the USA have shown that the social sciences and humanities are towards the left of the political spectrum, while among them, 'the more politically relevant disciplines—political science and, above all, sociology—appear to be the most liberal according to a number of independent surveys of academics in different fields' (S. M. Lipset and R. B. Dobson, 1972, p. 166). Similarly, according to Lipset, other surveys in Britain and Japan have shown that sociologists tend to be the most liberalist and left-of-centre (S. M. Lipset and E. C. Ladd Jr, 1972, p. 93). Liberal and leftist are of course relative to the standard of a particular political system. In contemporary China, sociologists are seen as the most rightist and bourgeois. Left or right, it appears fairly certain that sociologists in most societies tend to produce more political deviants and adversaries critical of the *status quo*. But this still begs the question. The answer, I believe, lies deeper than political affiliations. It rests on the *cultural* significance of the discipline. Sociology, as R. Robertson aptly depicts, constitutes the 'site of cultural tension' in modern societies (1972, p. 66).

To pursue this line of thought, let us begin by tracing the circumstances conducive to the emergence of a sociological consciousness. Sociology is usually the product of revolutionary changes in the social order. In France, as Durkheim reflected, 'there is no country where the old social organization has been uprooted more completely and where, consequently, in order to remake it, there is greater need for thought, that is, for science' (K. H. Wolff, 1960, p. 383). For Germany, Mannheim detected a similar situation: 'German sociology is the product of one of the greatest social dissolutions and reorganizations, accompanied by the highest form of self-consciousness and self-criticism' (K. Mannheim, 1953, p. 210). The case of China, as we have described, is no different. Traditionalism lost its hold. People were suddenly jolted with the realization that the old social arrangement was not a naturally prescribed order as they had been led to believe. But, as both Durkheim and Mannheim have argued, social change by itself does not engender sociology. It has to be accompanied by 'a veritàble faith in the power of reason' (Wolff, *op. cit.*), a 'highly developed capacity of objective scrutiny' (Mannheim, *op. cit.*, p. 211) which they have respectively found in their own philosophical traditions. Such a faith in the efficacy of science, or 'scientism', made its inroad into Chinese thought at the turn of this century (Kwok, 1965). The impact was evident on Chinese sociologists. Witness this pledge to reason by Fei Hsiao-t'ung (1948b, p. 88):

History is not always rational. But in any historical circumstances, there exists a rational solution. The rational development of history depends on the rational behaviour of men. One who is recognized as an 'academic' has the duty to point out the rational direction. But whether it can materialize into history or not, that should be left to the politician.

This commitment to reason has two important implications. First, the emergence of sociology appears to be part of what Weber called the 'disenchantment' of the modern world. Sociology waxes as religion, the foundation of most traditional cultures, wanes. Second, if the growth of sociology is arrested, it would mean that irrationality is on the rise. The embodiment of irrationality in modern society is often taken to be some form of ideology. Thus sociology is brought face to face with religion and ideology. This triple relationship usually produces great tension because they are so close to one another. It is their functional proximity that engenders conflict. When the Chinese sociologists fought for their survival under socialism with the argument that their subject resembled marxian social theory in many respects, they unwittingly inflicted a most damaging wound on themselves. They failed to profit from the insight of Karl Mannheim who pointed out how the principle of 'likes repel' operates in the field of political doctrines (1960, p. 215):

in political life one generally proceeds more sharply against the closely related opponent than against a distant one, because the tendency is much greater to glide over into his view, and consequently especial watchfulness must be exercised against this inner temptation. Communism, for example, fights more energetically against Revisionism than against conservatism.

Religion, ideology, and sociology are rooted 'in the basic fact that human social systems are systems of possible choice between valued alternatives' (B. Barber, 1971, p. 248). Since there is no objective reality as such that makes a particular form of social arrangement mandatory, alternative constructions of social reality are possible. Because of this, competing world-views, cognitive maps, or cultural systems may arise to provide symbolic interpretations, evaluations, and justifications of one choice as against another.

The proximity of religion and ideology is such a well-trodden path of analysis that it needs little elaboration. Numerous studies have viewed marxism as a form of religion, or 'civil religion' as it is some-times called. Maoism, especially the version prevalent during the Cultural Revolution, has been compared to a religious cult. A 1976 plenary assembly of the Spanish episcopacy shed interesting light on this interrelationship. In their *communiqué* the Spanish bishops described marxist socialism as 'surrounded by a certain halo of myth' which led to moral conflict for many Catholics engaging in labour activities. The bishops continued to say that they would consider socialism as a 'legitimate option' for their followers only if it upholds the transcendental value of the individual and dispenses with theories of class struggle, atheism, and the abolition of private property (*South China Morning Post* [Hong Kong], 1 March 1976, p. 3).

The bond between religion and sociology has received less atten-tion. The idea that sociology may be a substitute for religion was suggested by Auguste Comte who conceived of sociology as a 'religion of humanity'. One theme of Comte's work is the evolution-ary decline of the theological style of thinking and its cultural replacement by the scientific mode of thought. The social sciences, especially sociology, are the 'highest' among the hierarchy of sciences because they are the most complex and the most dependent for their emergence on the development of others (Robertson, 1972, p. 63; L. A. Coser, 1971, p. 9). Robert W. Friedrichs has analysed 'the priestly mode' of sociology at some length (1970, pp. 93–109). Empirically, the religious background of the early sociologists in the USA was very marked. The 'social gospel' formed one of their motivating forces. As Bramson observes, these early American sociologists, 'small town and farm boys almost to a man, faced these problems [the demands for a new social order] in moral terms inherited from their social and religious backgrounds. The reform philosophy had penetrated the backwoods, and those who stood to heed its moral message were predominantly from rural and religious milieu' (1961, p. 78). With the support of survey data, Alvin Gouldner asserts that this priestly connection has not yet been severed. Among 3,441 American sociologists who replied to a mailed questionnaire in 1964, Gouldner and Sprehe found more than one quarter of them had thought of becoming clergymen (Gouldner, 1971, p. 24). The linkage between religion, especially Christianity, and sociology appears to be rooted in a similar stance towards social life, the stance of 'being in but not of the world' (Robertson, 1972, p. 83). This religious attitude towards worldly events has its parallel in the methodological importance placed on detachment and objectivity ensured by some measure of psychic distance towards the objects of enquiry in sociology.

Radical critics have been insistent on exposing the ideological elements of academic sociology. Though one may have reservations about their tendency to 'over-ideologize' the subject, few would disagree that their assertion contains some measure of truth. Sociologists sometimes do use techniques bordering on a form of rhetoric, a mode of persuasion dressed in a scientific and quantitative veneer to induce popular belief and acceptance of their findings (A. J. Weigert, 1970, pp. 111–19). This affinity with ideology is more than technique and form. It reaches into the sphere of orientation and sentiment. The nature of ideology, according to Raymond Aron, involves (1957, p. 323):

> the longing for a purpose, for communion with the people, for something controlled by an idea and a will. The feeling of belonging to the security provided by a closed system in which the whole of history as well as one's own person find their place and their meaning; the pride of joining the past to the future in present action....

The intersection between universal history and individual biography and the effort to make sense of such an intersection is the essence of the sociological imagination conceived by C. W. Mills (1959). Bendix, commenting on Aron's definition, has found similar components in sociology 'in as much as scholarship involves a purpose, communion with people similarly engaged, and hence some feeling of belonging to a selected (if not elect) group' (Tiryakian, 1971, pp. 174–5). On the other hand, an ideological system necessarily incorporates some sociological elements. 'Ideology is a body of ideas', writes Talcott Parsons, 'that is at once empirical and evaluative in reference to actual and potential states of a social system. An ideology thus includes an empirically grounded diagnosis whose

111

degree of validity is, of course, an open question of the state of the system' (1969, p. 22). Realistic appraisal of social life is indispensable to an ideology, and ideologists of some calibre would typically subject their adversaries to sociological scrutiny. When the Chinese communists reassess confucianism, the perspective they employ is unmistakably that of the sociology of knowledge.

I have dwelt on the common features among religion, ideology and sociology at some length because I believe they are sufficiently similar to stand as potential substitutes for and competitors with one another. This threat of competition grown out of proximity has been revealed in a guide to readings compiled by Martin Shaw called *Marxism versus Sociology* (1974). Consistent with the title, Shaw argues that marxism constitutes a theoretical universe distinct from academic sociology. But he touches on the heart of the matter when he defines the purpose of his endeavour: 'Its message is that one does not need to be seduced by the sociological surrogate, however "marxised"' (*ibid.*, second page of the 'Introduction').

But we should not let the similarities overshadow the differences. The major dissimilarity that keeps sociology distinct from the other two is a commitment to analysis instead of justification. The distinction may be blurred in practice, but it is a real one in terms of norms and intentions. Ideally, sociology is concerned with the comprehension of the social world, not with the advocacy of the good or virtuous life. In an influential book, Peter Berger maintains that (1966, p. 15):

> Sociology is not a practice, but an attempt to understand.
> Certainly this understanding may have use for the practitioner...
> [but] there is nothing inherent in the sociological enterprise of
> trying to understand society that necessarily leads to this
> practice, or to any other....

Ideology and religion, on the other hand, have the preference for, and justification of, a particular form of society as their central concern. This difference in commitments leads to the intricate relationship between analysis and authority. One of the basic motifs of the sociological enterprise is myth-breaking. Practitioners are socialized to embrace the value of unearthing the 'true picture' of social life. But in order to establish political or religious authority in society, myths and legends are crucial. Thus clash ensues almost inevitably. Kenneth Boulding has put it best (1966, p. 97):

> One of the sources of legitimacy in any society is that the
> legitimate is simply not called into question. The moment an...
> legitimacy is called into question it is often very deeply
> threatened... but this is illegitimate in social science culture....

There is no guarantee whatever, therefore, that the pursuit of the subculture of the social sciences will not result in some deep conflicts with the fundamental values of other subcultures within the society.

Unlike the examination of natural objects, the act of social investigation cannot avoid having an impact on the objects it inquires into. Irrespective of his intentions, an investigator can alter people's definition of the situation and their behaviour by publishing his findings. Such an effect may be illustrated with the case of moral values (*ibid.*, p. 92):

There is likely to be an impact on the very ethical norms of the system . . . . The power of an ethical norm is a very complex function of its conformity with the existing value structure of society, perhaps with some ethical truth, and with the perception of the extent to which the norms are in fact obeyed. Hence knowledge about the extent to which norms are in fact obeyed may have a substantial impact on the degree to which the norms are accepted.

This recalls the controversy surrounding the two studies of village life conducted by Li Ching-han and Fei Hsiao-t'ung in 1957. These studies exposed certain hardships, both individual and local, created by the system of central planning and allocation of resources. What they described might well have existed objectively. But this is beside the point. Apparently it was the potential effect of these studies in creating discontent and corroding their political credibility that the communist leadership was keenly aware of and concerned about. By communicating the extent of hardship and difficulties, what was once regarded by individual villagers as a private trouble might be transformed into a public issue with the realization that similar hardships were shared by others. A social problem may be created and amplified by altering the public's image of social reality.

Since the aspiration to demolish social myths will lead to conflict with other 'subcultures', especially the political and religious orders, sociologists have to settle for some form of compromise in order to survive. The ideal of myth-breaking is frequently extolled in reverence but seldom practised in earnest. One mode of accommodation open to the sociological enterprise may be called encapsulation. This formula has numerous variations. But whether these variations be called 'idle curiosity', 'value-neutrality', 'objectivity', or 'disinterestedness', the message is basically the same. They amount to a declaration of a truce, a renunciation of worldly ambitions in exchange for institutional autonomy and a licence for

113

limited freedom of social inquiry. Obviously, encapsulation has its costs. 'The rationalization of sociology', remarked one critic of American sociology, 'threatens to alienate the field altogether from the study of society by converting it into a system of formal operations carried on primarily in response to internal professional pressure independently of an actual interest in social events' (Tiryakian, 1971, p. 363). The prevalence of technical jargons in western sociological circles is perhaps a part of the protective crust designed to ensure that findings only permeate gradually into public consciousness. By lessening the impact on public opinion, outside interference may be avoided. In Asia, such a concern is often more immediate. Heads of a sociology department in Singapore, for instance, tried in 1972 to discourage students from choosing sociology as a subject of study in order to avoid the displeasure of political leaders (*Singapore Times*, 16 December 1972):

> Sociology does not provide a social philosophy—an interpretation of this world in general, nor is it a venue to ventilate frustrations with one's own position in life. Sociology is by now a highly specialized and professionalized science with its own complicated theories, and methods which are handled by sophisticated reasoning and electronic computers alike.

The feasibility of this option of encapsulation depends on several factors. Foremost among them is the existence of a pluralistic tradition. In the feudal city-states of Western Europe, there was the political tradition of antitheses between church and state, and between state and society. Through the necessity of mutual adjustment and reconciliation, the spheres of influence of political and religious doctrines were more bounded, enabling intellectuals to have a better chance to carve niches for autonomous survival. But in many traditional East European and Asian countries, such dichotomies had seldom been acknowledged. Instead, a harmonious cosmic and socio-political order was upheld (S. N. Eisenstadt, 1973, p. 16). In the case of Imperial China, political authority and ideology were much more embracing and dominant. Religion had to be subservient to the polity to be tolerated (C. K. Yang, 1957, p. 285). Similarly, scholarship had long contented itself to play second fiddle *vis-à-vis* state ideology. Historically, the literati had seldom attained institutional autonomy. Their predicament is best expressed by Frederic Wakeman Jr: 'Scholars alone, acting as individuals, were respectably impotent. Scholars together, constituting a faction, were dubiously partisan' (1972, p. 41). Related to this past weakness of pluralistic elements was a definition of the intellectual role different from that of Western Europe. Self-esteem and integrity were built upon social commitment and responsibility. Scholarly virtue lay in the betterment of 'people's livelihood'. The value of detachment was seldom upheld as it seemed selfish and immoral. Therefore the pioneers of Chinese sociology did not employ the justification of understanding the mystery of social life as a valuable end in itself. Arguing in terms of the practical utility of their knowledge, they had forsaken the option of limited autonomy. But the last precondition for encapsulation adheres to the intellectual discipline itself. Facing the common political and cultural tradition, some subjects fare better in achieving a measure of autonomy. Psychology, for example, remains an independent academic subject in contemporary China while sociology fails to do so (R. Chin and A. S. Chin, 1965). The reason appears to be the capacity of the former to forge a more distinct academic identity for itself and obtain greater theoretical 'closure'. The disagreement and strife over the nature and scope of sociology do not strengthen its qualification for securing a place in the academies.

Another mode of accommodation for sociology is to assume a secondary interpretative function. When an ideology or religion claims a 'total' and monopolistic status, this is usually the only choice possible. I would argue that when the ideology is newly established and has yet to consolidate its position, the margin of tolerance for competition is particularly small. Under such circumstances, social inquiry surrenders its autonomy and identity to become an extension of the dominant cultural system. It acts as an interpreter or a theoretical broker, abandoning the critical and creative functions.

The third form of compromise, not mutually exclusive with the former two, is selective attention. In the case of encapsulated autonomy, not every aspect of society receives the same share of sociological attention. Generally analysis tends to be directed along the lines of least resistance in the power structure. The reflective among the sociological practitioners sometimes confess that the 'status inferiors' in society are over-researched while the 'status superiors' are rarely investigated. Critics of the discipline are quick to point out this weakness. Bourgeois empirical sociology, a Soviet writer once remarked, 'attempts to hide behind the scientific nature of its methods, and selects various exceedingly limited subject areas of investigation, thereby able to create the appearance of complete objectivity, total freedom from ideological influence....' (G. M. Andreeva, 1966, p. 341). And in the case of secondary interpretation, it is quite impossible that all areas are closed to investigations. No matter how 'total' the dominant ideology, there are bound to exist 'blind spots' and new developments with which it is incompetent to deal. One example is the study of the minorities in contemporary

115

China. It is just a question of the scope which selective attention is allowed.

How do we relate these options to the sociological scene in China? As far as theoretical and critical sociology is concerned, it appears to me that it is mainly devoted to secondary interpretations with a limited scope for selective attention. Is this going to remain or will it change in the near future? This would depend on the status of the political ideology. As the ideology is getting more secure in its hold on the population, it is conceivable that a greater part of the less controversial areas of social life may be open to selective attention. What about the prospect of encapsulated autonomy? As we have discussed, certain factors in the Chinese past may not be favourable to such a development unless two other conditions emerge. One is the possibility of the 'end of ideology' leading to the ascendance of sociology. We shall return to this point later. The other condition is the progress of sociology in other parts of the world in demonstrating its worth and attaining greater academic respectability. This will strengthen the candidacy of sociology for some measure of recognition in the Chinese institutions of higher learning.

So far we have dealt with the question of the relative absence of type A sociology in China, i.e. the theoretical, critical and institutionalized variety. Now let us turn to the type Z social research that is practical, non-professional and collectivistic. The adoption of such a variety in China is related to the problem of development. As an underdeveloped country, the popularization of social investigations conducted by a multitude of amateurs instead of the enhancement of research by a handful of professionals is perhaps a sensible use of available resources. It may be argued that China is making a virtue out of necessity by creating some kind of 'bare-foot sociologists'. The alternative is the situation in India where heavy investment in professional training yields a sociological enterprise that is elitist and restrictive in its impact. 'In spite of the considerable growth of sociology', admits one Indian practitioner, 'it has reached only a small section of the society. Most of the sociologists come from the upper castes, upper classes, and urban areas; the students of sociology are also drawn from almost the same sections of the society' (T. Fukutake and K. Morioka, 1974, pp. 302–3). Avoiding this tendency, the Chinese emphasis on popularization before enhancement, diffusion before innovation may be a more sensible and flexible strategy of assigning priorities for a developing country. The obvious cost of this emphasis is in technical standards of research. But as more resources are available, it is conceivable that the quality of social investigations will be improved to achieve greater accuracy and reliability.

But is the non-professional and non-institutionalized social

116

research practised in China today just a sign of underdevelopment? Here the convergence thesis is relevant (J. Weinberg, 1969; A. S. Feldman and W. E. Moore, 1965). Scholars subscribing to this idea assert that the process of industrialization creates specific needs. Differences in culture and social organization will be transcended as there is only a limited range of possible responses to fulfil such needs. One of these is the need for social information. Industrialization is usually accompanied by an increase in social differentiation and complexity. Knowledge about proliferating sub-groups and subcultures becomes more and more difficult to obtain. This poses problems especially for agencies such as the government because the successful execution of their tasks has to rely upon an accurate understanding and prediction of the behaviour of various groups in society. The increased emphasis on rational management of social affairs, the importance attached to bureaucracy as a problem-solving and goal-attaining mechanism in modern society underscore the need for systematic and reliable social information. Bauman has properly warned against the simplistic view that information is always welcome in a social system. He points out that the need for information is always selective, subject to power considerations. Social information and knowledge often become the basis of power and influence for various social groups. The demand for, and the absorption of, information varies with the configuration of competing social forces in a society. Nevertheless, he thinks that with increased industrialization, the foci of uncertainty will gradually come under expert management. He asserts that 'specialized bodies are necessary to make up for the natural shortcomings of spontaneous mechanism in information gathering' (1971, p. 30). Sociology, with its techniques of investigation, is one of these specialized bodies.

The Soviet experience lends some support to this convergence thesis. As we have already shown, the People's Republic of China followed the Soviet model quite closely in the early years and they had much in common in their treatment of sociology. In the Soviet Union, sociology as an academic subject and as a vocation had been suspended for several decades. Its formal resurrection came with the Twentieth Party Congress of the Soviet Communist Party held in 1956 to denounce Stalin. The formula justifying the revival was similar to that employed in China during the Hundred Flowers Movement. Basically, it was an attempt to define separate spheres of competence. Marxism–leninism would rule on the level of the direction and broad design of change, while social research would help on the level of concrete policy and details of implementation. Thus social investigations in both the Soviet Union and China were practically-oriented and eschewed theoretical

117

studies. But since the 1950s, social research in the USSR has moved towards increased specialization. The 1960 Party Programme called for the help of social scientists in constructing a communist society. Then the Twenty-Third Party Congress of 1966 recognized sociology as an independent discipline. Professional sociologists have been trained and they participated in successive meetings of the International Sociological Association since 1956 (E. A. Weinberg, 1974, p. 109; T. Parsons, 1965, pp. 121–5). Several reasons have been advanced to account for this re-emergence, and all point to significant trends in the development of Soviet society. 'The growth of sociology as a scientific discipline', argues David Lane in the view of the convergence hypothesis, 'reflects the Soviet elites' incapacity to solve, with their existing tools, the problem of a complex industrial order' (1970, p. 48). This results in a sort of bifurcation of elites into the technocrats and the ideocrats. Training in sociology becomes a legitimate channel for social ascent (Z. Katz, 1971, p. 23). The 'end of ideology' appears to be coming about in the Soviet Union in the sense that there is a decline in the dominance of ideology. As the regime is stabilized, and as reform and gradual change supersede revolution and sudden transformation, technical and 'objective' sociology becomes more attractive. Some amount of autonomy free from ideological interference is granted. Zev Katz has observed this tendency in a terminological change (*ibid.*, p. 23):

> In the process, Soviet sociological research has largely emancipated itself from the grip of dogmatic ideological terms and concepts to the point where one can now read articles or studies by Soviet sociologists without once encountering the old, outworn cliches. 'Building communism' has become 'socio-economic development'; instead of 'the system of proletarian dictatorship' or 'the state of the whole people', it is simply 'the political organization of society' to which the Soviet social scientist addresses himself . . . .

Associated with this ideological decline is a shift in the form of legitimation and social control. The preoccupation of the Soviet leadership in the post-stalinist era is to search for a more effective means of control with a greater reliance on persuasion and 'self-regulation' instead of coercion and force. This has been shown in the Soviet sociologists' considerable interest in cybernetic control. After a visit to the USSR in 1964, Parsons wrote that 'the strong Party emphasis on inculcating attitudes, as well as the problem of institutionalizing managerial authority in industrial enterprises, implies a primary interest in control in the cybernetic sense' (1965, p. 124).

This Soviet experience is of course a possible scenario for China as she industrializes. The embryonic blueprint has already been drafted by some Chinese intellectuals during the Hundred Flowers Movement. Though it has been shelved, the plan may still be acted upon in the future as the debate is only suspended and not resolved. The case for sociology as a speciality and vocation is quite a strong one. But social research performed by generalists in a collective manner may not be simply a passing phenomenon. Though industrialization may cause a convergence in *needs* and *functions*, institutional *forms* need not be the same. There are several reasons why China may be able to avoid the path of specialization in social inquiry. First, being a latecomer to industrialization, she has the chance to avoid the mistakes committed by the forerunners. The negative aspects of bureaucratization of modern society, such as the often unchecked powers of professionals, may warn future Chinese leadership against treading the same path. Second, an anti-professional orientation is contained in the 'amateur ideal' of the Chinese past as well as the communist future. Esteem and prestige for the traditional Chinese literati were secured through a generalist, humanistic education rather than technical training (J. R. Levenson, 1957, pp. 320–41). And in the utopia envisaged by Marx, the hero is not a technician with narrow expertise, but an all-round individual able to display various talents. Finally, the socialist mode of production may change the form of intellectual activity. As Chinese agriculture may be communized to increase production, is it impossible and undesirable to abolish private academic fields and to have a collectivization of the intellect? In all probability, sociology will grow in importance in tomorrow's China. But what form it will assume is still an open question.

Notes

Chapter 1 The growth of sociology in pre-Liberation China

1 See *She-hui-hsüeh chieh (Sociological World)*, vol. 9; and Yen-ta she-hui-hsüeh hui (ed.), 1933.

2 See M. Freedman (1974). I became aware of the sociological significance of de Groot and Granet through Professor Maurice Freedman's lectures and seminars in Oxford between 1973 and 1975. Just before his sudden death, Professor Freedman had completed an essay assessing the life and work of Granet as a sociologist (M. Granet, 1975, pp. 1–29). If his research on the western perception of Chinese religion had not been left unfinished, our knowledge of the early phase of Chinese sociology would have been greatly enriched.

3 These early translations from the Japanese have long been out of print and are unavailable to me; therefore I draw heavily on Sun Pen-wen (1931; 1949) and Wang Yü-ch'üan (1938) for information. According to a Chinese translation of a Japanese article on the history of the sociology department in the University of Tokyo, Japanese scholars at first also used two terms for sociology—*she-hui-hsüeh*, and *shih-t'ai-hsüeh* (literally, the study of the ways of the world). The most influential western sociologists in the early period of Japanese sociology were Herbert Spencer and F. H. Giddings (Ting Fu-yüan, 1943, pp. 77–96).

4 Liang ch'i-ch'ao, a famous Chinese scholar, had also used the term *ch'ün-hsüeh* in his 1902–3 essays (1930, vol. 6, p. 17; p. 36), but I incline to think that Liang followed the usage by Yen Fu since Yen had translated part of Spencer's book several years ago which was most probably read by Liang. And Liang, not knowing English himself, was unlikely to come into direct contact with western sociology and coined the Chinese name. As for the literal meaning of *ch'ün-hsüeh*, I prefer to interpret *ch'ün* as meaning 'human collectivities' instead of 'social organization' (Dubs, 1928, p. 137) or 'group' (Sun Pen-wen, 1949, p. 247) which appear to me to be too restrictive in connotation.

5 I have used H. H. Dubs's translation (1928, pp. 136–7) here but I have replaced the term 'social organization' with 'collectivities'.

120

6 Chou Tso-jen, a well-known modern prose writer, had recorded such an instance. While he attended the Kiangnan Naval Institute in 1901, a teacher took the term *she-hui* used by a student in his essays as referring to the traditional academies of private learning (1970, p. 100).

7 For example, Hsu Te-heng published an introductory text in 1928 based on articles written by Fouionnet and Mauss. Ou-yang Chün's book, referred to earlier, was another instance.

8 As a result of China's defeat by eight foreign powers in the Boxer Rebellion in 1900, a large indemnity of 450 million taels had to be paid to the powers. The USA took the lead in returning her share of the indemnity funds to China for cultural and educational purposes, followed by the Netherlands, Belgium and Great Britain.

9 English publications issued by the Institute included *Livelihood in Peiping, Factory Workers in Tangku, A Study of the Standard of Living of the Working Families in Shanghai, An Index of the Cost of Living in Peiping, Marketing of Cotton in the Province of Hopeh,* and *Wages and Labour Mobility in a Flour Mill in Tientsin.*

10 For an annotated bibliography of the major articles published in connection with this controversy, see Liu Chun-jo (1964, pp. 146–59).

11 The biographical details were drawn from his obituary published in *Quarterly Bulletin of Chinese Bibliography,* new series, vol. 1, no. 1, 1940, pp. 23–4.

12 See Lo Hung, 'The Attitude and Method of Rural Survey', in *Cheng-feng wen-ts'ung (A Collection of Essays on the Rectification Movement),* vol. 4, pp. 22–32. This is an interesting article because it is a marxist review comparing Mao Tse-tung's rural surveys with two village studies conducted by Fei Hsiao-t'ung and one other sociologist.

13 See Robert Redfield's 'Introduction' to Fei Hsiao-t'ung, *China's Gentry,* Chicago, University of Chicago Press, 1953, pp. 2–3. For an assessment of the political orientation of the intellectuals in the 1940s, see Suzanne Pepper, 'Socialism, Democracy, and Chinese Communism, A Problem of Choice for the Intelligentsia, 1945–49', in Chalmers Johnson (ed.), *Ideology and Politics in Contemporary China,* University of Washington Press, Seattle, 1973, pp. 161–218.

Chapter 2 Sociology under socialism

1 The role of sociology as envisaged in the integrated Institute of Social Sciences was shown in the following diagram:

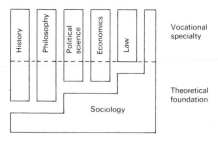

121

2 After the final revision of the manuscript was completed, I came across a book written by P'an Kuang-tan and Ch'üan Wei-t'ien (1952) giving a more extended treatment of the institution of *i-t'ien* and the process of land reform in southern Kiangsu.

3 Articles criticizing Liang had appeared in *Hsin chien-she* nos 7, 8, 9, 10 and 11, 1955.

Chapter 5   The four histories

1 Before the Socialist Education Movement, there had been efforts to compile materials on villages and industries, producing impressive documentary histories such as the study on the Nanyang Brothers Tobacco Company (1958). But, as far as I know, these documentary histories were not produced under the specific label of the 'four histories'. But for analytical purposes, we should perhaps broaden the definition of the 'four histories' to include these studies as well. In this case, I would agree with Greenblatt that the origin of the compilation activities may be traced to the late 1940s and that 'the movement is most accurately described as a sporadic and recurrent mobilization, over a period of nearly thirty years, of Chinese historical consciousness and historical resources in a variety of forms and for a variety of purposes' (1976, p. xvii).

2 In his series of articles on the four histories, Shih Ch'eng-chih mentioned that he intended to compile a bibliography of available works. Unfortunately, he died shortly afterwards. My inquiry at the University of California, Berkeley, where Shih had worked revealed that the bibliography had not taken shape before his death.

Bibliography

Works in Chinese

CHANG, CHEN-CHIEN, CH'EN, K'O-CHIEN, KAN MIN-CHUNG, and CH'EN K'O-HUN (1957) 'Fu-chien chu-yao ch'iao-ch'ü nung-ts'un ching-chi tan lun' ('A Study of the Rural Economy of the Principal Home Districts of the Fukien Overseas Chinese'), *HMTHHP*, no. 1, pp. 31–66.

CHANG, CH'I-YÜN (1954) *Chung-hua min-kuo ta-hsüeh chih (A Record of the Universities in the Republic of China)*, vols 1 and 2, Taipei, Chung-hua wen-hua ch'u-pan shih-yeh wei-yüan hui.

CHANG, YUNG (1957) *She-hui fa-chan kuei-lü chiang-hua (Talks on the Laws of Social Development)*, Shantung, Jen-min ch'u-pan she.

CHAO, CH'ENG-HSIN (1936) 'She-hui tiao-ch'a yü she-ch'ü yen-chiu' ('Social Surveys and Community Studies'), *She-hui shih-chieh* vol. 9, pp. 151–205.

CHAO-CHIA PENG TI PIEN-CH'IEN PIEN-HSIEH TSU (1976) *Chao-chia peng ti pien-ch'ien (The Transformation of Chao-chia Creek)*, Shanghai, Jen-min ch'u-pan she.

CHAO, WEI-PANG (1958) 'Fei Hsiao-t'ung teng shu ju kung-neng p'ai she-hui jen-lei-hsüeh ti fan-tung shih-chih' ('The Reactionary Nature of the Functional School of Social Anthropology Imported by Fei Hsiao-t'ung and Others'), *Ssu-ch'uan ta-hsüeh hsüeh-pao she-hui k'o-hsüeh pan,* nos 3 and 4, pp. 1–8.

CHAO, YU-FU, and LI, HAI (1965) 'Shih lun pien-hsieh ho yen-chiu "ssu-shih" ti chung-tai i-i' ('A tentative Discussion on the Importance of the Compilation and Research of the "Four Histories"'), *Li-shih yen-chiu,* no. 1, pp. 1–14.

CH'EN, CHIEN-TS'UNG (1882) *Chung-i chi-wen lu (Records of the Loyal and the Upright)*, reprinted in 1968, Taipei, Hua-wen shu-chü.

CH'EN, NIEN-PANG (1958) 'Chieh-ch'uan Fei Hsiao-t'ung ti "She-hui tiao-ch'a" ti fan-tung pen-chih' ('To Reveal the Reactionary Nature of Fei Hsiao-t'ung's "Social Investigations"'), *Yün-nan ta-hsüeh jen-wen k'o-hsüeh tsa-chih,* no. 1, pp. 11–18.

CH'EN, TA (1957) 'Chieh-yü, wan-hun yü hsin Chung-kuo jen-k'ou wen-t'i' ('Birth Control, Late Marriage, and the Population Problem of New China'), *HCS*, no. 5, pp. 1–15.

123

BIBLIOGRAPHY

CHENG, HSÜEH-CHIA (1965) *She-hui shih lun-chan ti ch'i-yin ho nei-jung (The Origin and Content of the Debate on Social History)*, Taipei, Chung-hua tsa-chih she.

CHIANG-NAN TSAO-CH'UAN CH'ANG SHIH PIEN-HSIEH TSU (1975) *Chiang-nan tsao-ch'uan ch'ang shih (The History of the Kiangnan Ship Building Factory)*, Shanghai, Jen-min ch'u-pan she.

CHIAO-YÜ-PU T'UNG-CHI SHIH (1936) *Erh-shih-san nien tu ch'üan-kuo kao-teng chiao-yü t'ung-chi (National Statistics on Higher Education in 1934)*, Shanghai, Shang-wu yin-shu kuan.

CHIEH-FANG SHE (1950) (ed.), *Cheng-feng wen-hsien (Documents on the Rectification Movement)*, Shanghai, Hsin-hua shu-tien.

CHIEH-FANG SHE (1952) (ed.), *She-hui fa-chan chien shih (A Brief History of Social Development)*, Peking, Jen-min ch'u-pan she.

CHIU, PO *et al.* (1962) *O-wen-k'o jen ti yüan-shih she-hui hsing-t'ai (The Primative Society of the Owenk People of the Border Regions of Inner Mongolia and Heilungkiang)*, Peking, Chung-hua ch'u-pan she.

CHOU, EN-LAI (1956) 'Kuan yü chih-shih fen-tzu wen-t'i ti pao-kao' ('Report on the Question of the Intellectuals'), *JMJP*, 30 January.

CHOU, SHU-LIN, LI, FU-T'UNG, and CHANG, SSU-CH'IEN (1957) 'T'ou shih "Ch'ung-fang Chiang Ts'un"' ('Looking through the Façade of "Chiang Ts'un Revisited"'), *Hsin Kuan-ch'a*, no. 15, pp. 9–11.

CHOU, TSO-JEN (1970) *Chih Tang hui-hsiang lu (The Memoir of Chou Tso-jen)*, Hong Kong, San-yü t'u-shu wen-chü kung-ssu.

CHOU, YANG (1963) 'Che-hsüeh she-hui k'o-hsüeh kung-tso che ti chan-tou jen-wu' ('The Combat Task of Philosophy and Social Science Workers'), *Hung-ch'i*, no. 24, pp. 1–30.

CHUANG, FU-LING (1963) 'P'i-p'an tzu-ch'an chieh-chi she-hui-hsüeh tsai chieh-chi ho chieh-chi tou-cheng wen-t'i shang ti miu-lun' ('A Critique of the Nonsense of Bourgeois Sociology on the Question of Class and Class Conflict'), *Hung-ch'i*, no. 9, pp. 14–20.

CHUANG, WEI-CHI, LIN, CHIN-CHIH, and KEUI, KUANG-HUA (1958) 'Fu-chien chin-chiang chuan-chü hua-ch'iao shih tiao-ch'a pao-kao' ('Investigations into the History of the Overseas Chinese of Chuanchou'), *HMTHHP*, no. 1, pp. 93–127.

CHUNG-KUO CH'ING-NIEN CH'U-PAN SHE (1965) 'Pien-chi ch'u-pan "ssu-shih" ti i-hsieh ti-wei' ('Some Thoughts on Editing and Publishing the "Four Histories"'), *JMJP*, 26 October.

CHUNG-KUO JEN-MIN TA-HSÜEH, CHI-HUA T'UNG-CHI HSI (1961) (ed.), *Mao Tse-tung lun tiao-ch'a yen-chiu (Mao Tse-tung on Investigation and Research)*, Hong Kong, San-lien shu-tien.

CHUNG-KUO K'O-HSÜEH YÜAN, SHANG-HAI CHING-CHI YEN-CHIU SO, SHANG-HAI SHE-HUI K'O-HSÜEH YEN-CHIU SO (1960) (ed.), *Nan-yang hsiung-ti yen-ts'ao kung-ssu shih liao (Historical Materials on the Nanyang Brothers' Tobacco Company)*, Shanghai, Jen-min ch'u-pan she.

CHUNG-KUO MIN-CHU T'UNG-MENG, CHUNG-YANG WEI-YÜAN HUI (1957) 'Kuan yü yu-kuan k'o-hsüeh t'i-chih wen-t'i ti chi tien i-chien' ('Several Suggestions on the Question of Our Scientific Enterprise'), *KMJP*, 9 June.

FEI, HSIAO-T'UNG (1948a) *Hsiang-t'u Chung-kuo (Rural China)*, Shanghai, Kuan-ch'a she.

124

FEI, HSIAO-T'UNG (1948b) *Hsiang-t'u ch'ung-chien (To Rebuild Rural China)*, Shanghai, Kuan-ch'a she.

FEI, HSIAO-T'UNG (1950a) *Wo che i-nien (This Year of Mine)*, Peking, San-lien shu-tien.

FEI, HSIAO-T'UNG (1950b) 'She-hui-hsüeh hsi tsen-yang kai-tsao' ('How to Reform Departments of Sociology'), *HCS*, vol. 2, no. 2, pp. 20–3.

FEI, HSIAO-T'UNG (1951) *Hsiung-ti min-tsu tsai Kuei-chou (Brother Nationalities in Kweichow)*, Peking, San-lien shu-tien.

FEI, HSIAO-T'UNG (1957a) 'Kuan yü she-hui-hsüeh, shuo chi-chü hua' ('A Few Words About Sociology'), *Wen-hui pao [Shanghai]*, 20 February.

FEI, HSIAO-T'UNG (1957b) 'Chih-shih fen-tzu ti tsao-ch'un tien-ch'i' ('The Early Spring Weather for Intellectuals'), *JMJP*, 24 March.

FEI, HSIAO-T'UNG (1957c) 'Ch'ung-fang Chiang Ts'un', *Hsin Kuan-ch'a*, no. 11, pp. 3–7; no. 12, pp. 11–14.

FEI, HSIAO-T'UNG (1957d) 'Hsiang jen-min fu-tsui' ('I Admit My Crime to the People'), *JMJP*, 13 July.

FEI, HSIAO-T'UNG, and LIN, YAO-HUA (1956a) 'Kuan yü shao-shu min-tsu tsu-pieh wen-t'i ti yen-chiu' ('A Study of the Ethnic Differences of the Minority Nationalities'), *JMJP*, 10 August; translated in *CB*, no. 430, 10 December, pp. 11–17.

FEI, HSIAO-T'UNG, and LIN, YAO-HUA (1956b) 'Kuan yü shao-shu min-tsu she-hui hsing-chih ti yen-chiu' ('A Study of the Societal Types of the Minority Nationalities'), *JMJP*, 14 August, translated in *CB*, no. 430, 10 December, pp. 18–25.

FEI, HSIAO-T'UNG, and LIN, YAO-HUA (1956c) 'Kuan yü shao-shu min-tsu wen-hua ho sheng-huo ti yen-chih' ('A Study of the Cultures and Ways of Life of the Minority Nationalities'), *JMJP*, 16 August; translated in *CB*, no. 430, 10 December, pp. 26–30.

FEI, HSIAO-T'UNG, and WU, HAN, *et al.* (1948) *Huang-ch'üan yü shen-ch'üan (Imperial Power and Gentry Power)*, Shanghai, Kuan-ch'a she.

HO, KANG-CH'IH (1937) *Chung-kuo she-hui shih wen-t'i lun-chan (Debates on the Problems of Chinese Social History)*, Shanghai, Sheng-huo shu-chü.

HO, LIEN-K'UEI (1955) 'Ssu-shih nien lai chih Chung-kuo min-tsu-hsüeh' ('Ethnological Study in China in the Past Four Decades'), *Chung-kuo min-tsu-hsüeh pao*, no. 1, pp. 1–20.

HSIA, HSIANG (1965) 'Hsieh ch'ün-chung ti li-shih, wei ch'ün-chung hsieh li-shih' ('To Write History of the Masses, for the Masses'), *Li-shih yen-chiu*, no. 5, pp. 1–10.

HSIA, YING (1961) 'Yang tiao-ch'a yen-chiu ti feng-ch'i yung-yüan fa-yang hsia ch'ü' ('Let the Style of Investigation and Research Continue and Spread Forever'), *JMJP*, 30 March.

HSU, YUNG-SHUN (1957) 'Ts'ung she-hui tiao-ch'a ju shou kai-chan she-hui-hsüeh ti kung-tso' ('To Begin Sociological Work with Social Investigations'), *HCS*, no. 7, pp. 47–8.

HSÜEH-HSI (1957) 'Kao-chi chih-shih fen-tzu t'an ma-lieh chu-i li-lun hsüeh-hsi' ('High-level Intellectuals on the Study of Marxism–Leninism'), *Hsüeh-hsi*, no. 11, pp. 9–12.

HSÜEH, MU-CH'AO (1957) 'Ti-i ko wu-nien chi-hua ch'i chien wo-kuo t'ung-chi kung-tso ti ch'u-pu ching-yen ho chin-hou jen-wu' ('The Initial Experience and the Future Task of Our Statistical Work After the First Five Year Plan'), *T'ung-chi kung-tso*, no. 21, pp. 1–15.

HU, CH'ING-CHÜN (1957) 'She-hui-hsüeh yü li-shih wei-wu chu-i ti kuan-hsi wen-t'i' ('On the Question of the Relation Between Sociology and Historical Materialism'), *HCS*, no. 7, pp. 46–7.

HU, SHENG, YÜ, KUANG-YÜAN, and WANG, HUI-TE (1951) *She-hui k'o-hsüeh chi-pen chih-shih chiang-tso (Lectures on the Fundamental Knowledge of the Social Sciences)*, Peking, Hsüeh-hsi tsa-chih she.

HUA, KANG (1949) *She-hui fa-chan shih kang (An Outline of the History of Social Development)*, Peking, San-lien shu-tien.

HUA, KANG (1952) 'Ssu-hsiang kai-tsao wen-t'i ta-wen' ('Questions and Answers on Thought Reform'), *HCS*, no. 1, pp. 1–6.

HUANG, WAN-LUN (1957) 'Po Fei Hsiao-t'ung tsai nung-ts'un wen-t'i shang ti fan-tung kuan-tien' ('To Criticize the Reactionary Viewpoint of Fei Hsiao-t'ung on Rural Problems'), *Hsüeh-hsi*, no. 18, pp. 12–14.

HUO, SUNG-LIN (1955) 'Tien-hsing wen-t'i shang-chüeh' ('A Discussion on the Question of Models'), *HCS*, no. 5, pp. 38–41.

HUNG, YEN-LIN (1956) *Tiao-ch'a yen-chiu yü kung-tso tsung-chieh (Investigation and Research and the Evaluation of Work)*, Peking, Jen-min ch'u-pan she.

HUNG, YEN-LIN (1961) 'Yu kuan tiao-ch'a yen-chiu ti i hsieh wen-t'i' ('Some Problems Concerning Investigation and Research'), *JMJP*, 18 April.

KUAN, FENG (1961) 'Tiao-ch'a yen-chiu ti tai-tu' ('The Attitude of Investigation and Research'), *Hung-ch'i*, no. 5, pp. 22–6.

'Kuan yü she-hui-hsüeh yen-chiu ti tui-hsiang ho nei-jung' ('On the Object and Content of Sociological Research'), *HCS* (1957) no. 7, pp. 40–6.

KUO, LO-CHI (1965) 'Ta cho ma-k'o-ssu chu-i chi-hao ti chu-kuan she-hui-hsüeh' ('Subjective Sociology Under the Banner of Marxism'), *HCS*, no. 1, pp. 14–21.

KUO, MO-JO (1957) 'She-hui k'o-hsüeh chieh fan yu-p'ai tou-cheng pi-ssü chin i-pu shen ju' ('The Anti-Rightist Struggle in the Field of the Social Sciences Must be Carried Further'), *JMJP*, 19 September.

LI, AN-CHE (1931) *I Li yü Li Chi chih she-hui-hsüeh ti yen-chiu (The Sociological Study of the Book of Etiquette and Ceremony and the Book of Rites)*, Shanghai, Shang-wu yin-shu kuan.

LI, CHING-HAN (1933) *Ting-hsien she-hui kai-k'uang tiao-ch'a (Survey of Social Conditions in Ting Hsien)*, Hopei, Chung-hua p'ing-min chiao-yü ts'u-chin hui.

LI, CHING-HAN (1957) 'Pei-ching chiao-chü hsiang-ts'un chia-ting sheng-huo ti chin-hsi' ('The Past and Present of Rural Family Life on the Outskirts of Peking'), *JMJP*, 1–3 February.

LI, JEN (1944?) 'Ju-ho chin-hsing nung-ts'un tiao-ch'a' ('How to Conduct Rural Surveys'), in *Cheng-feng wen-ts'ung (A Collection of Essays on the Rectification Movement)*, vol. 4, Hong Kong, Hung-min ch'u-pan she, pp. 14–21.

LI, PAI-KUAN, and CHU, KAI-MO (1956) 'Wu-chia mu-ch'iao nung-yeh sheng-ch'an ho-tso she ching-chi tiao-ch'a' ('An Economic Investigation of the Wu Family Bridge Agricultural Production Co-operative'), *HCS*, no. 2, pp. 11–19.

LIANG, CH'I-CH'AO (1930) *Yin-ping shih wen-chi ch'üan pien (Collected Essays of Liang Ch'i-ch'ao)*, Shanghai, Hsin-min shu-chü.

LIANG, CH'I-CH'AO (1976) 'K'ang Nan-hai ch'uan' ('Biography of K'ang Yu-wei'), in Chiang, Kuei-lin (ed.), *K'ang Nan-hai hsien-sheng i-chu hui-k'an (Collected Writings of K'ang Yu-wei)*, vol. 22, Taipei, Hung-yeh shu-chü.

LIU, TAO-SHENG (1959) 'She-hui k'o-hsüeh kung-tso che ti tang-ch'ien ti hsin k'o-t'i' ('The New Task Confronting the Social Sciences Workers'), *HCS*, no. 1, pp. 1–2.

LO, HUNG (1944?) 'Nung-ts'un tiao-ch'a ti tai-tu ho fang-fa' ('The Attitude and Method of Rural Survey'), in *Cheng-feng wen-ts'ung (A Collection of Essays on the Rectification Movement)*, vol. 4, Hong Kong, Hung-min ch'u-pan she, pp. 22–32.

LÜ, CHEN-YÜ (1940) *Chung-kuo she-hui shih chu wen-t'i (Issues in Chinese Social History)*, Shanghai, Keng-yün ch'u-pan she.

LU, HSÜN (1958) *Chao-hua hsi shih (Recollections)*, Hong Kong, San-lien shu-tien.

MA, HSÜ-LUN (1953) 'Kao-teng chiao-yü ti fang-chen, jen-wu wen-t'i' ('On the Direction and Task of Higher Education'), *Jen-min chiao-yü*, no. 36, pp. 12–14.

MA-LING-NO-SSU-CHI (Malinowski, B.), trans. by Fei Hsiao-t'ung (1944) *Wen-hua lun (What is Culture?)*, Chungking, Shang-wu ch'u-pan she.

MAO, TSE-TUNG (1967) *Mao Tse-tung ssu-hsiang wan-sui (Long Live the Thought of Mao Tse-tung)*, n.p.

MAO, TSE-TUNG (1969) *Mao Tse-tung ssu-hsiang wan-sui (Long Live the Thought of Mao Tse-tung)*, n.p.

MAO, TSE-TUNG (1970–72) *Mao Tse-tung chi (Collected Writings of Mao Tse-tung)*, Tokyo, Pei-wang she.

MO-ERH-KEN (Morgan, L. A.), trans. by Yang, Tung-shun, *et al.* (1972) *Ku-tai she-hui (Ancient Society)*, Peking, Shang-wu yin-shu kuan.

P'AN, CH'I (1951) 'Hsiang-hsi shou-shu min-tsu fang-wen tiao-ch'a pao-kao' ('An Investigation Report of Our Visit to the Minority Nationalities in Western Hunan'), in Chung-nan jen-min ch'u-pan she (ed.), *Chieh-fang liao ti Chung-nan ch'ü hsiung-ti min-tsu (The Liberated Brother Nationalities in the Chung-nan Area)*, Chung-nan, Jen-min ch'u-pan she, pp. 1–12.

P'AN, KUANG-TAN (1946) 'T'an Chung-kuo ti she-hui-hsüeh' ('On Chinese Sociology'), in P'an, *Tsu-yu chih lu (Road to Freedom)*, Shanghai, Shang-wu yin-shu kuan, pp. 270–5.

P'AN, KUANG-TAN (1950) 'Lun Chung-kuo fu-ch'üan tui chiu-ch'üan ti i-chih' ('On the Suppression of the Authority of the Maternal Uncle in the Patriarchal Society of China'), *HCS*, no. 5, pp. 42–3.

P'AN, KUANG-TAN, and CH'ÜAN, WEI-TIEN (1951) 'Ts'ung i-t'ien k'an Su-nan nung-ts'un ti feng-chien shih-li' ('To Examine the Feudal Influence in the Village of Southern Kiangsu from the Institution of the I-tien'), *HCS*, no. 5, pp. 27–32; no. 6, pp. 32–8.

P'AN, KUANG-TAN, and CH'ÜAN, WEN-TIEN (1952) *Su-nan t'u-ti kai-ko fang-wen chi (A visit to Southern Kiangsu on the Land Reform Movement)*, Peking, San-lien shu-tien.

P'AN, SHEN-NIEN (1957) 'Fen-sui tzu-ch'an chieh-chi she-hui-hsüeh fu-p'i ti yin-mou' ('To Destroy the Plot for the Comeback of Bourgeois Sociology'), *Hsin-hua pan-yüeh k'an*, no. 19, pp. 89–90.

SHANG-HAI KANG MA-T'OU TI PIEN-CH'IEN PIEN-HSIEH TSU (1975) *Shang-hai kang ma-t'ou ti pien-ch'ien (Changes in the Docks of Shanghai Harbour)*, Shanghai, Jen-min ch'u-pan she.

SHANG-HAI CH'I-I JEN-MIN KUNG-SHE SHIH PIEN-HSIEH TSU (1974) *Shang-hai Ch'i-i jen-min kung-she shih (A History of the Ch'i-i Commune in Shanghai)*, Shanghai, Jen-min ch'u-pan she.

SHANG-HAI SHE-HUI K'O-HSÜEH YÜAN, CHING-CHI YEN-CHIU SO (1965) *Shang-hai p'eng-hui chü ti pien-ch'ien (Changes in the Squatter Areas of Shanghai)*, Shanghai, Jen-min ch'u-pan she.

SHANG-HAI SHIH HUANG-P'U CH'Ü KO-MING WEI-YÜAN HUI HSIEH-TSO TSU (1976) *Shang-hai wai-t'an nan-ching lu shih-hua (Historical Notes on the Nanking Road of Shanghai)*, Shanghai, Jen-min ch'u-pan she.

SHEN, CHIH-YÜAN (1947) *She-hui k'o-hsüeh chi-ch'u chiang-tso (Lectures on the Foundation of the Social Sciences)*, Hong Kong, Chih-yüan shu-chü.

SHIH, CH'ENG-CHIH (1972) 'Shih lun "ssu-shih" yü "wen-ko"' ('A Tentative Discussion on the "Four Histories" and the "Cultural Revolution"'), *Ming-pao yüeh k'an*, vol. 6, no. 12, pp. 37–43.

SHIH, TUNG-HSIANG (1961) 'Tiao-ch'a yen-chiu shih ma-k'o-ssu chu-i ti ken-pen fang-fa' ('Investigation and Research is the Fundamental Method of Marxism'), *Hung-ch'i*, nos 9 and 10, pp. 1–10.

SSU-PIN-SAI (Spencer, H.), trans. by Yen, Fu (1927) *Ch'ün-hsüeh i-yen (The Study of Sociology)*, Shanghai, Shang-wu yin-shu kuan, 15th edn.

SU, K'O-CH'IN (1961) 'Chi nien lai shao-shu min-tsu she-hui li-shih tiao-ch'a yen-chiu kung-tso' ('Recent Year's Investigation and Research on Social Histories of the Nationalities'), *Min-tsu t'uan-chieh*, no. 5; trans in *SCMM*, no. 271, pp. 31–7.

SUN, PEN-WEN (1931) 'Chung-kuo she-hui-hsüeh chih kuo-ch'ü hsien-tsai chi chiang-lai' ('The Past, Present, and Future of Chinese Sociology'), in Chung-kuo she-hui-hsüeh she, (ed.), *Chung-kuo jen-k'ou wen-t'i (The Population Problem of China)*, Shanghai, Shih-chieh shu-chü, pp. 1–30.

SUN, PEN-WEN (1935) *She-hui-hsüeh yüan-li (Principles of Sociology)*, Shanghai Shang-wu yin-shu kuan.

SUN, PEN-WEN (1947) *Hsien-tai she-hui-hsüeh fa-chan shih (The History of the Development of Contemporary Sociology)*, Shanghai, Shang-wu yin-shu kuan.

SUN, PEN-WEN (1948) 'Erh-shih nien lai chih Chung-kuo she-hui-hsüeh she' ('The Chinese Sociological Society in the Past Twenty Years'), *She-hui-hsüeh hsün*, no. 8, pp. 1–2.

SUN, PEN-WEN (1957a) 'Kuan yü hsien-tai tzu-ch'an chieh-chi she-hui-hsüeh li-lun ti pen-chih ho nei-jung' ('On the Essence and Content of Contemporary Bourgeois Sociological Theories'), *Hsüeh-shu yüeh k'an*, no. 4, pp. 27–36.

SUN, PEN-WEN (1957b) 'Chien-chüeh fan-tui tzu-ch'an chieh-chi she-hui-hsüeh fu-p'i' ('Resolutely Oppose the Comeback of Bourgeois Sociology'), *Wen-hui pao [Shanghai]*, 4 October.

SUN, PEN-WEN (1958) 'P'i-p'an wo chiu-chu "She-hui-hsüeh yüan-li" ti tzu-ch'an chieh-chi ssu-hsiang' ('A Critique of the Bourgeois Thought of My Old Work "Principles of Sociology"'), *Che-hsüeh yen-chiu*, no. 6, pp. 41–5.

SUN, PEN-WEN (1972) 'Ch'i-nien lai ti she-hui-hsüeh' ('Sociology in the Past Seven Years'), *Ko-ming wen-hsien (Documents of the Revolution)*, no. 59, pp. 43–51.

SUN, TING-KUO (1957) 'Pi-hsü ch'e-ti p'i-p'an tzu-ch'an chieh-chi she-hui-hsüeh' ('Bourgeois Sociology Must be Thoroughly Criticized'), *HCS*, no. 9, pp. 1–5.

TAO, TE-LUN (1958) 'Yu-p'ai "she-hui-hsüeh chia" so ch'ui-hsü ti "she-hui tiao-ch'a" shih shih-mo huo-shih' ('What is the Nature of the "Social Research" Advocated by the Rightists "Sociologists"?'), *Hsüeh-hsi*, no. 4, pp. 11–13.

TENG, CHU-MIN (1949) *She-hui k'o-hsüeh ch'ang-shih chiang-hua (Talks on Common Social Scientific Knowledge)*, Hong Kong, Wen-hua kung-ying she.

TENG, CHU-MIN (1957) 'Ts'ung chieh-chi kuan-tien p'o hsi yu-p'ai fen-tzu ch'i-t'u k'uei-fu tzu-ch'an chieh-chi "she-hui ko-hsüeh" ti cheng-ch'h yin-mou' ('To Analyse from the Class Viewpoint the Rightist Political Plot of Attempting to Revive Bourgeois "Social Sciences"'), *HCS*, no. 11, pp. 21–6.

TING, FU-YÜAN (1943) 'Tung-ta she-hui-hsüeh shih' ('The History of the Development of Sociology in Tokyo University'), *She-hui k'o-hsüeh chi k'an (Pei-ta fa-hsüeh yüan)*, new series, vol. 2, no. 3, pp. 77–96.

TING, KENG-LIN (1957) 'Tsai ma-k'o-ssu lieh-ning chu-i ssu-hsiang chih-tao hsia, chi-chi kai-chan she-hui k'o-hsüeh ti yen-chiu' ('To Actively Promote the Study of Social Sciences Under the Guidance of Marxism–Leninism'), *Ssu-ch'uan ta-hsüeh hsüeh-pao she-hui k'o-hsüeh pan*, no. 4, pp. 1–10.

TING, WANG (1967) *Chung-kung wen-hua tai ko-ming tzu-liao hui-pien (A Collection of Materials on the Cultural Revolution of Communist China)*, Hong Kong, Ming-pao yüeh k'an.

TSUNG, CH'ÜN (1961) 'Shao-shu min-tsu kan-pu ti yai-lan' ('The Cradle of National Minority Cadres—Reminiscences of Yenan Nationalities College'), *Min-tsu t'uan-chieh*, nos 8–9, pp. 15–19; trans. in *SCMM*, no. 287, 13 November, pp. 29–35.

TU-ERH-K'O-HAI-MO (Durkheim, E.), trans. by Hsu, Te-heng (1925) *She-hui-hsüeh fang-fa lun (Les Régles de la méthode sociologique)*, Shanghai, Shang-wu yin-shu kuan.

TUNG, CHIEH (1957) 'Chien-li wu-ch'an chieh-chi jen-k'ou-hsüeh' ('To Establish Proletarian Demography'), *HCS*, no. 4, p. 1.

WANG, CHENG (1936) 'She-hui wen-t'i ti lien-huan hsin' ('Interrelations of Social Problems'), *She-hui-hsüeh k'an*, vol. 5, no. 1, pp. 89–101.

WANG, CH'ING-CHENG (1957) 'T'an she-hui-hsüeh ti ti-wei ho ch'ien-t'u' ('On the Status and Prospect of Sociology'), *HCS*, no. 4, p. 47.

WANG, KANG (1957) 'T'an tzu-ch'an chieh-chi she-hui-hsüeh ti fan-tung hsing' ('On the Reactionary Nature of Bourgeois Sociology'), *HCS*, no. 8, pp. 18–23.

WANG, KENG (1779) *Hui-t'u lieh-nü ch'uan (Illustrated Biographies of Heroic Women)*, Kyoto, reprinted by Chung-wen ch'u-pan she.

WANG, SHIH (1976) *Yen Fu ch'uan (Biography of Yen Fu)*, revised edn, Shanghai, Jen-min ch'u-pan she.

WANG, YA-NAN (1957) 'She lun ma-k'o-ssu chu-i ti jen-k'ou li-lun ho Chung-kuo jen-k'ou wen-t'i' ('To Elaborate on the Population Theory in Marxism and the Population Problem of China'), *HCS*, no. 5, pp. 16–17.

WANG, YEN-LI, *et al*. (1958) 'Kuan yü kao-chi nung-yeh she hsiang ch'üan-min so-yu chih kuo-t'u wen-t'i ti tiao-ch'a pao-kao', ('A Report on the Investigation into the Problem of Transition from High-level Co-operatives to the System of Ownership by the People'), *HCS*, no. 9, pp. 1–7.

WEI, WEI (1958) 'Fei Hsiao-t'ung, P'an Kuang-tan ti fan-tung ti wei-hsin chu-i p'i-p'an' ('A Critique of the Reactionary Idealism of Fei Hsiao-t'ung and P'an Kuang-tan'), *HCS*, no. 8, pp. 37–42.

WEN, I-WEN (1959) 'Man-huo ao-chien hsia ti Sun Pen-wen' ('The Sustained Persecution of Sun Pen-wen'), *Tsu-kuo chou k'an*, no. 317, pp. 13–7.

WU, CHIANG (1957) 'Kuan yü Fei Hsiao-t'ung, shuo chi-chü hua' ('A Few Words About Fei Hsiao-t'ung'), *Hsüeh-hsi*, no. 18, pp. 15–18.

WU, CHING-CH'AO (1955) 'P'i-p'an Liang Sou-ming ti hsiang-ts'un chien-she li-lun' ('A Critique of Liang Sou-ming's Rural Construction Theory'), *HCS*, no. 7, pp. 10–19.

WU, CHING-CH'AO (1957a) 'She-hui-hsüeh tsai hsin Chung-kuo hai yu t'i-wei ma?' ('Does Sociology Still Have a Place in New China?'), *HCS*, no. 1, p. 61.

WU, CHING-CH'AO (1957b) 'Chung-kuo jen-k'ou wen-t'i hsin lun' ('A New Discussion on the Population Problem of China'), *HCS*, no. 3, p. 1.

WU-HAN TA-HSÜEH CHENG-CHIH CHING-CHI-HSÜEH HSI (1972) 'Wo-men shih tsen-yang chieh-ho she-hui tiao-ch'a hsüeh-hsi cheng-shih ching-chi hsüeh ti' ('How We Studied Political Economy Through Social Investigations'), *Hung-ch'i*, no. 7, pp. 49–55.

YANG, CH'ING-K'UN (1972) 'Wu ai wu shih chien pu chen-li chih t'u' ('A Meeting with My Teachers Hsieh Ping-hsin and Wu Wen-tsao'), in Hua, Lo-keng, *et al.*, *Chung-kuo chih-shih fen-tzu chin yen lu (A Collection of Recent Interviews with Chinese Intellectuals)*, Hong Kong, Kuang-yü ch'u-pan she, pp. 54–61.

YANG, K'UN (1942) 'Ko-lan-yen yen-chiu tao-lun' ('An Introduction to Granet's Researches'), *Kuo-li Pei-ching ta-hsüeh fa-hsüeh yüan she-hui k'o-hsüeh chi k'an*, vol. 1, no. 3, pp. 33–48; vol. 1, no. 4, pp. 15–54.

YANG, LI-WEN (1965) 'Kuan yü pien-hsieh ts'un-shih ti chi-ko wen-t'i ti ch'u-pu t'an-t'ao' ('An Initial Discussion on Several Problems Concerning the Compilation of Village Histories'), *HCS*, no. 3, pp. 23–30.

YANG, PO (1959) 'Tsen-yang tso tien-hsing tiao-ch'a' ('How to Conduct Model Surveys'), *Chi-hua yü t'ung-chi*, no. 1, pp. 36–7; no. 2, pp. 36–7; no. 3, pp. 24–5; no. 4, pp. 40–1; no. 5, pp. 36–7.

YEN, HSIN-CHE (1936) 'Sheng-huo ch'eng-tu yen-chiu fang-fa t'ao-lun' ('Method of Studying the Standard of Living'), *She-hui-hsüeh k'an*, vol. 5, no. 1, pp. 57–88.

YEN-TA SHE-HUI-HSÜEH HUI (1933) *P'ai-k'o she-hui-hsüeh lun-wen chi (A Collection of Essays on R. E. Park's Sociology)*, Peking, Yen-ching ta-hsüeh she-hui-hsüeh hui.

YO, WEI (1965) 'Lun she-hui ching-chi ti tiao-ch'a yen-chiu' ('On Social and Economic Investigations and Research'), *Ching-chi yen-chiu*, no. 6, pp. 43–51.

130

YÜAN, FANG (1957) 'Kai-chan wo-kuo kung-jen chieh-chi chuang-huang ti tiao-ch'a yen-chiu' ('To Start Investigations and Research on the Working Class of Our Country'), *HCS*, no. 6, pp. 18–20.

Works in English

ALBROW, MARTIN (1970) 'The Role of the Sociologist as a Professional: the Case of Planning', in Paul Halmos (ed.), *The Sociology of Sociology*, Sociological Review monograph no. 16, University of Keele, pp. 1–19.

AL-QAZZAZ, AYAD (1972) 'Sociology in Underdeveloped Countries—a Case Study of Iraq', *Sociological Review*, vol. 20, no. 1, pp. 93–103.

ANDREEVA, G. M. (1966) 'Bourgeois Empirical Sociology Seeks a Way out of Its Crisis', trans. in *Soviet Sociology*, vol. 2, no. 1, 1963, pp. 61–7; abstracted in *Sociological Abstract*, vol. 14, p. 341.

APTER, D. (1965) *The Politics of Modernization*, University of Chicago Press.

ARON, RAYMOND (1957) *The Opium of the Intellectuals*, New York, Norton.

ARON, RAYMOND (1965) *Main Currents in Sociological Thought*, vol. 1, London, Weidenfeld & Nicolson.

BARBER, B. (1971) 'Function, Validity and Change in Ideological System', in B. Barber and A. Inkeles, (eds), *Stability and Social Change*, Boston, Little & Brown, pp. 244–62.

BAUMAN, ZYGMUNT (1971) 'Uses of Information: When Social Information Becomes Desired', *Annals*, vol. 393, pp. 20–31.

Behavioral and Social Sciences Survey Committee (1969) *The Behavioral and Social Sciences: Outlook and Needs*, Englewood Cliffs, New Jersey, Prentice-Hall.

BENDIX, REINHARD (1970) *Embattled Reason: Essays on Social Knowledge*, New York, Oxford University Press.

BERGER, PETER (1966) *Invitation to Sociology*, Harmondsworth, Penguin.

BERGER, PETER (1969) (ed.), *Marxism and Sociology*, New York, Appleton-Century-Crofts.

BERGER, PETER and LUCKMANN, THOMAS (1966) *The Social Construction of Reality*, New York, Doubleday.

BIRCH, CYRIL (1963) 'Chinese Communist Literature: The Persistence of Traditional Form', *China Quarterly*, no. 13, pp. 74–91.

BOORMAN, HOWARD L. and BOORMAN, RICHARD C. (1967–71) (eds) *Biographical Dictionary of Republican China*, 4 vols. New York and London, Columbia University Press.

BOTTOMORE, T. B., and RUBEL, M. (1963) (eds) *Karl Marx: Selected Writings in Sociology and Social Philosophy*, Harmondsworth, Penguin Books.

BOULDING, KENNETH (1966) *The Impact of the Social Sciences*, New Jersey, Rutgers University Press.

BRAMSON, LEON (1961) *The Political Context of Sociology*, Princeton University Press.

BRYANT, C. G. A. (1972) 'Sociology and Socialism in Poland', *Social Research*, vol. 39, no. 1, pp. 102–33.

BUCK, JOHN L. (1937) *Land Utilization in China*, Shanghai, Commercial Press.

BURGESS, J. S. (1928) *The Guilds of Peking,* New York, Columbia University Press.

BURKI, SHADHID JAVED (1965) *A Study of Chinese Communes,* Cambridge, Mass., Harvard University, East Asian Research Center.

BURNS, TOM (1969) (ed.), *Industrial Man,* Harmondsworth, Penguin.

CH'EN HAN-SENG (1933) 'The Present Agrarian Problem in China', preliminary paper prepared for the Fifth Biennial Conference of the IPR, Shanghai, Chinese Institute of Pacific Relations.

CH'EN HAN-SENG (1936) *Landlord and Peasant in China: A Study of the Agrarian Crisis in South China,* New York, International Publishers; reprinted in 1973, Westport, Hyperion Press.

CH'EN HAN-SENG (1939) *Industrial Capital and Chinese Peasants: A Study of the Livelihood of Chinese Tobacco Cultivators,* Shanghai, Kelly & Walsh.

CH'EN HAN-SENG (1948) 'Agrarian Reform in China', *Far Eastern Survey,* vol. 17, no. 4, pp. 41–3.

CH'EN HAN-SENG (1949) *Frontier Land System in Southernmost China,* New York, Institute of Pacific Relations.

CHEN, THEODORE H. E. (1960) *Thought Reform of the Chinese Intellectuals,* Hong Kong University Press.

CHIN, ROBERT and CHIN, AI-LI S. (1965) *Psychological Research in Communist China,* Cambridge, Mass., MIT Press.

CHOW, TSE-TSUNG (1960) *The May Fourth Movement: Intellectual Revolution in Modern China,* Cambridge, Mass., Harvard University Press.

CHYNE, W. Y. (1936) *Handbook of Cultural Institutes in China,* Shanghai, Chinese National Committee on Intellectual Co-operation; reprinted in 1967, Taipei, Ch'eng-wen Publishing Co.

COLEMAN, JAMES (1971) 'Conflicting Theories of Social Change', *American Behavioral Scientist,* vol. 14, no. 5, pp. 633–50.

COOPER, GENE (1973) 'An Interview with Chinese Anthropologists', *Current Anthropology,* vol. XIV, pp. 480–2.

CORBETT, CHARLES HODGE (1963) *Lingnan University,* New York, Trustees of Lingnan University.

COSER, LEWIS ALFRED (1971) *Masters of Sociological Thought,* New York, Harcourt Brace Jovanovich.

CROOK, DAVID and CROOK, ISABEL (1966) *The First Year of Yangyi Commune,* London, Routledge & Kegan Paul.

CURTIS, JAMES E., and PETRAS, JOHN W. (1972) 'The Sociology of Sociology, Some Lines of Inquiry in the Study of the Discipline', *Sociological Enquiry,* vol. 13, no. 2, pp. 197–209.

DAY, CLARENCE BURTON (1955) *Hangchow University: A Brief History,* New York, United Board for Christian Colleges in China.

DUBS, HOMER H. (1928) (trans.), *The Works of Hsüntze,* London, Arthur Probsthain.

EDWARDS, DWIGHT W. (1959) *Yenching University,* New York, United Board for Christian Higher Education in Asia.

EISENSTADT, S. N. (1973) 'Continuity and Reconstruction of Tradition', *Daedalus,* vol. 102, no. 1, pp. 1–28.

FEI, HSIAO-TUNG (1939) *Peasant Life in China,* London, Routledge & Kegan Paul.

FEI, HSIAO-TUNG (1945a) *Earthbound China, A Study of Rural Economy in Yunnan*, University of Chicago Press.

FEI, HSIAO-TUNG (1945b) 'Review of Chao Chao-kuo's *One Month in Yenan*', *Pacific Affairs*, vol. 18, no. 4, pp. 392–3.

FEI, HSIAO-TUNG (1946) 'Peasantry and Gentry: An Interpretation of Chinese Social Structure and Its Changes', *Americal Journal of Sociology*, vol. 52, no. 1, pp. 1–17.

FEI, HSIAO-TUNG (1953) *China's Gentry*, University of Chicago Press.

FEI, HSIAO-TUNG (1956) 'Old Friends and a New Understanding', *People's China*, no. 11, pp. 12–17.

FEI, HSIAO-TUNG and LIN, YUEH-HWA (1957) 'Ways of Life Among China's Minorities', *China Reconstructs*, no. 4, pp. 18–22.

FELDMAN, A. S., and MOORE, W. E. (1965) 'Are Industrial Societies Becoming Alike?', in A. W. Gouldner, and S. M. Miller (eds), *Applied Sociology*, New York, Free Press, pp. 260–5.

FEUERWERKER, ALBERT (1968) (ed.), *History in Communist China*, Cambridge, Mass., MIT Press.

FISCHER, GEORGE (1967) (ed.), *Science and Ideology in Soviet Society*, New York, Atherton.

FOKKEMAN, D. W. (1966) 'Chinese Criticism of Humanism: Campaign Against the Intellectuals 1964–1965', *China Quarterly*, no. 26, pp. 68–81.

FREEDMAN, MAURICE (1962) 'Sociology in and of China', *British Journal of Sociology*, vol. 13, pp. 106–16.

FREEDMAN, MAURICE (1963) 'A Chinese Phase in Social Anthropology', *British Journal of Sociology*, vol. 14, pp. 1–19.

FREEDMAN, MAURICE (1974) 'On the Sociological Study of Chinese Religion', in Arthur P. Wolf (ed.), *Religion and Ritual in Chinese Society*, Stanford University Press, pp. 19–41.

FRIED, MORTON H. (1954) 'Community Studies in China', *Far Eastern Quarterly*, vol. 14, no. 1, pp. 11–36.

FRIED, MORTON H. (1958) 'China', in J. S. Roucek (ed.), *Contemporary Sociology*, New York, Philosophical Library, pp. 993–1012.

FRIEDRICHS, R. W. (1970) *A Sociology of Sociology*, New York, Free Press.

FUKUTAKE, T., and MORIOKA, K. (1974) (eds), *Sociology and Social Development in Asia*, University of Tokyo Press.

GAMBLE, SYDNEY (1954) *Ting Hsien, A North China Rural Community*, New York, Institute of Pacific Relations.

GEDDES, WILLIAM ROBERT (1963) *Peasant Life in Communist China*, Ithaca, Society for Applied Anthropology.

GEERTZ, CLIFFORD (1964) 'Ideology as a Cultural System', in David Apter (ed.), *Ideology and Discontent*, London, Collier-Macmillan.

GELLNER, ERNEST (1970) 'Concepts and Society', in Dorothy Emmet, and Alastair MacIntyre (eds), *Sociological Theory and Philosophical Analysis*, London, Macmillan, pp. 115–49.

GJESSING, GUTORM (1957) 'Chinese Anthropology and New China's Policy Toward her Nationalities', *Acta Sociologica*, vol. 2, pp. 45–67.

GOLDMAN, LUCIEN (1969) *The Human Sciences and Philosophy*, London, Cape.

GOLDMAN, MERLE (1967) *Literary Dissent in Communist China*, Cambridge, Mass., Harvard University Press.

133

GOULDNER, ALVIN WARD (1971) *The Coming Crisis of Western Sociology,* London, Heinemann.

GRANET, MARCEL (1975) *The Religion of the Chinese People,* translated, edited and with an introduction by Maurice Freedman, Oxford, Basil Blackwell.

GRAY, JACK (1972) 'The Chinese Model: Some Characteristics of Maoist Policies for Social Change and Economic Growth', in Alec Nove, and D. M. Nuti (eds), *Socialist Economics,* Harmondsworth, Penguin, pp. 491–510.

GREENBLATT, SYDNEY L. (1972) 'Editor's Introduction', *Chinese Sociology and Anthropology,* vol. 4, no. 3, pp. 171–4.

GREENBLATT, SYDNEY L. (1976) (ed.), *The People of Taihang: An Anthology of Family Histories,* New York, International Arts and Sciences Press.

GROSS, EDWARD (1972) 'Universities and the Shape of Sociological Ideas', *Pacific Sociological Review,* vol. 1, pp. 6–29.

HOLLANDER, PAUL (1967) 'The Dilemma of Soviet Sociology', in Alex Simirenko (ed.), *Soviet Sociology,* London, Routledge & Kegan Paul, pp. 306–26.

HOROWITZ, DAVID (1971) *Radical Sociology,* San Francisco, Canfield Press.

HOROWITZ, IRWIN (1965) (ed.), *The New Sociology,* New York, Oxford University Press.

HSU, FRANCIS, L. K. (1944) 'Sociological Research in China', *Quarterly Bulletin of Chinese Bibliography,* vol. 4, nos 1–4, pp. 12–25.

HSU, FRANCIS, L. K. (1961) 'Anthropological Sciences', in S. H. Gould (ed.), *Sciences in Communist China,* Washington, American Association for the Advancement of Science, pp. 129–57.

HSU, I-T'ANG (1944) 'Ethnological Research in China', *Quarterly Bulletin of Chinese Bibliography,* no. 4, pp. 27–33.

HSU, LEONARD S. (1927a) 'Chinese Sources in General Sociology', *CSPSR,* vol. 11, no. 1, pp. 14–27.

HSU, LEONARD S. (1927b) 'The Teaching of Sociology in China', *CSPSR,* vol. 11, no. 3, pp. 373–89.

HU, SHIH (1931) 'Hu Shih', in Albert Einstein *et al., Living Philosophies,* New York, Simon & Schuster, pp. 235–63.

HUANG, PHILIP C. C. (1975) 'Analyzing the Twentieth Century Chinese Countryside: Revolutionary versus Western Scholarship', *Modern China,* vol. 1, no. 2, pp. 132–60.

INKELES, ALEX (1965) *What is Sociology? An Introduction to the Discipline and Profession,* New Delhi, Prentice-Hall of India (Private) Ltd.

ISRAEL, JOACHIM (1972) 'Is a Non-normative Social Science Possible?', *Acta Sociologica,* vol. 15, no. 1, pp. 69–89.

Joint Research Publications Service (trans.) (1962) *Ethnography and National Minorities in Communist China,* Washington, US Department of Commerce.

KAHN, HAROLD L. (1965) 'Some Mid-Ch'ing Views on the Monarchy', *Journal of Asian Studies,* vol. 24, no. 2, pp. 229–43.

KANEKO, MITSURU (1958) 'The Present Situation of Chinese Sociology', *Japanese Sociological Review,* pp. 107–8, abstracted in *Sociological Abstract,* vol. 11, no. 4 (1963), p. 214.

KATZ, ZEV (1971) 'Sociology in the Soviet Union', *Problem of Communism,* vol. 20, pp. 22–40.

KENNEDY, NEVILLE T., JR (1957) 'The Chinese Democratic League', *Papers on China,* vol. 7, pp. 136–75.

KLEIN, DONALD W., and CLARK, ANNE B. (1971) *Biographic Dictionary of Chinese Communism, 1921–1965,* Cambridge, Mass., Harvard University Press.

KULP, DANIEL HARRISON, II (1925) *Country Life in South China: The Sociology of Familism, Vol. 1: Phenix Village, Kwangtung, China,* New York, Teachers College, Columbia University; reprinted in 1966, Taipei, Ch'eng-wen Publishing Co.

KWOK, D. W. Y. (1965) *Scientism in Chinese Thought, 1900–1950,* New Haven and London, Yale University Press.

LANE, DAVID (1970) 'Ideology and Sociology in the USSR', *British Journal of Sociology,* vol. 21, pp. 43–51.

LAU, CHONG-CHOR (1974) 'Non-professional Social Research in Communist China: 1968–1970', mimeo. paper, Social Research Centre, Chinese University of Hong Kong.

LEONG, Y. K., and TAO, L. K. (1915) *Village and Town Life in China,* London, Allen & Unwin.

LEVENSON, JOSEPH R. (1967) '"History" and "Value": The Tension of Society: Evidence from Painting', in John K. Fairbank (ed.), *Chinese Thought and Institutions,* University of Chicago Press, pp. 320–41.

LEVENSON, JOSEPH R. (1967) '"History" and "Value": The Tension of Intellectual Choice in Modern China', in Arthur F. Wright (ed.), *Studies in Chinese Thought,* University of Chicago Press, pp. 146–94.

LEVENSON, JOSEPH R. (1972) 'Communist China in Time and Space: Roots and Rootlessness', *China Quarterly,* no. 39, pp. 3–6.

LEWIS, J. W. (1963) *Leadership in Communist China,* Ithaca, Cornell University Press.

LI, AN-CHE (1938) 'Notes on the Necessity of Field Research in Social Science in China', *Yenching Journal of Social Studies,* vol. 1, no. 6, pp. 122–7.

LI, CHOH-MING (1962) *The Statistical System of Communist China,* Berkeley, University of California Press.

LI, S. K. (1966) 'Social Sciences in Communist China', *American Behavioral Scientist,* vol. 1, no. 8, pp. 3–7.

LI, YU-NING (1971) *The Introduction of Socialism into China,* New York, Columbia University Press.

LIPSET, S. M., and DOBSON, R. B. (1972) 'The Intellectual as Critic and Rebel', *Daedalus,* vol. 101, no. 3, pp. 137–98.

LIPSET, S. M. and LADD, E. C. JR (1972) 'The Politics of American Sociologists', *American Journal of Sociology,* vol. 78, no. 1, pp. 67–101.

LIU, CHUN-JO (1964) *Controversies in Modern Chinese Intellectual History: An Analytical Bibliography of Periodical Articles Mainly of the May Fourth and Post-May Fourth Era,* Cambridge, Mass., Harvard University, East Asian Research Center.

LOWE, DONALD M. (1970) 'A Review Article: Marx and China, A Disparity of Two Worlds', *China Quarterly,* no. 41, pp. 114–21.

LUTZ, J. G. (1971) *China and the Christian Colleges, 1850–1950,* Ithaca, Cornell University Press.

135

BIBLIOGRAPHY

MACFARQUHAR, RODERICK (1960) (ed.), *The Hundred Flowers*, London, Atlantic Books.

MACFARQUHAR, RODERICK (1974) *The Origins of the Cultural Revolution, Vol. 1: Contradictions Among the People 1956–1957*, New York, Columbia University Press.

MANNHEIM, KARL (1953) *Essays on Sociology and Social Psychology*, London, Routledge & Kegan Paul.

MANNHEIM, KARL (1960) *Ideology and Utopia*, London, Routledge & Kegan Paul.

MAO, TSE-TUNG (1965) *Selected Works of Mao Tse-Tung*, vols 1–4, Peking, Foreign Languages Press.

MAO, TSE-TUNG (1971) *Selected Readings from the Works of Mao Tse-tung*, Peking, Foreign Languages Press.

MAO, TSE-TUNG (1977) *Selected Works of Mao Tse-tung*, vol. 5, Peking, Foreign Languages Press.

MARCUSE, HERBERT (1958) *Soviet Marxism: A Critical Analysis*, London, Routledge & Kegan Paul.

MERTON, ROBERT K. (1968) *Social Theory and Social Structure*, New York, Free Press, enlarged edn.

MERTON, ROBERT K. (1972) 'Insiders and Outsiders: A Chapter in the Sociology of Knowledge', *American Journal of Sociology*, vol. 78, no. 1, pp. 9–47.

MESKILL, J. M. (1970) 'The Chinese Genealogy as a Research Source', in Maurice Freedman (ed.), *Family and Kinship in Chinese Society*, Stanford University Press, pp. 139–62.

MILLS, C. WRIGHT (1959) *The Sociological Imagination*, New York, Oxford University Press.

MIRSKY, JONATHAN (1972) 'China After Nixon', *Annals*, vol. 402, pp. 84–106.

MOL, HANS (1971) 'The Dysfunctions of Sociological Knowledge', *The American Behavioral Scientist*, vol. 6, pp. 221–3.

MOLODTSOV, V. S. (1959) 'Philosophy, Sociology, Logic and Psychology: Teaching of Social Sciences in the Higher Education Establishment of the USSR', *International Social Science Journal*, vol. 11, pp. 176–84.

MOSELEY, GEORGE (1966) *The Party and the National Question in China*, Cambridge, Mass., MIT Press.

MUNRO, DONALD (1971) 'The Malleability of Man in Chinese Marxism', *China Quarterly*, no. 48, pp. 609–40.

MYRDAL, JAN (1965) *Report from a Chinese Village*, London, Heinemann.

NANCE, W. B. (1956) *Soochow University*, New York, United Board for Christian Colleges in China.

NEEDHAM, JOSEPH (1954) *Science and Civilization in China, Vol. 1: Introductory Orientations*, London, Cambridge University Press.

NEWELL, WILLIAM H. (1952) 'Modern Chinese Sociologists', *Sociological Bulletin*, vol. 1, no. 2, pp. 89–94.

NISBET, ROBERT ALEXANDER (1967) *The Sociological Tradition*, London, Heinemann.

O'HARA, ALBERT R. (1961) 'The Recent Development of Sociology in China', *American Sociological Review*, vol. 26, no. 6, pp. 928–9.

136

OKSENBERG, MICHEL (1969) 'Sources and Methodological Problems in the Study of Contemporary China', in A. Doak Barnett (ed.), *Chinese Communist Politics in Action,* Seattle, University of Washington Press, pp. 577–606.

OKSENBERG, MICHEL (1974) 'Method of Communication Within the Chinese Bureaucracy', *China Quarterly,* no. 57, pp. 1–39.

ORLANS, HAROLD (1971) 'The Political Uses of Social Research', *Annals,* vol. 393, pp. 28–35.

PARSONS, TALCOTT (1965) 'An American Impression of Sociology in the Soviet Union', *American Sociological Review,* vol. 30, pp. 121–5.

PARSONS, TALCOTT (1969) 'The Intellectuals: A Social Role Category', in P. Rieff (ed.), *On Intellectuals,* New York, Doubleday, pp. 3–24.

PEPPER, SUZANNE (1973) 'Socialism, Democracy, and Chinese Communism: A Problem of Choice for the Intelligentsia, 1945–49', in Chalmers Johnson (ed.), *Ideology and Politics in Contemporary China,* Seattle, Washington University Press, pp. 161–218.

POPPER, KARL (1969) *The Poverty of Historicism,* London, Routledge & Kegan Paul.

PRYBYLA, J. S. (1975) 'Notes on Chinese Higher Education, 1974', *China Quarterly,* no. 62, pp. 271–96.

RICHMAN, BARRY MARTIN (1969) *Industrial Society in Communist China,* New York, Random House.

ROBERTSON, ROLAND (1972) 'The Sociocultural Implications of Sociology: A Reconnaisance', in J. J. Nossiter, A. H. Hanson, and S. Rokkan (eds), *Imagination and Precision in the Social Sciences,* London, Faber & Faber, pp. 59–95.

ROSS, ROBERT, and STAINES, GRAHAM L. (1972) 'The Politics of Analysing Social Problems', *Social Problems,* vol. 20, no. 1, pp. 18–40.

RUSSELL, BERTRAND (1968) *Unpopular Essays,* London, Allen & Unwin.

SANCHEZ, A. R. (1974) 'Social Science and Social Criticism in China from 1930 to 1949 with special reference to Agrarian Problems', University of Oxford, unpublished B. Litt. thesis.

SANCHEZ, A. R. and WONG, S. L. (1974) 'On "An Interview with Chinese Anthropologists"', *China Quarterly,* no. 60, pp. 775–90.

SCHRAM, STUART (1974) *Mao Tse-tung Unrehearsed,* Harmondsworth, Penguin.

SCHURMANN, FRANZ (1970) *Ideology and Organization in Communist China,* Berkeley, University of California Press, 2nd edn, enlarged.

SCHWARTZ, BENJAMIN (1954) 'A Marxist Controversy on China', *Far Eastern Quarterly,* vol. 13, pp. 143–53.

SCHWARTZ, BENJAMIN (1964) *In Search of Wealth and Power: Yen Fu and the West,* Cambridge, Mass., Harvard University Press.

SCHWARTZ, H. G. (1973) 'The Treatment of Minorities', in Michel Oksenberg (ed.), *China's Developmental Experience,* New York, Academy of Political Science, pp. 193–207.

SHAW, MARTIN (1974) *Marxism versus Sociology,* London, Pluto Press.

SHIH, KUO-HENG (1944) edited and translated by Fei Hsiao-t'ung and Francis L. K. Hsu, *China Enters the Machine Age,* Cambridge, Mass., Harvard University Press.

137

SHIROKOGOROFF, S. M. (1942) 'Ethnographic Investigation of China', *Folklore Studies*, vol. 1, pp. 1–8.

SIMIRENKO, ALEX (1967) (ed.), *Soviet Sociology*, London, Routledge & Kegan Paul.

Singapore Times (1972) 'Students Warned on Sociology Course', 16 December.

SKINNER, G. WILLIAM (1951) 'The New Sociology in China', *Far Eastern Quarterly*, vol. 10, no. 8, pp. 365–71.

SNOW, EDGAR (1971) *Red China Today: The Other Side of the River*, Harmondsworth, Penguin.

SNOW, EDGAR (1972) *Red Star over China*, revised and enlarged edn, Harmondsworth, Penguin.

SOLOMON, RICHARD H. (1971) *Mao's Revolution and the Chinese Political Culture*, Berkeley, Calif., and London, University of California Press.

SPRENKEL, OTTO B. VAN DER (1950) (ed.), *China: Three Views*, London, Turnstile Press.

SUN PEN-WEN (1949) 'Sociology in China', *Social Forces*, vol. 27, no. 3, pp. 247–51.

TAO, L. K. (1925) 'A Note on the Bibliography of Chinese Sociology', *CSPSR*, vol. 9, no. 1, pp. 52–5.

THOMAS, JOHN N. (1974) *The Institute of Pacific Relations: Asian Scholar and American Politics*, University of Washington Press.

TIRYAKIAN, E. (1971) (ed.), *The Phenomenon of Sociology*, New York, Appleton-Century-Crofts.

TOWNSEND, JAMES R. (1969) 'Revolutionizing Chinese Youth: A Study of Chung-kuo Ch'ing-nien', in A. D. Barnett (ed.), *Chinese Communist Politics in Action*, University of Washington Press, pp. 447–76.

TREADGOLD, DONALD W. (1973) *The West in Russia and China, Vol. 2: China 1582–1949*, London, Cambridge University Press.

UHALLEY, STEPHEN, JR (1966) 'The "Four Histories" Movement: A Revolution in Writing China's Past', *Current Scene*, vol. 4, no. 2, pp. 1–10.

Union Research Institute (1970) *Who's Who in Communist China*, Hong Kong, Union Research Institute.

VAN SLYKE, LYMAN P. (1967) *Enemies and Friends: The United Front in Chinese Communist History*, Stanford University Press.

VEBLEN, THORSTEIN (1972) 'Idle Curiosity in Society', in Barry Baines (ed.), *Sociology of Science*, Harmondsworth, Penguin, pp. 321–30.

WAKEMAN, FREDERIC, JR (1972) 'The Price of Autonomy: Intellectuals in Ming and Ching Politics', *Daedalus*, vol. 101, no. 2, pp. 35–70.

WANG, YÜ-CHÜAN (1938) 'The Development of Modern Social Science in China', *Pacific Affairs*, vol. 11, no. 3, pp. 345–62.

WANG, Y. C. (1966) *Chinese Intellectuals and the West, 1872–1949*, Chapel Hill, University of North Carolina Press.

WEIGERT, ANDREW J. (1970) 'The Immoral Rhetoric of Scientific Sociology', *American Sociologist*, vol. 5, no. 2, pp. 111–19.

WEINBERG, ELIZABETH ANN (1974) *The Development of Sociology in the Soviet Union*, London, Routledge & Kegan Paul.

WEINBERG, JAN (1969) 'The Problem of the Convergence of Industrial

Societies: A Critical Look at the State of a Theory', *Comparative Studies in Society and History*, vol. 11, pp. 1–5.

WEN, SHIH (1963) 'Political Parties in Communist China', *Asian Survey*, vol. 3, pp. 157–64.

WEN, SHUN CHI (1970) 'Liang Shu-ming and Chinese Communism', *China Quarterly*, no. 41, pp. 74–91.

WEST, PHILIP (1976) *Yenching University and Sino-Western Relations, 1910–1952*, Cambridge, Mass., Harvard University Press.

WITTFOGEL, KARL A. (1955) 'Review of Fei Hsiao-tung's *China's Gentry*', *Encounter*, January, pp. 78–80.

WOLFF, KURT (1960) (ed.), *Emile Durkheim, 1858–1917*, Columbus, Ohio State University Press.

WONG, SIU-LUN (1975) 'Social Inquiries in the People's Republic of China', *Sociology*, vol. 9, no. 3, pp. 459–76.

WU, WEN-TSAO (1932) 'Review of *Systematic Sociology*', *CSPSR*, vol. 16, pp. 336–7.

YANG, C. K. (1957) 'The Functional Relationship Between Confucian Thought and Chinese Religion', in John Fairbank (ed.), *Chinese Thought and Institutions*, University of Chicago Press, pp. 269–90.

YANG, C. K. (1959) *A Chinese Village in Early Communist Transition*, Cambridge, Mass., MIT Press.

YEN, CHUNG-CHIANG (1967) 'Folklore Research in Communist China', *Asian Folklore Studies*, vol. 26, no. 2, pp. 1–62.

YEN, W. W. (1928) 'China Foundation for the Promotion of Education and Culture', *CSPSR*, vol. 12, no. 2, pp. 426–9.

YOUNG, L. C. (1974) 'Mass Sociology: The Chinese Style', *American Sociologist*, vol. 9, pp. 117–25.

INDEX

Routledge Social Science Series

Routledge & Kegan Paul   London, Henley and Boston

39 Store Street, London WC1E 7DD
Broadway House, Newtown Road, Henley-on-Thames,
Oxon RG9 1EN
9 Park Street, Boston, Mass. 02108

Contents

Authors wishing to submit manuscripts for any series in this catalogue should send them to the Social Science Editor, Routledge & Kegan Paul Ltd, 39 Store Street, London WC1E 7DD

● *Books so marked are available in paperback*
All books are in Metric Demy 8vo format (216 × 138mm approx.)

International Library of Sociology

General Editor   John Rex

GENERAL SOCIOLOGY

Barnsley, J. H. The Social Reality of Ethics. *464 pp.*
Belshaw, Cyril. The Conditions of Social Performance. *An Exploratory Theory. 144 pp.*
Brown, Robert. Explanation in Social Science. *208 pp.*
● Rules and Laws in Sociology. *192 pp.*
Bruford, W. H. Chekhov and His Russia. *A Sociological Study. 244 pp.*
Cain, Maureen E. Society and the Policeman's Role. *326 pp.*
●**Fletcher, Colin.** Beneath the Surface. *An Account of Three Styles of Sociological Research. 221 pp.*
Gibson, Quentin. The Logic of Social Enquiry. *240 pp.*
Glucksmann, M. Structuralist Analysis in Contemporary Social Thought. *212 pp.*
Gurvitch, Georges. Sociology of Law. *Preface by Roscoe Pound. 264 pp.*
Hodge, H. A. Wilhelm Dilthey. *An Introduction. 184 pp.*
Homans, George C. Sentiments and Activities. *336 pp.*
Johnson, Harry M. Sociology: *a Systematic Introduction. Foreword by · Robert K. Merton. 710 pp.*
●**Keat, Russell,** and **Urry, John.** Social Theory as Science. *278 pp.*
Mannheim, Karl. Essays on Sociology and Social Psychology. *Edited by Paul Kecskemeti. With Editorial Note by Adolph Lowe. 344 pp.*
Systematic Sociology: *An Introduction to the Study of Society. Edited by J. S. Erös and Professor W. A. C. Stewart. 220 pp.*
Martindale, Don. The Nature and Types of Sociological Theory. *292 pp.*
●**Maus, Heinz.** A Short History of Sociology. *234 pp.*
Mey, Harald. Field-Theory. *A Study of its Application in the Social Sciences. 352 pp.*
Myrdal, Gunnar. Value in Social Theory: *A Collection of Essays on Methodology. Edited by Paul Streeten. 332 pp.*
Ogburn, William F., and **Nimkoff, Meyer F.** A Handbook of Sociology. *Preface by Karl Mannheim. 656 pp. 46 figures. 35 tables.*
Parsons, Talcott, and **Smelser, Neil J.** Economy and Society: *A Study in the Integration of Economic and Social Theory. 362 pp.*
Podgórecki, Adam. Practical Social Sciences. *About 200 pp.*
●**Rex, John.** Key Problems of Sociological Theory. *220 pp.*
Sociology and the Demystification of the Modern World. *282 pp.*
●**Rex, John** (Ed.) Approaches to Sociology. *Contributions by Peter Abell, Frank Bechhofer, Basil Bernstein, Ronald Fletcher, David Frisby, Miriam Glucksmann, Peter Lassman, Herminio Martins, John Rex, Roland Robertson, John Westergaard and Jock Young. 302 pp.*
Rigby, A. Alternative Realities. *352 pp.*
Roche, M. Phenomenology, Language and the Social Sciences. *374 pp.*

Sahay, A. Sociological Analysis. *220 pp.*

Simirenko, Alex (Ed.) Soviet Sociology. *Historical Antecedents and Current Appraisals. Introduction by Alex Simirenko. 376 pp.*

Strasser, Hermann. The Normative Structure of Sociology. *Conservative and Emancipatory Themes in Social Thought. About 340 pp.*

Urry, John. Reference Groups and the Theory of Revolution. *244 pp.*

Weinberg, E. Development of Sociology in the Soviet Union. *173 pp.*

FOREIGN CLASSICS OF SOCIOLOGY

●**Durkheim, Emile.** Suicide. *A Study in Sociology. Edited and with an Introduction by George Simpson. 404 pp.*

●**Gerth, H. H.,** and **Mills, C. Wright.** From Max Weber: *Essays in Sociology. 502 pp.*

●**Tönnies, Ferdinand.** Community and Association. (*Gemeinschaft und Gesellschaft.) Translated and Supplemented by Charles P. Loomis. Foreword by Pitirim A. Sorokin. 334 pp.*

SOCIAL STRUCTURE

Andreski, Stanislav. Military Organization and Society. *Foreword by Professor A. R. Radcliffe-Brown. 226 pp. 1 folder.*

Carlton, Eric. Ideology and Social Order. *Preface by Professor Philip Abrahams. About 320 pp.*

Coontz, Sydney H. Population Theories and the Economic Interpretation. *202 pp.*

Coser, Lewis. The Functions of Social Conflict. *204 pp.*

Dickie-Clark, H. F. Marginal Situation: *A Sociological Study of a Coloured Group. 240 pp. 11 tables.*

Glaser, Barney, and **Strauss, Anselm L.** Status Passage. *A Formal Theory. 208 pp.*

Glass, D. V. (Ed.) Social Mobility in Britain. *Contributions by J. Berent, T. Bottomore, R. C. Chambers, J. Floud, D. V. Glass, J. R. Hall, H. T. Himmelweit, R. K. Kelsall, F. M. Martin, C. A. Moser, R. Mukherjee, and W. Ziegel. 420 pp.*

Johnstone, Frederick A. Class, Race and Gold. *A Study of Class Relations and Racial Discrimination in South Africa. 312 pp.*

Jones, Garth N. Planned Organizational Change: *An Exploratory Study Using an Empirical Approach. 268 pp.*

Kelsall, R. K. Higher Civil Servants in Britain: *From 1870 to the Present Day. 268 pp. 31 tables.*

König, René. The Community. *232 pp. Illustrated.*

●**Lawton, Denis.** Social Class, Language and Education. *192 pp.*

McLeish, John. The Theory of Social Change: *Four Views Considered. 128 pp.*

Marsh, David C. The Changing Social Structure of England and Wales, 1871-1961. *288 pp.*

Menzies, Ken. Talcott Parsons and the Social Image of Man. *About 208 pp.*

4

●**Mouzelis, Nicos.** Organization and Bureaucracy. *An Analysis of Modern Theories. 240 pp.*

Mulkay, M. J. Functionalism, Exchange and Theoretical Strategy. *272 pp.*

Ossowski, Stanislaw. Class Structure in the Social Consciousness. *210 pp.*

●**Podgórecki, Adam.** Law and Society. *302 pp.*

Renner, Karl. Institutions of Private Law and Their Social Functions. *Edited, with an Introduction and Notes, by O. Kahn-Freud. Translated by Agnes Schwarzschild. 316 pp.*

SOCIOLOGY AND POLITICS

Acton, T. A. Gypsy Politics and Social Change. *316 pp.*

Clegg, Stuart. Power, Rule and Domination. *A Critical and Empirical Understanding of Power in Sociological Theory and Organisational Life. About 300 pp.*

Hechter, Michael. Internal Colonialism. *The Celtic Fringe in British National Development, 1536–1966. 361 pp.*

Hertz, Frederick. Nationality in History and Politics: *A Psychology and Sociology of National Sentiment and Nationalism. 432 pp.*

Kornhauser, William. The Politics of Mass Society. *272 pp. 20 tables.*

●**Kroes, R.** Soldiers and Students. *A Study of Right- and Left-wing Students. 174 pp.*

Laidler, Harry W. History of Socialism. *Social-Economic Movements: An Historical and Comparative Survey of Socialism, Communism, Co-operation, Utopianism; and other Systems of Reform and Reconstruction. 992 pp.*

Lasswell, H. D. Analysis of Political Behaviour. *324 pp.*

Martin, David A. Pacifism: *an Historical and Sociological Study. 262 pp.*

Martin, Roderick. Sociology of Power. *About 272 pp.*

Myrdal, Gunnar. The Political Element in the Development of Economic Theory. *Translated from the German by Paul Streeten. 282 pp.*

Wilson, H. T. The American Ideology. *Science, Technology and Organization of Modes of Rationality. About 280 pp.*

Wootton, Graham. Workers, Unions and the State. *188 pp.*

CRIMINOLOGY

Ancel, Marc. Social Defence: *A Modern Approach to Criminal Problems. Foreword by Leon Radzinowicz. 240 pp.*

Cain, Maureen E. Society and the Policeman's Role. *326 pp.*

Cloward, Richard A., and **Ohlin, Lloyd E.** Delinquency and Opportunity: *A Theory of Delinquent Gangs. 248 pp.*

Downes, David M. The Delinquent Solution. *A Study in Subcultural Theory. 296 pp.*

Dunlop, A. B., and **McCabe, S.** Young Men in Detention Centres. *192 pp.*

Friedlander, Kate. The Psycho-Analytical Approach to Juvenile Delinquency: *Theory, Case Studies, Treatment. 320 pp.*

Glueck, Sheldon, and **Eleanor.** Family Environment and Delinquency. *With the statistical assistance of Rose W. Kneznek. 340 pp.*

5

Lopez-Rey, Manuel. Crime. *An Analytical Appraisal. 288 pp.*
Mannheim, Hermann. Comparative Criminology: *a Text Book. Two volumes. 442 pp. and 380 pp.*
Morris, Terence. The Criminal Area: *A Study in Social Ecology. Foreword by Hermann Mannheim. 232 pp. 25 tables. 4 maps.*
Rock, Paul. Making People Pay. *338 pp.*
● **Taylor, Ian, Walton, Paul,** and **Young, Jock.** The New Criminology. *For a Social Theory of Deviance. 325 pp.*
● **Taylor, Ian, Walton, Paul,** and **Young, Jock** (Eds). Critical Criminology. *268 pp.*

SOCIAL PSYCHOLOGY

Bagley, Christopher. The Social Psychology of the Epileptic Child. *320 pp.*
Barbu, Zevedei. Problems of Historical Psychology. *248 pp.*
Blackburn, Julian. Psychology and the Social Pattern. *184 pp.*
● **Brittan, Arthur.** Meanings and Situations. *224 pp.*
Carroll, J. Break-Out from the Crystal Palace. *200 pp.*
● **Fleming, C. M.** Adolescence: Its Social Psychology. *With an Introduction to recent findings from the fields of Anthropology, Physiology, Medicine, Psychometrics and Sociometry. 288 pp.*
● The Social Psychology of Education: *An Introduction and Guide to Its Study. 136 pp.*
● **Homans, George C.** The Human Group. *Foreword by Bernard DeVoto. Introduction by Robert K. Merton. 526 pp.*
● Social Behaviour: *its Elementary Forms. 416 pp.*
● **Klein, Josephine.** The Study of Groups. *226 pp. 31 figures. 5 tables.*
Linton, Ralph. The Cultural Background of Personality. *132 pp.*
● **Mayo, Elton.** The Social Problems of an Industrial Civilization. *With an appendix on the Political Problem. 180 pp.*
Ottaway, A. K. C. Learning Through Group Experience. *176 pp.*
Plummer, Ken. Sexual Stigma. *An Interactionist Account. 254 pp.*
● **Rose, Arnold M.** (Ed.) Human Behaviour and Social Processes: *an Interactionist Approach. Contributions by Arnold M. Rose, Ralph H. Turner, Anselm Strauss, Everett C. Hughes, E. Franklin Frazier, Howard S. Becker, et al. 696 pp.*
Smelser, Neil J. Theory of Collective Behaviour. *448 pp.*
Stephenson, Geoffrey M. The Development of Conscience. *128 pp.*
Young, Kimball. Handbook of Social Psychology. *658 pp. 16 figures. 10 tables.*

SOCIOLOGY OF THE FAMILY

Banks, J. A. Prosperity and Parenthood: *A Study of Family Planning among The Victorian Middle Classes. 262 pp.*
Bell, Colin R. Middle Class Families: *Social and Geographical Mobility. 224 pp.*

Burton, Lindy. Vulnerable Children. *272 pp.*

Gavron, Hannah. The Captive Wife: *Conflicts of Household Mothers.* *190 pp.*

George, Victor, and **Wilding, Paul.** Motherless Families. *248 pp.*

Klein, Josephine. Samples from English Cultures.
1. Three Preliminary Studies and Aspects of Adult Life in England. *447 pp.*
2. Child-Rearing Practices and Index. *247 pp.*

Klein, Viola. The Feminine Character. *History of an Ideology. 244 pp.*

McWhinnie, Alexina M. Adopted Children. *How They Grow Up. 304 pp.*

● **Morgan, D. H. J.** Social Theory and the Family. *About 320 pp.*

● **Myrdal, Alva,** and **Klein, Viola.** Women's Two Roles: *Home and Work.* *238 pp. 27 tables.*

Parsons, Talcott, and **Bales, Robert F.** Family: Socialization and Inter-action Process. *In collaboration with James Olds, Morris Zelditch and Philip E. Slater. 456 pp. 50 figures and tables.*

SOCIAL SERVICES

Bastide, Roger. The Sociology of Mental Disorder. *Translated from the French by Jean McNeil. 260 pp.*

Carlebach, Julius. Caring For Children in Trouble. *266 pp.*

George, Victor. Foster Care. *Theory and Practice. 234 pp.*
Social Security: *Beveridge and After. 258 pp.*

George, V., and **Wilding, P.** Motherless Families. *248 pp.*

● **Goetschius, George W.** Working with Community Groups. *256 pp.*

Goetschius, George W., and **Tash, Joan.** Working with Unattached Youth. *416 pp.*

Hall, M. P., and **Howes, I. V.** The Church in Social Work. *A Study of Moral Welfare Work undertaken by the Church of England. 320 pp.*

Heywood, Jean S. Children in Care: *the Development of the Service for the Deprived Child. 264 pp.*

Hoenig, J., and **Hamilton, Marian W.** The De-Segregation of the Mentally Ill. *284 pp.*

Jones, Kathleen. Mental Health and Social Policy, 1845-1959. *264 pp.*

King, Roy D., Raynes, Norma V., and **Tizard, Jack.** Patterns of Residential Care. *356 pp.*

Leigh, John. Young People and Leisure. *256 pp.*

● **Mays, John.** (Ed.) Penelope Hall's Social Services of England and Wales. *About 324 pp.*

Morris, Mary. Voluntary Work and the Welfare State. *300 pp.*

Nokes, P. L. The Professional Task in Welfare Practice. *152 pp.*

Timms, Noel. Psychiatric Social Work in Great Britain (1939-1962). *280 pp.*

● Social Casework: *Principles and Practice. 256 pp.*

Young, A. F. Social Services in British Industry. *272 pp.*

7

SOCIOLOGY OF EDUCATION

Banks, Olive. Parity and Prestige in English Secondary Education: a Study in Educational Sociology. *272 pp.*

Bentwich, Joseph. Education in Israel. *224 pp. 8 pp. plates.*

●**Blyth, W. A. L.** English Primary Education. *A Sociological Description.*
 1. Schools. *232 pp.*
 2. Background. *168 pp.*

Collier, K. G. The Social Purposes of Education: *Personal and Social Values in Education. 268 pp.*

Dale, R. R., and **Griffith, S.** Down Stream: *Failure in the Grammar School. 108 pp.*

Evans, K. M. Sociometry and Education. *158 pp.*

●**Ford, Julienne.** Social Class and the Comprehensive School. *192 pp.*

Foster, P. J. Education and Social Change in Ghana. *336 pp. 3 maps.*

Fraser, W. R. Education and Society in Modern France. *150 pp.*

Grace, Gerald R. Role Conflict and the Teacher. *150 pp.*

Hans, Nicholas. New Trends in Education in the Eighteenth Century. *278 pp. 19 tables.*

● Comparative Education: *A Study of Educational Factors and Traditions. 360 pp.*

●**Hargreaves, David.** Interpersonal Relations and Education. *432 pp.*

● Social Relations in a Secondary School. *240 pp.*

Holmes, Brian. Problems in Education. *A Comparative Approach. 336 pp.*

King, Ronald. Values and Involvement in a Grammar School. *164 pp.*
 School Organization and Pupil Involvement. *A Study of Secondary Schools.*

●**Mannheim, Karl,** and **Stewart, W. A. C.** An Introduction to the Sociology of Education. *206 pp.*

Morris, Raymond N. The Sixth Form and College Entrance. *231 pp.*

●**Musgrove, F.** Youth and the Social Order. *176 pp.*

●**Ottaway, A. K. C.** Education and Society: An Introduction to the Sociology of Education. *With an Introduction by W. O. Lester Smith. 212 pp.*

Peers, Robert. Adult Education: *A Comparative Study. 398 pp.*

Pritchard, D. G. Education and the Handicapped: *1760 to 1960. 258 pp.*

Stratta, Erica. The Education of Borstal Boys. *A Study of their Educational Experiences prior to, and during, Borstal Training. 256 pp.*

Taylor, P. H., Reid, W. A., and **Holley, B. J.** The English Sixth Form. *A Case Study in Curriculum Research. 200 pp.*

SOCIOLOGY OF CULTURE

Eppel, E. M., and **M.** Adolescents and Morality: *A Study of some Moral Values and Dilemmas of Working Adolescents in the Context of a changing Climate of Opinion. Foreword by W. J. H. Sprott. 268 pp. 39 tables.*

●**Fromm, Erich.** The Fear of Freedom. *286 pp.*

● The Sane Society. *400 pp.*

Mannheim, Karl. Essays on the Sociology of Culture. *Edited by Ernst Mannheim in co-operation with Paul Kecskemeti. Editorial Note by Adolph Lowe. 280 pp.*

Weber, Alfred. Farewell to European History: *or The Conquest of Nihilism. Translated from the German by R. F. C. Hull. 224 pp.*

SOCIOLOGY OF RELIGION

Argyle, Michael and **Beit-Hallahmi, Benjamin.** The Social Psychology of Religion. *About 256 pp.*

Glasner, Peter E. The Sociology of Secularisation. *A Critique of a Concept. About 180 pp.*

Nelson, G. K. Spiritualism and Society. *313 pp.*

Stark, Werner. The Sociology of Religion. *A Study of Christendom.*
Volume I. *Established Religion. 248 pp.*
Volume II. *Sectarian Religion. 368 pp.*
Volume III. *The Universal Church. 464 pp.*
Volume IV. *Types of Religious Man. 352 pp.*
Volume V. *Types of Religious Culture. 464 pp.*

Turner, B. S. Weber and Islam. *216 pp.*

Watt, W. Montgomery. Islam and the Integration of Society. *320 pp.*

SOCIOLOGY OF ART AND LITERATURE

Jarvie, Ian C. Towards a Sociology of the Cinema. *A Comparative Essay on the Structure and Functioning of a Major Entertainment Industry. 405 pp.*

Rust, Frances S. Dance in Society. *An Analysis of the Relationships between the Social Dance and Society in England from the Middle Ages to the Present Day. 256 pp. 8 pp. of plates.*

Schücking, L. L. The Sociology of Literary Taste. *112 pp.*

Wolff, Janet. Hermeneutic Philosophy and the Sociology of Art. *150 pp.*

SOCIOLOGY OF KNOWLEDGE

Diesing, P. Patterns of Discovery in the Social Sciences. *262 pp.*

●**Douglas, J. D.** (Ed.) Understanding Everyday Life. *370 pp.*

●**Hamilton, P.** Knowledge and Social Structure. *174 pp.*

Jarvie, I. C. Concepts and Society. *232 pp.*

Mannheim, Karl. Essays on the Sociology of Knowledge. *Edited by Paul Kecskemeti. Editorial Note by Adolph Lowe. 353 pp.*

Remmling, Gunter W. The Sociology of Karl Mannheim. *With a Bibliographical Guide to the Sociology of Knowledge, Ideological Analysis, and Social Planning. 255 pp.*

Remmling, Gunter W. (Ed.) Towards the Sociology of Knowledge. *Origin and Development of a Sociological Thought Style. 463 pp.*

Stark, Werner. The Sociology of Knowledge: *An Essay in Aid of a Deeper Understanding of the History of Ideas. 384 pp.*

URBAN SOCIOLOGY

Ashworth, William. The Genesis of Modern British Town Planning: *A Study in Economic and Social History of the Nineteenth and Twentieth Centuries. 288 pp.*

Cullingworth, J. B. Housing Needs and Planning Policy: *A Restatement of the Problems of Housing Need and 'Overspill' in England and Wales. 232 pp. 44 tables. 8 maps.*

Dickinson, Robert E. City and Region: *A Geographical Interpretation 608 pp. 125 figures.*
The West European City: *A Geographical Interpretation. 600 pp. 129 maps. 29 plates.*
● The City Region in Western Europe. *320 pp. Maps.*

Humphreys, Alexander J. New Dubliners: *Urbanization and the Irish Family. Foreword by George C. Homans. 304 pp.*

Jackson, Brian. Working Class Community: *Some General Notions raised by a Series of Studies in Northern England. 192 pp.*

Jennings, Hilda. Societies in the Making: *a Study of Development and Redevelopment within a County Borough. Foreword by D. A. Clark. 286 pp.*

●**Mann, P. H.** An Approach to Urban Sociology. *240 pp.*

Morris, R. N., and **Mogey, J.** The Sociology of Housing. *Studies at Berinsfield. 232 pp. 4 pp. plates.*

Rosser, C., and **Harris, C.** The Family and Social Change. *A Study of Family and Kinship in a South Wales Town. 352 pp. 8 maps.*

●**Stacey, Margaret, Batsone, Eric, Bell, Colin,** and **Thurcott, Anne.** Power, Persistence and Change. *A Second Study of Banbury. 196 pp.*

RURAL SOCIOLOGY

Haswell, M. R. The Economics of Development in Village India. *120 pp.*

Littlejohn, James. Westrigg: *the Sociology of a Cheviot Parish. 172 pp. 5 figures.*

Mayer, Adrian C. Peasants in the Pacific. *A Study of Fiji Indian Rural Society. 248 pp. 20 plates.*

Williams, W. M. The Sociology of an English Village: *Gosforth. 272 pp. 12 figures. 13 tables.*

SOCIOLOGY OF INDUSTRY AND DISTRIBUTION

Anderson, Nels. Work and Leisure. *280 pp.*

●**Blau, Peter M.**, and **Scott, W. Richard.** Formal Organizations: *a Comparative approach. Introduction and Additional Bibliography by J. H. Smith. 326 pp.*

Dunkerley, David. The Foreman. *Aspects of Task and Structure. 192 pp.*

Eldridge, J. E. T. Industrial Disputes. *Essays in the Sociology of Industrial Relations. 288 pp.*

Hetzler, Stanley. Applied Measures for Promoting Technological Growth. *352 pp.*
Technological Growth and Social Change. *Achieving Modernization. 269 pp.*

Hollowell, Peter G. The Lorry Driver. *272 pp.*

●**Oxaal, I., Barnett, T.**, and **Booth, D.** (Eds). Beyond the Sociology of Development. *Economy and Society in Latin America and Africa. 295 pp.*

Smelser, Neil J. Social Change in the Industrial Revolution: *An Application of Theory to the Lancashire Cotton Industry, 1770–1840. 468 pp. 12 figures. 14 tables.*

ANTHROPOLOGY

Ammar, Hamed. Growing up in an Egyptian Village: *Silwa, Province of Aswan. 336 pp.*

Brandel-Syrier, Mia. Reeftown Elite. *A Study of Social Mobility in a Modern African Community on the Reef. 376 pp.*

Dickie-Clark, H. F. The Marginal Situation. *A Sociological Study of a Coloured Group. 236 pp.*

Dube, S. C. Indian Village. *Foreword by Morris Edward Opler. 276 pp. 4 plates.*
India's Changing Villages: *Human Factors in Community Development. 260 pp. 8 plates. 1 map.*

Firth, Raymond. Malay Fishermen. *Their Peasant Economy. 420 pp. 17 pp. plates.*

Gulliver, P. H. Social Control in an African Society: a Study of the Arusha, Agricultural Masai of Northern Tanganyika. *320 pp. 8 plates. 10 figures.*
Family Herds. *288 pp.*

Ishwaran, K. Tradition and Economy in Village India: *An Interactionist Approach.*
Foreword by Conrad Arensburg. 176 pp.

Jarvie, Ian C. The Revolution in Anthropology. *268 pp.*

Little, Kenneth L. Mende of Sierra Leone. *308 pp. and folder.*
Negroes in Britain. *With a New Introduction and Contemporary Study by Leonard Bloom. 320 pp.*

Lowie, Robert H. Social Organization. *494 pp.*

Mayer, A. C. Peasants in the Pacific. *A Study of Fiji Indian Rural Society. 248 pp.*

Meer, Fatima. Race and Suicide in South Africa. *325 pp.*

Smith, Raymond T. The Negro Family in British Guiana: *Family Structure and Social Status in the Villages. With a Foreword by Meyer Fortes. 314 pp. 8 plates. 1 figure. 4 maps.*
Smooha, Sammy. Israel: Pluralism and Conflict. *About 320 pp.*

SOCIOLOGY AND PHILOSOPHY

Barnsley, John H. The Social Reality of Ethics. *A Comparative Analysis of Moral Codes. 448 pp.*
Diesing, Paul. Patterns of Discovery in the Social Sciences. *362 pp.*
●**Douglas, Jack D.** (Ed.) Understanding Everyday Life. *Toward the Reconstruction of Sociological Knowledge. Contributions by Alan F. Blum. Aaron W. Cicourel, Norman K. Denzin, Jack D. Douglas, John Heeren, Peter McHugh, Peter K. Manning, Melvin Power, Matthew Speier, Roy Turner, D. Lawrence Wieder, Thomas P. Wilson and Don H. Zimmerman. 370 pp.*
Gorman, Robert A. The Dual Vision. *Alfred Schutz and the Myth of Phenomenological Social Science. About 300 pp.*
Jarvie, Ian C. Concepts and Society. *216 pp.*
●**Pelz, Werner.** The Scope of Understanding in Sociology. *Towards a more radical reorientation in the social humanistic sciences. 283 pp.*
Roche, Maurice. Phenomenology, Language and the Social Sciences. *371 pp.*
Sahay, Arun. Sociological Analysis. *212 pp.*
Sklair, Leslie. The Sociology of Progress. *320 pp.*
Slater, P. Origin and Significance of the Frankfurt School. *A Marxist Perspective. About 192 pp.*
Smart, Barry. Sociology, Phenomenology and Marxian Analysis. *A Critical Discussion of the Theory and Practice of a Science of Society. 220 pp.*

International Library of Anthropology

General Editor Adam Kuper

Ahmed, A. S. Millenium and Charisma Among Pathans. *A Critical Essay in Social Anthropology. 192 pp.*
Brown, Paula. The Chimbu. *A Study of Change in the New Guinea Highlands. 151 pp.*
Gudeman, Stephen. Relationships, Residence and the Individual. *A Rural Panamanian Community. 288 pp. 11 Plates, 5 Figures, 2 Maps, 10 Tables.*
Hamnett, Ian. Chieftainship and Legitimacy. *An Anthropological Study of Executive Law in Lesotho. 163 pp.*
Hanson, F. Allan. Meaning in Culture. *127 pp.*
Lloyd, P. C. Power and Independence. *Urban Africans' Perception of Social Inequality. 264 pp.*

Pettigrew, Joyce. Robber Noblemen. *A Study of the Political System of the Sikh Jats. 284 pp.*

Street, Brian V. The Savage in Literature. *Representations of 'Primitive' Society in English Fiction, 1858–1920. 207 pp.*

Van Den Berghe, Pierre L. Power and Privilege at an African University. *278 pp.*

International Library of Social Policy

General Editor Kathleen Jones

Bayley, M. Mental Handicap and Community Care. *426 pp.*

Bottoms, A. E., and **McClean, J. D.** Defendants in the Criminal Process. *284 pp.*

Butler, J. R. Family Doctors and Public Policy. *208 pp.*

Davies, Martin. Prisoners of Society. *Attitudes and Aftercare. 204 pp.*

Gittus, Elizabeth. Flats, Families and the Under-Fives. *285 pp.*

Holman, Robert. Trading in Children. *A Study of Private Fostering. 355 pp.*

Jones, Howard, and **Cornes, Paul.** Open Prisons. *About 248 pp.*

Jones, Kathleen. History of the Mental Health Service. *428 pp.*

Jones, Kathleen, with **Brown, John, Cunningham, W. J., Roberts, Julian,** and **Williams, Peter.** Opening the Door. *A Study of New Policies for the Mentally Handicapped. 278 pp.*

Karn, Valerie. Retiring to the Seaside. *About 280 pp. 2 maps. Numerous tables.*

Thomas, J. E. The English Prison Officer since 1850: *A Study in Conflict. 258 pp.*

Walton, R. G. Women in Social Work. *303 pp.*

Woodward, J. To Do the Sick No Harm. *A Study of the British Voluntary Hospital System to 1875. 221 pp.*

International Library of Welfare and Philosophy

General Editors Noel Timms and David Watson

● **Plant, Raymond.** Community and Ideology. *104 pp.*

● **McDermott, F. E.** (Ed.) Self-Determination in Social Work. *A Collection of Essays on Self-determination and Related Concepts by Philosophers and Social Work Theorists. Contributors: F. P. Biestek, S. Bernstein, A. Keith-Lucas, D. Sayer, H. H. Perelman, C. Whittington, R. F. Stalley, F. E. McDermott, I. Berlin, H. J. McCloskey, H. L. A. Hart, J. Wilson, A. I. Melden, S. I. Benn. 254 pp.*

Ragg, Nicholas M. People Not Cases. *A Philosophical Approach to Social Work. About 250 pp.*

● **Timms, Noel,** and **Watson, David** (Eds). Talking About Welfare. *Readings in Philosophy and Social Policy. Contributors: T. H. Marshall, R. B. Brandt, G. H. von Wright, K. Nielsen, M. Cranston, R. M. Titmuss, R. S. Downie, E. Telfer, D. Donnison, J. Benson, P. Leonard, A. Keith-Lucas, D. Walsh, I. T. Ramsey. 320 pp.*

Primary Socialization, Language and Education

General Editor   Basil Bernstein

Adlam, Diana S., *with the assistance of Geoffrey Turner and Lesley Lineker.* Code in Context. *About 272 pp.*

Bernstein, Basil. Class, Codes and Control. *3 volumes.*
  1. *Theoretical Studies Towards a Sociology of Language. 254 pp.*
  2. *Applied Studies Towards a Sociology of Language. 377 pp.*
● 3. *Towards a Theory of Educatiomal Transmission. 167 pp.*
Brandis, W., and **Bernstein, B.** Selection and Control. *176 pp.*
Brandis, Walter, and **Henderson, Dorothy.** Social Class, Language and Communication. *288 pp.*

Cook-Gumperz, Jenny. Social Control and Socialization. *A Study of Class Differences in the Language of Maternal Control. 290 pp.*
●**Gahagan, D. M.,** and **G. A.** Talk Reform. *Exploration in Language for Infant School Children. 160 pp.*

Hawkins, P. R. Social Class, the Nominal Group and Verbal Strategies. *About 220 pp.*

Robinson, W. P., and **Rackstraw, Susan D. A.** A Question of Answers. *2 volumes. 192 pp. and 180 pp.*

Turner, Geoffrey J., and **Mohan, Bernard A.** A Linguistic Description and Computer Programme for Children's Speech. *208 pp.*

Reports of the Institute of Community Studies

●**Cartwright, Ann.** Parents and Family Planning Services. *306 pp.*
  Patients and their Doctors. *A Study of General Practice. 304 pp.*
Dench, Geoff. Maltese in London. *A Case-study in the Erosion of Ethnic Consciousness. 302 pp.*
●**Jackson, Brian.** Streaming: *an Education System in Miniature. 168 pp.*
Jackson, Brian, and **Marsden, Dennis.** Education and the Working Class: *Some General Themes raised by a Study of 88 Working-class Children in a Northern Industrial City. 268 pp. 2 folders.*
Marris, Peter. The Experience of Higher Education. *232 pp. 27 tables.*
  Loss and Change. *192 pp.*
Marris, Peter, and **Rein, Martin.** Dilemmas of Social Reform. *Poverty and Community Action in the United States. 256 pp.*

Marris, Peter, and Somerset, Anthony. African Businessmen. *A Study of Entrepreneurship and Development in Kenya. 256 pp.*

Mills, Richard. Young Outsiders: *a Study in Alternative Communities. 216 pp.*

Runciman, W. G. Relative Deprivation and Social Justice. *A Study of Attitudes to Social Inequality in Twentieth-Century England. 352 pp.*

Willmott, Peter. Adolescent Boys in East London. *230 pp.*

Willmott, Peter, and Young, Michael. Family and Class in a London Suburb. *202 pp. 47 tables.*

Young, Michael. Innovation and Research in Education. *192 pp.*

● Young, Michael, and McGeeney, Patrick. Learning Begins at Home. *A Study of a Junior School and its Parents. 128 pp.*

Young, Michael, and Willmott, Peter. Family and Kinship in East London. *Foreword by Richard M. Titmuss. 252 pp. 39 tables.*
    The Symmetrical Family. *410 pp.*

Reports of the Institute for Social Studies in Medical Care

Cartwright, Ann, Hockey, Lisbeth, and Anderson, John L. Life Before Death. *310 pp.*

Dunnell, Karen, and Cartwright, Ann. Medicine Takers, Prescribers and Hoarders. *190 pp.*

Medicine, Illness and Society

General Editor W. M. Williams

Robinson, David. The Process of Becoming Ill. *142 pp.*

Stacey, Margaret, *et al.* Hospitals, Children and Their Families. *The Report of a Pilot Study. 202 pp.*

Stimson, G. V., and Webb, B. Going to See the Doctor. *The Consultation Process in General Practice. 155 pp.*

Monographs in Social Theory

General Editor Arthur Brittan

● Barnes, B. Scientific Knowledge and Sociological Theory. *192 pp.*

Bauman, Zygmunt. Culture as Praxis. *204 pp.*

● Dixon, Keith. Sociological Theory. *Pretence and Possibility. 142 pp.*

Meltzer, B. N., Petras, J. W., and Reynolds, L. T. Symbolic Interactionism. *Genesis, Varieties and Criticisms. 144 pp.*

● Smith, Anthony D. The Concept of Social Change. *A Critique of the Functionalist Theory of Social Change. 208 pp.*

Routledge Social Science Journals

The British Journal of Sociology. *Editor – Angus Stewart; Associate Editor – Leslie Sklair. Vol. 1, No. 1 – March 1950 and Quarterly. Roy. 8vo. All back issues available. An international journal publishing original papers in the field of sociology and related areas.*

Community Work. *Edited by David Jones and Marjorie Mayo. 1973. Published annually.*

Economy and Society. *Vol. 1, No. 1. February 1972 and Quarterly. Metric Roy. 8vo. A journal for all social scientists covering sociology, philosophy, anthropology, economics and history. All back numbers available.*

Religion. Journal of Religion and Religions. *Chairman of Editorial Board, Ninian Smart. Vol. 1, No. 1, Spring 1971. A journal with an interdisciplinary approach to the study of the phenomena of religion. All back numbers available.*

Year Book of Social Policy in Britain, The. *Edited by Kathleen Jones. 1971. Published annually.*

Social and Psychological Aspects of Medical Practice

Editor   Trevor Silverstone

Lader, Malcolm. Psychophysiology of Mental Illness. *280 pp.*

● **Silverstone, Trevor,** and **Turner, Paul.** Drug Treatment in Psychiatry. *232 pp.*

Printed in Great Britain by
Lowe & Brydone Printers Limited, Thetford, Norfolk